MULTICULTURAL EDUCATION SERIES

James A. Banks, Series Editor

WITHDRAWN

Thriving
in the
Multicultural
Classroom

PRINCIPLES AND PRACTICES FOR EFFECTIVE TEACHING

Mary Dilg

FOREWORD BY VIVIAN GUSSIN PALEY

Teachers College, Columbia University
New York and London

For Fivvie, beloved

The excerpt of the interview with Sandra Cisneros in chapter 5 is reprinted by permission of Susan Bergholz Literary Services, New York. All rights reserved. Copyright by Sandra Cisneros.

Published by Teachers College Press, 1234 Amsterdam Avenue, New York, NY 10027

Library of Congress Cataloging-in-Publication Data

Dilg, Mary.
 Thriving in the multicultural classroom : principles and practices for effective
teaching / Mary Dilg ; foreword by Vivian Gussin Paley.
     p. cm. — (Multicultural education series)
 Includes bibliographical references and index.
 ISBN 0-8077-4390-9 (cloth : alk. paper) — ISBN 0-8077-4389-5 (pbk. : alk. paper)
   1. Multicultural education—United States. 2. Effective teaching—United States.
3. Education, Secondary—Social aspects—United States—Case studies. I. Title.
II. Multicultural education series (New York, N.Y.)

LC1099.3.D56 2003
370.117—dc21
                                                                    2003050764

ISBN 0-8077-4389-5 (paper)
ISBN 0-8077-4390-9 (cloth)

Printed on acid-free paper
Manufactured in the United States of America

10 09 08 07 06 05 04 03   8 7 6 5 4 3 2 1

Contents

Series Foreword

The nation's deepening ethnic texture, interracial tension and conflict, and the increasing percentage of students who speak a first language other than English make multicultural education imperative in the 21st century. The U.S. Census Bureau (2000) estimated that people of color made up 28% of the nation's population in 2000 and predicted that they would make up 38% in 2025 and 47% in 2050.

American classrooms are experiencing the largest influx of immigrant students since the beginning of the 20th century. About a million immigrants are making the United States their home each year (Martin & Midgley, 1999). More than seven and one-half million legal immigrants settled in the United States between 1991 and 1998, most of whom came from nations in Latin America and Asia (Riche, 2000). A large but undetermined number of undocumented immigrants also enter the United States each year. The influence of an increasingly ethnically diverse population on the nation's schools, colleges, and universities is and will continue to be enormous.

Forty percent of the students enrolled in the nation's schools in 2001 were students of color. This percentage is increasing each year, primarily because of the growth in the percentage of Latino students (Martinez & Curry, 1999). In some of the nation's largest cities and metropolitan areas, such as Chicago, Los Angeles, Washington, D.C., New York, Seattle, and San Francisco, half or more of the public school students are students of color. During the 1998–1999 school year, students of color made up 63.1% of the student population in the public schools of California, the nation's largest state (California State Department of Education, 2000).

Language and religious diversity is also increasing among the nation's student population. Sixteen percent of school-age youth lived in homes in which English was not the first language in 1990 (U.S. Census Bureau, 2000). Harvard professor Diana L. Eck (2001) calls the United States the "most religiously diverse nation on earth" (p. 4). Most teachers now in the classroom and in teacher education programs are likely to have students from diverse ethnic, racial, language, and religious groups in their classrooms during their careers. This is true for both inner-city and suburban teachers.

An important goal of multicultural education is to improve race relations and to help all students acquire the knowledge, attitudes, and skills needed to participate in cross-cultural interactions and in personal, social, and civic action that will help make our nation more democratic and just. Multicultural education is consequently as important for middle-class White suburban students as it is for students of color who live in the inner-city. Multicultural education fosters the public good and the overarching goals of the commonwealth.

The major purpose of the *Multicultural Education Series* is to provide preservice educators, practicing educators, graduate students, scholars, and policy makers with an interrelated and comprehensive set of books that summarizes and analyzes important research, theory, and practice related to the education of ethnic, racial, cultural, and language groups in the United States and the education of mainstream students about diversity. The books in the *Series* provide research, theoretical, and practical knowledge about the behaviors and learning characteristics of students of color, language minority students, and low-income students. They also provide knowledge about ways to improve academic achievement and race relations in educational settings.

The definition of multicultural education in the *Handbook of Research on Multicultural Education* (Banks & Banks, 2001) is used in the *Series:* "Multicultural education is a field of study designed to increase educational equity for all students that incorporates, for this purpose, content, concepts, principles, theories, and paradigms from history, the social and behavioral sciences, and particularly from ethnic studies and women studies" (p. xii). In the *Series,* as in the *Handbook,* multicultural education is considered a "metadiscipline."

The dimensions of multicultural education, developed by Banks (2001) and described in the *Handbook of Research on Multicultural Education,* provide the conceptual framework for the development of the books in the *Series.* They are: *content integration, the knowledge construction process, prejudice reduction, an equity pedagogy,* and *an empowering school culture and social structure.* To implement multicultural education effectively, teachers and administrators must attend to each of the five dimensions of multicultural education. They should use content from diverse groups when teaching concepts and skills, help students to understand how knowledge in the various disciplines is constructed, help students to develop positive intergroup attitudes and behaviors, and modify their teaching strategies so that students from different racial, cultural, language, and social-class groups will experience equal educational opportunities. The total environment and culture of the school must also be transformed so that students from diverse groups will experience equal status in the culture and life of the school.

Although the five dimensions of multicultural education are highly interrelated, each requires deliberate attention and focus. Each book in the series focuses on one or more of these dimensions, although each book deals with all of them to some extent because of the highly interrelated characteristics of these dimensions.

This incisive and engaging book is a source of inspiration and hope in these troubled times. The emphasis on testing, standards, and accountability that is mandated in most states compels many teachers to focus on narrow and basic skills in reading, writing, and math. In too many classrooms testing and test preparation are replacing teaching and learning. Research by Audrey L. Amrein and David C. Berliner (2002) indicates that the emphasis on testing and accountability is having detrimental affects on student learning. Because of the ways in which accountability is being conceptualized and implemented, the professional role of teachers is being fractured and minimized. Many teachers are becoming, in the words of Henry Giroux (1988), "deskilled."

The national focus on basic skills and testing is diverting attention from the broad liberal education that students need to live and function effectively in a multicultural nation and world. It is essential that all students acquire basic literacy and numeracy skills. However, as Mary Dilg documents in this informative and needed book, students also need the knowledge, skills, and values that will enable them to live, interact, and make decisions with fellow citizens from different racial, ethnic, cultural, language, and religious groups.

Students also need to acquire the knowledge and skills that will enable them to understand and to come to grips with their own ethnic and cultural identities. Dilg reveals how difficult this essential process can be for the adolescents she describes in this book with the eye of an insightful anthropologist and the heart of a compassionate teacher. She not only makes it clear that teachers need to facilitate the identity quests of adolescents, she also uses vivid examples to illustrate how she engages her students in powerful discussions to help them clarify their racial, ethnic, and cultural affiliations.

I commend this book to both teachers and teacher educators because it has several unique, important, and helpful characteristics that help to bridge the gap between theory and practice. Dilg belies the often-heard and insidious statement that teachers do not see the color or race of their students. She not only describes the rich racial, ethnic, and language differences of her students, she illustrates why teachers must "see" and acknowledge these differences in order to respond to them in culturally sensitive and appropriate ways. Teachers who do not "see" the racial and ethnic characteristics of their students, as the research by Schofield (2003) indicates, will not only fail to respond to the cultural needs and struggles of the students of color in their classes, but are likely to unwittingly discriminate against them.

Dilg explicates how essential but difficult it is for teachers to create empowering classroom learning communities made up of students who come from very different groups and neighborhoods. Her rich and thick descriptions of the homes and neighborhoods from which her students come are skillful and informative. She illustrates how she and her students construct multicultural learning communities in the classroom by creating empowering environments in which students take risks and reveal their experiences with racial privilege, racism, rejection, cultural conflicts, and personal struggles and triumphs. Student voices, which are too rarely revealed in the professional literature for teachers, are a significant part of this book.

Dilg's inviting prose, wisdom, keen insight, and compassion inform and grace every page of this timely and significant book. My hope is that this book will give voice to caring and gifted teachers who are unsung, as well as inspire and give hope to new teachers who are entering a noble but greatly undervalued profession that can transform lives and affect eternity.

James A. Banks
Series Editor

REFERENCES

Amrein, A. L., & Berliner, D. C. (2002). High-stakes testing, uncertainty, and student learning. *Education Policy Analysis Archives, 10*(8). [On-line]. Retrieved February 14, 2003, from http://eppa.asu.edu/eppa/v10n18/.

Banks, J. A. (2001). Multicultural education: Historical development, dimensions, and practice. In J. A. Banks & C. A. M. Banks (Eds.), *Handbook of research on multicultural education* (pp. 3–24). San Francisco: Jossey-Bass.

Banks, J. A., & Banks, C. A. M. (Eds.) (2001). *Handbook of research on multicultural education.* San Francisco: Jossey-Bass.

California State Department of Education. (2000). [On line]. Retrieved March 11, 2003, from http://data1.cde.ca.gov/dataquest.

Eck, D. L. (2001). *A new religious America: How a "Christian country" has become the world's most religiously diverse nation.* New York: HarperSanFrancisco.

Giroux, H. A. (1988). *Teachers as intellectuals: Toward a critical pedagogy of learning.* Granby, MA: Bergin & Garvey Publishers.

Martin, P., & Midgley, E. (1999). Immigration to the United States. *Population Bulletin, 54*(2), 1–44. Washington, DC: Population Reference Bureau.

Martinez, G. M., & Curry A. E. (1999, September). *Current population reports: School enrollment—social and economic characteristics of students* (update). Washington, DC: U. S. Census Bureau.

Riche, M. F. (2000). America's diversity and growth: Signposts for the 21st century. *Population Bulletin, 55*(2), 1–43. Washington, DC: Population Reference Bureau.

Schofield, J. W. (2003). The colorblind perspective in school: Causes and consequences. In J. A. Banks & C. A. M. Banks (Eds.), *Multicultural education: Issues and perspectives* (4th ed., revised, pp. 247–267). New York: Wiley.

U.S. Census Bureau. (2000). *Statistical abstract of the United States* (120th edition). Washington, DC: U.S. Government Printing Office.

Foreword

Young children begin school with scant interest in each other's background and circumstances. They exhibit, instead, a great curiosity about the scope of everyone's imagination. "I'm Luke Skywalker. Who are you?" they ask upon first meeting. As the culture of fantasy play unfolds into character and plot, "pretend" has the power to place every child into a shared universe of myth and metaphor, and the roles one chooses become part of the group's story. It is a true glimpse into our potential for a democratic spirit. The instinctive desire to hear every voice and observe as many different behaviors as possible is, to the children, the whole point of being in school.

By first and second grade, however, the process of separation has begun. The "who are you?" is suddenly determined by other standards, and the group seems to turn away from certain children. Are you a fast learner or too slow to respond? Are you swift afoot or too clumsy for the game? Do we value your experiences or speak only of other ways of being or looking? The clues accumulate from grade to grade: some voices are heard constantly and others are barely audible; certain students automatically join the inner circle while others seem destined for the outsider's role.

Mary Dilg is not content to play this game. She and the diverse group of high school students in her courses are inventing a new set of rules—or, more accurately, returning to the one that made sense at the start of school life: the certainty that every person has a role to play and a story to tell.

Fantasy play is replaced by works of literature and film, by poetry and prose, all representing the wide variety of experiences in the world. The subtexts of race, culture, religion, and even neighborhood are not melted down to abstract, covert symbols, but used to provide a common language whereby students are better able to explain things about themselves, ideas and opinions they have learned in silence.

No voice is allowed to dominate in this mostly White classroom, nor are words permitted to hurt or offend. Yet how does one know which words or stories or poems shock and anger another person? This too becomes a goal in her courses: to find the words that honor individual sensitivities even as we push further into the groups' discoveries and conflicts.

Is this not a dangerous notion that Mary Dilg proposes? Wouldn't it be safer to continue the practice of talking *around* racial and cultural issues? Safety is important to Ms. Dilg. She willingly describes her own errors as she searches for ways to become an honest broker in what is often an unexplored territory. Her students, who are White, Black, Latino, Asian, Middle-Eastern, and those who identify themselves in other ways, attempt to speak seriously of delicate issues in each other's presence; if safety is an overriding concern, we see that the classroom seems safer when its inhabitants no longer must hide behind a façade designed by others in order to be accepted into the full membership.

To read this book is, of necessity, to change one's perspective. No matter what courses we teach or at which grade level, we cannot help but reexamine the question that sends so many children into hiding: Are my experiences valued, or is it only other ways of being or looking or achieving that matter to my teacher and classmates?

Mary Dilg's splendid narrative, filled with the voices of students trying to explain who they are, demonstrates that it is never too early nor too late to open up our classrooms and learn to include every child as an equal participant. This is surely a basic requirement for all discussions of race and culture, but beyond that, is the foundation of good teaching itself.

To thrive in a classroom, children must be helped to remove the brand of the outsider and speak with the authority of those who belong. In the model Ms. Dilg presents, students and teachers are not afraid to make mistakes. This is the beginning of all learning.

Vivian Gussin Paley

Acknowledgments

Administrators and colleagues at the Francis W. Parker School in Chicago have supported this work for over a decade. Dr. Daniel Frank, Dr. Donald Monroe, Dr. Joseph Ruggiero, and Gene Gross have created a school unusual in its wisdom and support of children and in being a space in which the processes of teaching and learning remain the focus of constant inquiry. Their generosity in providing a yearlong sabbatical leave and an enrichment grant made possible a period of uninterrupted time, crucial for completing the manuscript. As was true with my first book, Robert Merrick, chairman of the History Department, friend, and teaching partner, made this work possible. Our shared commitment to working with adolescents dealing with issues of race and culture in the classroom became a central involvement of my professional life. Colleagues have shared my enthusiasm for research and writing; their friendship and vivacity allow for good cheer and the thrill of intellectual discovery on a daily basis. My students' animation, trust, candor, intellectual curiosity, and openness helped me to learn more about cross-cultural teaching and learning each day. They are what all of the work is about.

Writer residencies through the Ragdale Foundation in Lake Forest, Illinois, and the Vermont Studio Center in Johnson, Vermont, offered a special time and place to work. Their founders and their staffs have created magical environments for artists to work in solitude and community.

Dr. James Banks of the University of Washington and Brian Ellerbeck, Wendy Schwartz, Aureliano Vazquez, Ami Norris, and others at Teachers College Press remain the ideal mediators between writer and reader—safety nets under the high-wire act of writing.

My parents gave me the freedom and an education that would allow me to eventually gain some understanding of the social environment of my childhood. My family, Russ, Aynsley, and Justin Vandenbroucke, have inspired and supported my love for children and my wish to do what I can to make education the fully engaging and satisfying process it ought to be in students' lives.

A Way of Seeing

In Jacques Doillon's luminous and haunting film *Ponette* (1998), the audience watches a child attempt to come to terms with the death of her mother in a car accident. Placed by her father with relatives when he must return to work, Ponette is essentially left on her own to try to understand why her mother has gone—and where—and what that means. In the weeks following the accident, her emotions are buffeted not only by the loss of her mother but by the contrary explanations offered by well-meaning relatives and by cavalier classmates who cover their own fears about her situation with jesting and taunts. All of those surrounding Ponette offer opinions about her loss and how she should behave in its wake. From theories emerging from Catholic doctrine to teasing by her playmates, Ponette is hurled from one belief system to another. Ultimately, in desperation, she takes herself down the hill to her mother's grave where, digging through the soil with her own hands, she comes to understand the meaning of death. Then and only then, we are led to believe, can she go forward with her young life.

Emerging with a friend from the darkened Chicago theater into the bright-light afternoon, I am surprised by my own response to the film, a response dominated not by the oversweeping sadness at the heart of the film but rather with thoughts of teaching. And more particularly, with thoughts of learning. To what degree each day do the adolescents I teach experience a feeling of being buffeted by myriad perspectives as they attempt to understand their world, even as they are simultaneously attempting to build and understand their own selves?

OF CULTURES AND CONFUSION

One aspect of this confusing world our students are trying to comprehend—linked in its own way to dimensions of tragedy—is cross-cultural relations in this multicultural nation. As someone who has worked with

1

students in urban public and private schools throughout the country for over 25 years, I know that students struggle, sometimes profoundly and often in silence, with racial and cultural dynamics in this race-conscious society. I know, too, that these dynamics affect significant aspects of their schooling, and that this is a burden that adds to the already difficult process of building meaning in a world that may appear at times incomprehensible and full of contradictions.

To work closely with adolescents in this country today is to know how deeply issues of race and culture are unresolved. How wrong are the legions of adults who, comforted by memories of the civil rights movement, declare, "We've taken care of that." Our students, in ways many would find hard to imagine, face cruelty, loss, harassment, exclusion, and uncertainty stemming from a nation divided, one in which adults have decided to reward the members of some cultures at the expense of others. Looking at our country through the eyes of its children offers us, at times, a sobering vision.

Doubly frustrating for me as a teacher is the fact that the voices of these students and their real and troubling experiences and concerns are so little known beyond the tables of their lunchrooms or the halls of their schools. Historically, we are a nation little concerned with the voices of adolescents. Often the brunt of jokes, they are an age group broadly maligned, feared, avoided. Even their own parents openly express "dread" about the arrival of the teenage years. The stories of adolescents' lives, the stories of their confusions and needs, have little access to public forums, and even those in the circles closest to them—those within their families or schools—too often mistrust and silence them. One effect of our lack of a meaningful connection with these young adults, however, is that we may miss the ways in which they can educate us not only about themselves, but also about our own selves.

Pressing issues of race and culture that surround us, as well as the students' lives I witness each day, however, have drawn me ever closer to working directly with these issues in my classroom—initially in bringing to my classes works of literature by members of cultures not broadly taught in American schools, and then through teaching a team-taught elective course that explores issues as they emerge from or transcend specific cultures. Taking this approach has resulted in a personal and professional journey filled with its own questions as I have tried to become a better teacher in classrooms of students from many different cultures.

Repeatedly, classroom moments have led me to attempt to understand specific factors at work in teaching and learning across cultural lines, lines that have gained their depth and distinctiveness not recently through the "tribalism" of the politicized young, but through the effects of years of deliberate decisions at the highest levels of formal and informal policy-making in this country. In schools today, teachers and students inherit the effects of years of widespread prejudice and discrimination and of the wide gaps that separate one culture from another.

It was with a growing awareness of the challenges of cross-cultural teaching and learning that I began to observe my students as they came together to study the works of writers, historians, filmmakers, sociologists, and psychologists from multiple cultures, and, as they addressed directly in their discussions and writing, the issues those materials raise. What those observations suggest is that a series of factors lie at the heart of cross-cultural teaching and learning. Understanding those factors may enable us to be more effective as teachers and less intimidated by the challenges of classroom teaching today.

One cluster of factors accompanies students into the classroom: the nature of the journey each student takes between home and school, the presence of history, and the role of racial or cultural identity. An additional cluster of factors emerges once class begins: the need for a broad range of materials and approaches in teaching; the nature of multifaceted discussions; a shift in the nature of authority; the impact of curriculum and pedagogy; and the potential for complexity, volatility, or controversy tied to a single lesson. Additional factors can be observed over time as a course unfolds: the uniqueness of each group of students, the significance of sequence in curriculum design, and the emotional highs and lows of examining issues related in some way to race or culture across racial or cultural lines.

Given the sensitivity of acknowledging or working with issues of race or culture in the classroom, however, it is perhaps important to describe the context in which an awareness of these factors emerged, as well as the ways in which they may prove useful.

ON MILIEU AND METHODS

My understanding of these factors emerged from working with multicultural groups of adolescents in required and elective English and history courses in an urban private progressive high school in Chicago. The high school, with a population of 310 students, is part of a Junior Kindergarten–12 school of approximately 900 students, many of whom enter in preschool. Other students enter during the middle school years, and another cluster of students enters at the beginning of high school, grade 9. Twenty-one percent are students of color. The school supports the use of a broad range of materials in creating inviting and challenging experiences with learning, especially as those materials include and reflect the experiences of individuals from multiple cultures. The school values having students discuss openly and with each other the complicated and volatile issues that surround them and that influence their lives and interactions with each other. And, grounded in the principles of progressive educators, the school emphasizes thoughtful exploration of the processes of teaching and learning as well as a commitment to humanitarian and democratic ideals.

In a multicultural society that has decided that "race matters" (West, 1993), the processes of teaching and learning are unavoidably tied to issues of race and culture. Consistent with observations by Janet Helms (1990) and Beverly Tatum (1997), the atmosphere of racism pervasive in American society seeps into schools and becomes an inevitable, if unwanted, influence. Schools cannot keep that atmosphere at bay at the schoolhouse door. Teachers and students must then attempt to build cohesive multicultural communities and support gestures toward the common good in the face of pressures that replicate some of the worst tendencies of the larger culture beyond the school itself.

Although observations in these chapters emerged from particular courses in a specific urban high school, research, anecdotal evidence, and courses and faculty development workshops I have offered for public and private elementary, middle, and high school teachers from schools with both White and student of color majority enrollments suggest that the factors described here are widespread and reflect the effects of a race- and culture-conscious society on classroom dynamics. These cross-cultural dynamics reflect the ways in which living in a race-conscious society informs and influences the spirit and nature of interactions in a classroom community.

Much of the information in these chapters comes from listening to students discuss readings and films, as well as aspects of their own and each other's lives, in high school English and history courses, in particular, a team-taught interdisciplinary elective course for seniors called "Issues of Race and Culture," an elective course for juniors and seniors on Chicago writers, a required course for sophomores on classic and contemporary fiction, and a required course for freshmen focusing on literary genres and on ideas relating to self and community. Most of the student observations in these essays emerged in discussions, assigned writings, or student journals in these courses.

The fact that all of my courses are discussion-based allows me to hear students talking regularly with each other about issues important in their lives. All of my courses also involve extensive writing in which students are encouraged to develop their voices and perspectives and to write about aspects of texts or human experience that are important to them. The combination of these factors has meant that I have been close to students' conversations and writings on topics of interest to them, including issues related to race and culture, for many years.

In Issues of Race and Culture, students from multiple cultures regularly engage in discussing and writing about racial and cultural issues. Students keep journals in which they respond to course readings, discussions, guest speakers, or films, or any racial or cultural issue emerging in the classroom, school, or beyond. Because many of the student observations used here originated in these journals, they reflect students' private, candid, written responses to issues that surround them, rather than observations offered in the public give-and-take of classroom conversations.

While many schools may not have courses designed to directly address issues of race and culture, and thus draw out more vividly, constantly, and intensely cross-cultural dynamics related to studying, discussing, and writing about those issues, in all classrooms of students from multiple racial or cultural backgrounds, students and teachers are negotiating with each other complex cross-cultural dynamics. Further, the multicultural nature of student populations suggests the benefits of drawing on materials from multiple cultures. Studying and responding to such materials, however, generates additional complex classroom moments related to race or culture.

Many of my students are quoted throughout this book, and in each case, their racial or cultural identity is included. There will be readers who decry the cultural labeling throughout these chapters. Why is it necessary to indicate that a student is a "young Black male" or a "young Latina"? Once I would have agreed. But I know from experience that given the race consciousness of our society, our own racial or cultural identities as teachers and the racial or cultural identities of our students are at times central factors in classroom dynamics. Understanding that fact and understanding the effects of that fact have helped me understand better not only my students but central challenges in cross-cultural teaching and learning. Personal details have been altered to protect the privacy of the students, and, in many instances, general descriptors such as "Latino" or "Asian American" have been used instead of more specific designations for the same reason. Students' names are pseudonyms. "Black" and "White" are capitalized where they are used to refer to populations. In direct quotations, original racial and cultural identifiers as well as capitalization have been maintained. The word race as used throughout is understood to be a social-historical-political concept (Andersen & Collins, 1995, p. 61; Omi & Winant, 1986), and culture as the history, language, customs, values, traditions, or worldview of a particular group at a particular time. The use of "we" in reference to classroom activities refers to my teaching partner and me in our work together in the team-taught elective course on racial and cultural issues.

I am neither a sociologist, anthropologist, nor formal educational researcher. The dynamics described and analyzed here are those I have observed in interactions among students from multiple cultures as they have come together in my urban classrooms. Finding similar dynamics discussed by formal researchers offered clarity on dynamics I myself was observing, as well as ways of thinking about, managing, and addressing them as they emerge in day-to-day activities among my students. *Thriving in the Multicultural Classroom* draws on years of classroom experience as well as vital, published, formal educational research. *Thriving in the Multicultural Classroom* is by a teacher, for teachers.

Contemporary racial and cultural dynamics make it essential that an author writing about those dynamics situate herself in a social context. I am a White high school English teacher who was born and raised in the Jim Crow South of a Southern mother and a Northern father, with regular intervals spent living in the New York metropolitan area and New England. As a child, I saw what segregation did to adults and to children, Black and White. I did not understand most of what unfolded around me, but I learned early the sweeping contradiction between "authority" and morality. I heard adults say one thing in the face of a reality that, I could see in front of me, was something quite different. I watched White adults conduct themselves as if Blacks in their midst were invisible or worse. I was surrounded by pervasive malignant factors that prohibited anyone from feeling a sense of belonging across cultural lines. In the midst of that milieu I enjoyed a relationship with a Black woman that—as best such a relationship could in that time and place—transcended, even as it was rooted in, much of what surrounded us. Memories of that relationship became an organizing principle of my life. As I look across the classroom at my students each year, I vow to support experiences that reflect the richness of cross-cultural relationships, not the tainted and crippled cross-cultural relationships that so broadly populated the American South of the 1950s and 1960s.

There are those who say that White educators should not take on the study of multicultural education, and particularly should not write about it, but the demographic reality is that the majority of teachers are White, even in many schools where the majority of students are students of color. Students in American classrooms represent an increasingly diverse population, while those going into teaching remain overwhelmingly White. According to one study, "In 1982, approximately one of four schoolchildren were students of color. If current trends continue, that figure will increase to nearly one out of two by 2020" (Shaw, 1996, p. 328). In contrast, teachers of color make up 9.3% of teachers nationally ("Who's In," 1998). The situation will most likely not improve in the near future, since 85% of students in undergraduate teacher preparation programs are white females (Gursky, 2002). Such disparities exist in public and private schools, in cities, and in suburbs. Currently, private schools in New York City, for example, report an enrollment of 20.8% students of color and a "paucity" of teachers of color (Randolph Carter, quoted in Archibold, 1999, pp. A1, A35). Additionally, immigrants today are increasingly moving to the suburbs: "Suburbs are on their way to becoming the most common place of residence for Hispanic Americans and Asian Americans, the groups that make up most of the country's foreign-born population," whether that trend is appearing in suburbs close to Washington, D.C. or Fargo, North Dakota (Brad Edmondson, quoted in Engebretson, 2000, p. 15). Multicultural education is a fact of American life.

All of us—White teachers and teachers of color—face challenges in meeting the needs of the students before us in multicultural classrooms. "A grammar school teacher in California may now have students from fifty-four language groups in her class, as does one grammar school teacher I know," explains Richard Rodriguez. "How shall she teach such an assembly anything singular?" (1997, p. 68). In one national study of over 4,000 public school teachers, only one in five indicated they felt well qualified to teach in today's classroom with students from diverse backgrounds (Honan, 1999).

FACTORS IN CROSS-CULTURAL TEACHING AND LEARNING

Factors of cross-cultural teaching and learning explored in this book might reflect in some ways an observation in Asian Indian philosophical parables: that there are elements beneath the surface and unseen—as well as those we perceive—that make the whole more complex. The factors described here reveal in certain ways the inner workings of a multicultural group of students. They allow us to see into and beneath the surface of an always complex and often perplexing picture. They describe patterns that may be apparent or submerged but that shape the experience in a classroom in visible and significant ways. They provide a map of sorts for reading classroom dynamics that result from living in a race- and culture-conscious society.

Describing these factors is a way of trying to understand the pressure points, the subterranean and overt pressures that inform daily interactions and gestures in the multicultural classroom, and to clarify what may help teachers and students in the face of those dynamics. Descriptions of these factors represent starting points; explorations of each of these factors can and should be taken further in additional research. These factors are at work in any classroom, but they may emerge and be experienced more intensely in a multicultural classroom. And they may exist more openly in classes that touch on, directly or indirectly, materials or issues tied in some way to race or culture. Individually, each of these factors may be familiar to the classroom teacher; the following chapters offer a way of thinking about multiple factors working simultaneously, their interrelatedness and their impact on teaching and learning. Description and analysis of each factor is accompanied by a discussion of ways in which we as teachers may respond to that factor to create a fuller, more satisfying classroom experience for our students and for ourselves.

The journey between home and school taken by each of our students influences the way they experience and contribute to their days in a multicultural school. Focusing on the students themselves, chapter 1, From Home to School and Home Again, describes and analyzes factors that shape that journey: the effects of growing up in race- or culture-conscious homes and neighborhoods, challenges with finding a comfortable fit in the school community, negotiating satisfactorily the process of students learning about themselves and each other, and navigating successfully the distance between the world of home and the world of school. The challenge of the school and the teacher is to understand and support students in their daily journeys between home and school and to facilitate a comfortable fit for all students in the school environment.

Chapter 2, The Presence of History, examines the impact of multiple histories that accompany students and teacher into the classroom. Students' and teachers' histories influence who they are and what they know, what they bring to and take from classroom materials, how they experience classroom pedagogy and discussions, and how they experience themselves and each other. The weight of history has the power to support or to derail the best intentions for a class. Understanding the impact of history in the classroom can lead to deeper and richer experiences for students and teacher.

In a nation that remains conscious of racial or cultural identity, students' racial or cultural identities are significant aspects of their lives by the time they enter schools, and they can affect in powerful and lasting ways what unfolds there. Chapter 3, The Role of Racial or Cultural Identity, examines multiple facets of students' emerging identities in the multicultural classroom, as well as challenges students face in meeting the expectations of others, dealing with the weight of prejudice, and finding a comfortable fit in a society where racial or cultural designations continue to affect daily lives. Knowing how and to what degree our students' experiences are complicated by issues tied to racial and cultural identities can enable us to take a more thoughtful approach to aspects of classroom life, from taking roll until our students leave us.

Chapter 4, Multifaceted Discussions, explores the nature of discussions in classrooms of students from multiple cultures. Students in multicultural classrooms want to know more about each other but are often uncertain how to engage in conversations that would help them to do so. The use of language, the multiple conflicting perspectives that emerge, the emotions such conversations trigger, and the stresses on individual partici- pants all offer challenges for students and teachers. Providing a safe envi- ronment and support for each individual's voice as well as for the group as a whole can promote discussions that enable students and teachers to think more broadly about the world around us.

Multicultural school communities and multifaceted discussions in those communities invite a broader way of thinking about authority in the classroom. Chapter 5, Authority Shared and Shifting, examines that form of authority. The complex nature of issues tied in one way or another to racial and cultural histories and identities results in multiple, contrasting, authoritative points of view emerging in the multicultural classroom. Moreover, authority about such issues will be found not only with the teacher or the work of known scholars and artists, but with students, tied to their life experiences. This broad base of knowledge will result in a nat- urally occurring, shared and shifting locus of authority in working with issues across cultural lines in the classroom. Anticipating, recognizing, and supporting this shared and shifting authority can result in a fuller explo- ration of issues as well as the nurturing of emerging authority in those of the next generation.

In Chapter 6, Anatomy of a Failure: The Impact of Curriculum/The Power of Pedagogy, analysis of a series of moments in a course on Chicago writers reveals the complexity of knowledge construction in a multicultur- al classroom in a racialized society. Several bodies of existing knowledge merge in a classroom as teacher and students convene to build new knowl- edge. All of those knowledge bases and the way in which new knowledge is constructed are influenced by aspects of culture and power. Understanding the ways in which culture and power support or impinge upon teaching and learning can help teachers engage in a more thoughtful approach to curriculum and pedagogy.

Creating a course syllabus grounded in multiple cultures grows out of an understanding of how we learn and why we read, the private and pub- lic experience of reading, and the ways in which cultural identities are relat- ed to reading, writing, and learning. Chapter 7, A Breadth of Materials: Reading Within and Across Cultural Lines, suggests that multicultural reading lists reflect overarching values espoused by classic and contempo- rary humanists, enable students to satisfy their yearnings for exploring both what is familiar and what is new, and draw together students from multiple cultures in the classroom. While this chapter focuses on teaching literature, similar thinking about curriculum can broaden the base of explorations in other disciplines as well.

The needs of students and the challenges of the multicultural classroom invite consideration of a "pedagogy of belonging." A pedagogy of belonging reflects: understanding the pressures and choices that can divide us in the multicultural classroom, the importance of thoughtful planning, understanding and drawing on the power resident in a multicultural group of students, understanding what might be expected in the flow of a course, and creating a supportive environment. Principles and practices advocated in Chapter 8, A Pedagogy of Belonging: Toward a Pedagogy of Multiculturalism, draw on classroom experience as well as the work of leading educators throughout the century: John Dewey, Francis W. Parker, Vivian Gussin Paley, Sonia Nieto, Geneva Gay, Gloria Ladson-Billings, Beverly Tatum, bell hooks, and others.

SERVING OUR STUDENTS

Understanding factors in cross-cultural teaching and learning can help us to better serve the students who come before us as well as the families who entrust us with their children, and to savor the joys and the challenges of working with students in the multicultural classroom. Being aware of such factors can enable us to support our students in their journeys from confusion toward some measure of clarity about issues that often surround them and that affect them in their daily lives at school and beyond. In so doing, perhaps we can offer them a more fruitful and less painful search for understanding than the one experienced by young Ponette in the French countryside at the grave of her mother.

*   *   *

At a celebration at Bard College of Chinua Achebe's 70th birthday, the writer was asked that playful, long-posed question: "If you were stuck on a desert island, what book would you take with you?" Without hesitation, Mr. Achebe replied, "Toni Morrison's *Beloved*" (1987), and proceeded to describe the ways in which that novel continues to haunt the Black world. Ms. Morrison herself was a participant in the celebration that day, and, offered the same question, she answered, "I'd like to write the book I'd like to read" (Sengupta, 2000, pp. B1, B6).

Thriving in the Multicultural Classroom is a book I needed over the years as I moved in and out of multicultural classrooms knowing I was not adequately understanding or meeting the needs of the students before me. Repeatedly, I wondered how I could understand—and therefore anticipate and better address—complex dynamics among my students unfolding in front of me on a daily basis. This is the book I wanted to read.

PART I

Understanding the Multicultural Classroom: Supporting Our Students

CHAPTER 1

From Home to School and Home Again

Two hours before school starts each morning, LaShandra hoists on her backpack, says goodbye to her mother, and heads out the door. She will take two buses and the El from her apartment on Chicago's predominantly Black West Side to her independent school on the city's predominantly White Near North Side. Vanessa steps out of her house in the Latino neighborhood of Pilsen on the city's South West Side. And Jackson boards a bus on the West Side and begins his own long journey across town. An hour later, Dong descends from his high-rise in the West Loop and hops a city bus for the 20-minute ride uptown. Almost two hours after LaShandra has left home, Joshua, Justin, Tameka, and Erica leave their homes and apartments on the city's Near North Side for a short walk to the sleek red brick building of their high school. By 8:00 A.M., all of these students have dumped jackets into lockers and, with slamming metal doors echoing behind them, taken their places, along with their other classmates, at tables next to each other in the first class of their day. I look out over these students, some barely awake at this hour, although the day has begun long ago for some of them, and hope that today, together, we can make their journey between home and school a good one, a worthwhile one, a journey that will serve to take them, individually and collectively, farther along where they wish to travel in the longer journey of their lives. I hope that somehow we can traverse in some meaningful way the chasms that divide our lives by night and sliver our days with challenges in this multicultural and segregated city.

JOURNEYING BETWEEN HOME AND SCHOOL

What years of observations and conversations with these and other students have shown is that their daily journeys from home to school and

home again in some not insignificant measure influence the way in which
they experience and contribute to their days at school. All of these students
bring to school the hopes and expectations that a good education can make
a difference in the arc of a life. Those hopes and expectations will be buffeted by the effects of living in a race-conscious society. By the time these
students take their seats next to one another, each of them has been educated, in one way or another, to be race-conscious and to interact with each
other in ways that reflect, acknowledge, respond to, or perpetuate historical and current tensions as well as patterns of thinking and interacting
across racial and cultural lines. For many of them, their teachings at home,
consciously or unconsciously, will have reinforced and perpetuated negative attitudes toward cultural groups other than their own as well as
instructed them in ways of navigating the multicultural terrain of their city.
Their multiple cultural backgrounds and identities will leave them trying to
understand and assess the role of language in their own and each other's
lives and the ways in which language relates to family, peers, the community of their home, and the community of their school. They enter school
each morning aware of the divided nature of their surrounding neighborhoods. All of these factors provide the backdrop for their movement
between the two worlds they inhabit for their day-to-day lives as students:
the world of home and the world of school. For some students, these two
worlds are contiguous, twin worlds almost, reflecting broadly overlapping
values, priorities, and assumptions. Other students travel each day between
widely separate and discrete worlds.

Once in school, students will find that the cultural mix of their school
yields an alternately comfortable and strained coexistence and intermingling among students from multiple cultural backgrounds, brightened by
sustained connection and support, and darkened by moments of tension or
hostility between individuals or groups. The experience of the student in a
cultural minority in his or her school setting—no matter what that cultural identity is—will be different than the experience of the child who is in a
cultural majority. Especially for those students who are members of minority cultures within the school, there will be an ongoing drama surrounding
fitting in and being left out. And all of the students will wrestle with fitting
together: What is one willing or able to do to fit in? And what is one willing or able to do to reach out?

As students return home each afternoon, they carry with them the
residue of the day. The natural process of human development assures that
these students return home day after day slightly different from the individuals who waved goodbye in the morning. They bring into the doors of
their homes each afternoon the expectations of teachers, administrators,
and peers, and their education will shift the way they think about home,

family, friends, neighborhood, language, and community. In some cases, that understanding will lead to a greater measure of clarity about their lives outside of school. In some cases, their growing understanding of the cultural complexity of the world they have inherited will produce no small measure of pain as they regularly traverse cultural borders. In other cases, their changing lives will bring them closer to those they leave behind each morning.

Some of the students before me this morning will have a difficult one or two or four years. For a few, movement between home and school will collapse altogether under the weight of diverging worlds. For most, however, that movement will be sustained, and the goodbyes of mornings in their neighborhoods will yield to a last goodbye to those of us at school, as they begin the longer journey into their nascent adult lives. Whether or not these students' times with me and with others in this school succeed in enriching their lives and launching them with satisfaction and pride into young adulthood depends in part on the sensitivity and knowledge I can gain and act on in relation to their complex daily journeys between home and school.

HOME

A Race-Conscious Society/A Race-Conscious Home

In one way or another, all of these students bring into the classroom the effects of living in a race-conscious society and a society that also views racial or cultural identity hierarchically. They learn of racism and they learn the effects of racism through what they hear at home, what they see, and what they are taught.

They hear and see racist attitudes and behaviors in those closest to them, echoing Gordon Allport's notion that prejudice is often "not taught," but "caught" (1958, p. 285). Racism is not limited to those from a particular culture, but spreads across the home lives of students from multiple cultures. Our students observe racism in the words of grandparents, mothers or fathers, relatives or friends. They tell us of an uncle's prejudices about Jews and Latinos. They tell us of a mother who says, "You sound like a Jew." Or a father who says, "I'm so sick of these Puerto Ricans." They see disgust on the faces of parents at the sight of an interracial couple, and parents who decry the influence of Blacks on their daughter, who is Guatemalan. They see friends engage in name-calling and bigotry.

Caught between the need to remain close and connected to those they love and to accommodate their yearnings for cultural harmony, students often attempt to justify or rationalize what they have heard or seen. And

so they speak or write of such moments in the context of frustration, justi-
fication, or rationalization. "My sister wasn't racist, but I think sometimes
she did things that were racist," or "I really believe my grandfather did not
mean to be offensive, but he was." Or of a friend, "He knows his remarks
are wrong, he's not trying to be a racist. His friends just don't care." "They
are not bad people," another student says of his friends, "they just don't
care if they offend other people. They're just trying to be funny." Once students observe such behavior, they are in positions of having to ignore or
respond to the moment. As one student explained, "It's hard to accept what
my dad says and does. Should I correct him?" Or the student who said,
"We all laughed at my cousin's racist jokes. But then I thought, 'Is that
wrong?'" Or as another said after witnessing a friend's mother make a public racist remark, "I was too uncomfortable to say anything to her, but now
I see her differently." Students are coming to school schooled in racism.

Beyond bearing witness to racist attitudes and gestures, students' voices also reflect diametrically opposed experiences with the power of race.
For some, race is tied to power exerted over them. For others, racial identity yields power.

Many of these students have lived with and observed the effects of
racism day after day. Many students of color speak of parents being mis-
treated by salesclerks, or of themselves constantly being followed in department stores. They speak of being insulted on the street with names and gestures—the White woman clutching her purse tighter in front of the young
Black male—of hearing ethnic slurs as they walk by. One young Latina
remembered why her mother, after moving from Mexico, had quit school
before reaching high school: "She hated being Mexican, hated having a
strong accent. She was feared, taunted, the whole works. Let's face it, kids
can be so cruel! And they were, they got to her. She stopped going. And
tended to the housework."

Other students describe living in a sheltered White world. They have
never been made fun of; never felt the effects of discrimination; never been
ostracized, followed, teased, or harassed because of their cultural identity.
For some White students, the protection of their racial status extends well
beyond the confines of home and school. Some students describe feeling
part of a sheltered network from East Coast to West Coast comprised of
families and friends who share similar types of schools, offices, and futures,
and never feel the effects of discrimination. As some students realize and
explain, because they have grown up safe from feeling the effects of racism,
they find it hard to understand or relate at all to the experiences of classmates for whom the power of racism may be a daily factor in their lives.

In some instances, students' relationships with those from other cultures are complicated by issues of class and of their having come to know

individuals from other cultures through those individuals' employment in their parents' homes as babysitters or domestic helpers. When this is the case, attempting to speak in public of what, to them, may have been experienced as a close and caring relationship across cultural lines, may not at all be experienced the same way by classmates. Describing such relationships may underscore distances among students along lines of both culture and class.

While some students experience racial or cultural dynamics in the worlds of their homes that may make it more challenging for them to relate comfortably across racial or cultural lines in school, other students grow up with a deeply felt satisfaction with role models in the home for relating across cultural divides. Students describe parents whose actions in the neighborhood or political or social arenas distinguish them as committed to working for deepening and bettering cross-cultural relations. But they are noted, in a way, because they are noteworthy. And this, too, suggests the consciousness of racial divisions surrounding these students.

Lessons from Home

In addition to what they learn in hearing and observing moments tied to race or culture, many of these students leave home carrying multiple overt lessons concerning race and culture.

For some, those lessons center on the importance of inclusive thinking and behavior, of reaching out to include those not like oneself on a daily basis.

For others, the lessons focus on ways of thinking to ease the challenges that may lie ahead. One young biracial woman likened the effect of reading an essay on "White privilege" (McIntosh, 1998) in our course on racial and cultural issues to conversations with her own mother as her mother readied her to face a world at times unwelcoming both to women and to people of color.

Students have also been taught ways of thinking about and moving around their city, and one effect of this will be the attitudes toward each other they bring into school each day. They have been taught, by loving and thoughtful parents, to lock their car doors, to understand which are the "good" neighborhoods and which are the "bad," and where they may and should not travel. Some of them have been taught to distrust Whites, others to fear or to feel uneasy about—in one way or another—Asian Americans, African Americans, or Latinos.

Although through their teachings parents are attempting to give their children guidelines for urban safety and road maps for living their lives, those same guidelines often perpetuate negative ways of thinking across cultures. This serves to widen the gaps among classmates from different cultures as students come together in classrooms and hallways. The people they have been "taught" to fear or resent are now their classmates, and students must adjust and reorient their thinking to overcome the messages they have been given from home.

Consider the following series of observations about Cabrini Green, a public housing project not far from our school. Cabrini Green, now in the process of being torn down, is a cluster of high-rises on the city's North Side. Although once surrounded by flower gardens, today, from the street, the grounds of Cabrini Green appear barren, edges of some windows are lined with broken glass, an occasional tattered curtain dangles into space, and some doors are barricaded with plywood. Within blocks of Cabrini Green lies some of the city's most expensive real estate, to the north and to the south. Many of our students traveling between their homes and downtown go past the projects. Raised by their parents to steer clear of the projects for reasons of safety, they come to hold a fearful curiosity about them. They have learned they are not to go there, a place associated with violence, drugs, and danger.

But for a number of our students, Cabrini Green is home. In school, students raised to fear Cabrini will come to hear about another side of life in the high-rises. But their prejudices about the place are well formed before they get to know their classmates or hear of their lives. For one young Black woman, the fourth-floor hallway at Cabrini is the scene of many of her fondest childhood memories. One day, she reads a paper about home to her class. Her memories tumble forward: jumping rope, making best friends, buying cooling summer sweets from a neighbor, even the best place for a secret kiss. She remembers teaching friends to skate there, times listening to music, and playing make-believe. This young woman also remembers the darker moments: a playmate shot in the head in her apartment by an errant bullet coming from the hallway, and the friend who was raped in one corner. After the projects were slated for destruction, many of the families were moved out. Her family, she tells us, enjoys being in a "better neighborhood." But she herself misses the hallway of her childhood at Cabrini. The room is quiet after her reading. She has left her classmates with new lessons to think about.

What these students' lessons from home suggest is that our students have already been educated, to a degree, about certain aspects of life in a race-conscious society. Some of those lessons will facilitate their day-to-day lives in a multicultural school community, and some of those lessons will make their days in their multicultural school more difficult, for themselves and others. Students have been taught lessons that bring with them, consciously or inadvertently, a practice of prejudice or racism, no matter which culture is the culture of home. Many of our students know this, and they know that the lessons they have learned in this area are hard ones to move beyond. As one White student explained, her instructions for moving around in the city have left her with distinct biases. As a result, she recognizes that her public stands against racism operate in contradiction to the racism, she says, she will probably always carry within her as a result of her upbringing, however geared for her well-being or however well-intentioned it was. Or as another White student wrote, "Even though high school is the end of one stage of development and college is the beginning of another, people are pretty set in their ways by the time they escape the influence of their parents."

Neighborhood Worlds

Beyond the direct lessons from home these students bring to school, students also bring to school an accumulated awareness of the divided nature of surrounding neighborhoods and communities, in some ways related to race and culture, and these divides affect students in personal and significant ways. One of the ways these divides affect them personally is the degree to which they characterize the students' own movement around the city, and this in turn affects their relationships in school. Students quickly learn—beyond the teachings of their parents—where they feel comfortable, where they are welcome and where they are not.

For one young Black student and his Latina friend, neighborhood divides precluded his feeling comfortable visiting her at home. Here they both speak of what they know:

> *Young Black male:* In my neighborhood, on Chicago's South West Side, the blacks and Latinos are divided. There are train tracks between 21st and 22nd Street; 21st on back are blacks and 22nd on up are Latinos. If you're black it's dangerous to cross the tracks to the Latino side and it's the same for Latinos. This is so serious that people have gotten hurt, shot and even killed. For me, I don't cross the tracks often, and one reason is because I don't understand why there is so much tension between the two minorities.

> *Young Latina:* I asked a friend of mine to come to my house this weekend. His response was, "Man, I can't go over there. I'm black." I felt so frustrated. He seriously thinks he'll get shot and killed if he came to my house. That is utterly ridiculous. He told me this story about a friend of his who got shot not too far from my house. I have never come across any type of violence in my neighborhood. Gangs

and drugs do not bother me here. People assume that because [of where I live], I dodge bullets every time I leave my house. That is so ignorant. My home is my home and it angers me that people who do not know any better assume the worst of my home. What angers me even more is that my friend was scared to come into my neighborhood. Just because he's black, that is no reason he should not be able to come into my neighborhood. Isn't segregation illegal or something? It's not fair that he can't come to my house because of the color of my skin.

For one Asian-American student, the knowledge of neighborhood cultural divides came through outings in her Latino neighborhood or daily bus rides. "[At the back of the bus], a black girl says to a guy, 'Look, that Chinese girl is looking at your crazy self.' I got aggravated because I live in a Latino neighborhood. And growing up I heard little kids say, 'Look at that Chinese girl.' I'm not some kind of exotic animal that is on display. But I didn't do anything. I just stared out the window. Done it so much, I recognize all of the buildings and streets I pass by."

Other students note specific activities associated, in their minds, with one neighborhood or another. For one biracial student, a scene she saw unfolding in the back of a McDonald's in a Black neighborhood would not have happened in a White neighborhood. The scene consisted of, she recalled, three young White people "visiting the ghetto," a concealed bag—later found to contain all the elements for smoking heroin—and policemen seeing the moment but turning away. A Black student described the day he lost a close friend: "My friend was murdered around the corner from my house. Not only was his body sitting out there for two hours, but when the police finally showed up, they just dumped him in the back of the wagon." According to this student, that would never have happened in a White neighborhood.

Other students say they "play it safe" and note that they've never even been to the South Side or the West Side—known to be neighborhoods predominantly of people of color—and so, as one White student surmised, it's probably hard for the people who live there to come to my neighborhood. White students and students of color express reservations about being in one another's neighborhoods after dark.

For others, knowledge of neighborhoods beyond their own comes vicariously—through the movies, videos, or music. For one White student, this occurred through seeing a film on "the hood," an event that precipitated an emotional walk home wrapped in the arms of his father and a keen awareness of the benefits of his own neighborhood set in stark relief against the images of the film. For another White student, as he explained, his journeys into distant neighborhoods came through the lyrics of hip-hop and rap. Music brought him, he said, an inside perspective on urban trauma from the safety of his affluent suburban home.

These students' knowledge—vicarious or otherwise—of the differences in their city's neighborhoods establishes a context through which they greet and come to know—or not know—their classmates. Their knowledge of the neighborhoods from which their classmates come predisposes them to reach out to each other or to hang back. And this can lead to tensions, misunderstanding, and isolation.

The Community of Home and the Community of School

Although these students have learned something of the multiple communities that characterize their city, for many of them it will be two communities that concern them the most: the community of their home and the community of their school. It will be these two worlds that, potentially, contribute the most to the ways in which they experience their life at school.

For some students at our independent school, there is barely a thread's-width difference between the community of their home and that of the school. They roll out of bed at 7:45 A.M., wolf down breakfast, and sprint across the street to class. The local hangouts they frequent during lunchtime are the same ones they're drawn to on the weekend. Some can run home between classes if they forget a paper. And many of their parents are neighbors, if not friends.

For other students, leaving each day the neighborhood of their home for the neighborhood of the school means losing touch with family, relatives, friends, and the community where they've been raised. For some it means traveling each day between two different worlds. For some it feels like living two different lives and not fully inhabiting either.

For one Black student, leaving his own neighborhood and attending a predominantly White school caused his Black friends at home to reject him, leaving him feeling as though he was dangling between two worlds with little sense of belonging to either. For one young Chinese-American student, friends at school were almost all White, but when he went to church all of his friends were Chinese. He felt like he lived two lives, "one as an almost white person, and the other as a full-fledged Chinese." According to some students, the students who live "sheltered lives" in the neighborhood surrounding the school will never understand the dynamics of their neighborhoods across town, dynamics they themselves sometimes find it difficult to return to at the end of the day. For still others, the journey itself between home and school poses its own challenges as students chart routes to avoid the territory of hostile gangs or neighborhoods where they know kids like them are not only not welcome, but are in danger. To make their daily journey across town more acceptable, some sport haircuts that readmit them to the neighborhood, and others have resorted to changing clothes as they enter and leave school.

The effects of such distances extend into after-school hours as students from neighborhoods across town experience their classmates' reluctance to come to their homes in neighborhoods unfamiliar to them, or the difficulty of staying for evening activities if it means long bus and El rides home late at night. One young Latina remembered, years later, the effects of such moments as she was bused to a predominantly White elementary school from kindergarten through second grade: "Not one of my friends came over from school. I was told their parents did not want to drive them to 'that' neighborhood. I was told repeatedly that it was a bad neighborhood to drive to. I was never taken to their houses because we had no car and my mother was usually at work. I discovered how segregated the city of Chicago really was."

One young Black woman recalled such experiences during her high school years. School friends rarely asked her out. Neighborhood friends drifted away, knowing she was often at school. Eventually her world divided between seeing White friends during the week and Black friends on the weekend. Such social bifurcation left her trying to find a sense of self that would allow her to feel happy in each world. Another Black student suggested one way to hold onto both worlds, but doing so was, for him, not without conscious effort: "When I came [here], I held on to my identity and continue to do so. If you are a willful person, you will be able to hold on to your heritage. If not, you may get caught in the wave."

Perhaps one Asian-American student expressed the challenges of this daily journey the fullest. He found comfort in the familiarity of an essay by Christian Neira, a New York Latino who left his home in public housing to attend a preparatory school downtown. Neira writes in his essay, "Trying to live in two different worlds, one is in peril of not belonging to either of them. One is left in a state of confusion" (1988, p. 337). For our student, trying to belong to two very different communities meant trying to adapt to both, taking on characteristics of one that might not fit the other, and eventually wondering whether he was the person he was at home or the person he was at school, not an easy question for adolescents already uncertain enough about who they are and who they are becoming.

Useful in understanding what each of our students may be experiencing in this regard is the work of Phelan, Davidson, and Yu, who describe four patterns of relationship between home and school: 1) "Congruent Worlds/Smooth Transitions," in which students move easily between two similar worlds; 2) "Different Worlds/Border Crossings Managed," in which students develop successful strategies to navigate the different worlds of home and school; 3) "Different Worlds/Border Crossings Difficult," in which students find the necessary adjustment between their different worlds of home and school to be difficult, uncomfortable, and possible only in certain situations that tend to minimize the distance and discomfort; and 4) "Different Worlds/Borders Impenetrable," in which students find the necessary adjustment between two different worlds of home and school so difficult as to create "stress and anxiety," or, eventually, to be impossible (1993, pp. 59–85). And as Stonequist explains, "Wherever there are cultural transitions and cultural conflicts there are marginal personalities," and these individuals may experience tension and discomfort (1937, p. 4, quoted in Suarez-Orozco & Suarez-Orozco, 1993, p. 115). For students who cannot successfully manage the transition between the worlds of home and school, the consequences can be significant. There is the danger of landing in a netherworld belonging to neither; they will fall "outside of both worlds" (S. Lee, 1996, p. 104). Or those "for whom the conflict is simply too great are expelled or drop out, either physically or psychologically" (Nieto, 1996, p. 286).

Beyond influencing the way students experience their schooling, themselves, and each other, relationships between the worlds of home and school can also result in placing some students at an advantage over others. "Some students reach the schoolhouse door with the officially sanctioned language, culture, and background experiences," Nieto explains, "and they are therefore more privileged from the very outset to succeed in the school setting" (1999, p. 33). The nature of a student's relationship between home and school can also affect what goes on directly between teacher and student: In instances of considerable difference between the culture of home and the culture of school, "teachers can easily misread students' aptitudes, intent, or abilities" because of variations in styles of communication. Or they may use teaching techniques or approaches to discipline incompatible with practices in the community (Delpit, 1995, p. 167).

In the face of these challenges, we must remember that "all children come to school motivated to enlarge their worlds. [We must] enter their world in order to aid them and . . . to build bridges between two worlds, not walls" (Sarason, 1990, p. 164, quoted in Phelan, Davidson, & Yu, 1993, p. 52). Further, some students who can learn how to navigate successfully two different worlds can eventually become "creative agents . . . able to contribute to the solution of the conflict of races and cultures" (Stonequist, 1937, p. 15, quoted in Suarez-Orozco & Suarez-Orozco, 1993, p. 115).

Questions of Language

Another effect of the divisions our students experience tied to race or culture as they move between home and school is a complex relationship with language. Language can define, divide, embarrass, exclude, draw together, or isolate students and those around them at home and at school. Those who come to school speaking English as their first language may struggle with the academic demands of their courses in foreign language, but for other students, challenges tied to language push much deeper.

Those who speak English as their second language will be asked repeatedly, through their experiences, to clarify their relationship to language. What does it mean to speak my first language? What does it mean not to speak my first language? Why should I hide or develop my first or second language? For some students, language becomes another element of culture to assert or to defend, to reveal with pride or to hide. Pressures and quandaries relating to language can be considerable. Language is tied to identity and to status: "In a society where one language, English, has more prestige than another, and where 'success' is judged in terms of attaining proficiency in that language as a means of assimilating to the mainstream culture, [it will be harder to maintain the language of home]" (Villanueva, 1997, p. 76). In our predominantly White school, students for whom Spanish is their first language have recalled with emotion being embarrassed to speak on the pay phone in the hall for fear other students would hear them speaking Spanish to their mothers. One Filipino spoke movingly of the growing distance he is experiencing at home as his Tagalog has become blended with English. As a result, he can no longer fully communicate with his father, and this leaves him worried: Does his father understand him? Does his father feel disconnected from him?

Or consider the words of this young Black woman who has given much thought to the notion of Black dialect:

> As I got off the phone I thought about something. As I said something to a family member, I realized that my voice had changed, rather my dialect and the way I spoke was different than when I was talking on the phone with my friend, and at [school] for that matter. This caused me to question something about myself. Is *not* speaking [or] using standard, conventional "white" dialect wrong? Does doing so make others perceive you as "ignorant" or "ghetto" if you choose to speak that way around them? At home, I also most often use standard English dialect, but why isn't it vice versa with my using black vernacular [at school]?

After hearing Cornell West speak, I was profoundly moved, not solely by his intellect, but by his lack of restraint with the use of b[lack] v[ernacular]. He was succinct, with multiple illuminating ideas, but he didn't adhere at all times to standard English dialect, which is something I admire immensely. I guess it's because it defies stereotypes of blacks not knowing how to use standard English and speak well and utilize [a respected] vocabulary.

Cultural identity and societally-viewed identity, then, go hand and hand and should not be too far a skip from one another. One shouldn't have to split [oneself] into two, racially, to fit in or be accepted amongst one's peers. I should be able to say something in front of two different [ethnic] groups, and feel equally comfortable with them both.

Will a student fall to the pull of assimilationist pressure to let a dialect or native language recede in public life, or will that language become a powerful symbol of cultural identity and therefore be embraced and asserted with pride? For many students, at least at this stage of their lives, that question has no easy response.

What is significant here is that such moments reflect students attempting to create an acceptable sense of self (Fordham, 1999) within the pressures of a larger context and to function successfully in two cultural contexts. For teachers, the challenge is to "understand the *meaning* of [adolescent] linguistic practices" (p. 287), and to support students in maintaining a relationship to language that enables them to be "successful in two languages and two cultural environments" (Fordham, 1999; Villanueva, 1997, p. 78).

Language can also, students feel, be used to exclude each other. "When I am at a friend's house who has a different cultural background," one White student explained, "they speak a different language while I'm around. This is a form of segregation. It always singles me out. I feel uncomfortable, and not good. It is unfair, because if I spoke Hebrew or German in my house while I had a guest over, [the guest] would be uncomfortable as well." Similarly, students' accents or lack of linguistic skills can result in their being taunted or excluded (S. Lee, 1996).

Language may also be tied to a hesitant and fragile relationship to the drone of words that makes up any given day in a school, resulting in academic, social, and psychological difficulties: fatigue, confusion, insult, or disorientation. After a morning meeting in which his advisor had spent time helping the small group of students understand a recent tragedy in the community—the suicide of a former student—one young man from Russia, but attending school here, said to another teacher, "My advisor spent the whole time talking about dead people." Many of us for whom English is our first language can only vaguely understand the level of confusion and lack of comprehension some of our students may be experiencing on a daily basis, hour after hour, as teachers' and students' words fill the air with concepts, formulas, and observations.

And what of the wishes of these students' parents: Is Japanese or Russian or Tagalog or Spanish the language to be revered, to be held onto as the private language of intimacy, as Richard Rodriguez so eloquently describes in *Hunger of Memory* (1982), or is it to be set aside for movement into mainstream American life? And how does the student reconcile those yearnings of his or her parents with the day-to-day challenges he or she must confront alone in the English-speaking world of the classroom, the cafeteria, and the locker room?

SCHOOL

When our students pass through the doors of the school and our classroom each morning from their multiple neighborhoods and cultural backgrounds, what will they find? What will be the nature of their experience there?

In multicultural school communities, most students will find an uneasy coexistence and intermingling among students from multiple cultures. Multicultural school communities are, simply, more complex than are those school communities that are more culturally homogeneous. But they are also, potentially, much richer in experience for all of us. Several distinct challenges await students and adults in the school whose population includes students from multiple cultural backgrounds. Students whose cultural identity places them in the minority—no matter what their specific cultural identity may be—will face a series of challenges on a day-to-day basis in school, especially surrounding issues of finding a comfortable fit in a school in which many of the other students come from cultural backgrounds different from their own. Students in a cultural majority will have a responsibility to reach out to those in the cultural minority to create an inclusive community. And all students in the school community will face the challenge of "fitting together."

Students do not automatically build a cohesive multicultural community within the school, and much confusion exists among the students surrounding questions of integration, segregation, assimilation, and separatism. For some cultural-minority students who choose to integrate, developing close relationships with those in the cultural majority appears smooth and satisfying; others meet with less success. Still others feel a need to carve out a social niche that allows them to live a more public expression of their cultural identity, and sometimes the result of that choice is to construct more distance between themselves and others. For students in the cultural minority, finding a comfortable fit can absorb much of their emotional energy. For all of the students, there will be constant questions surrounding belonging. As minority-culture and majority-culture students work out the dynamics of their smaller and larger groups, there will be little constancy in the ways in which students work out a fit with each other.

The danger for any of our students is that the fit between the individual and larger community fails to develop, and the student moves into a zone of social and psychological isolation. Throughout their years together, however, there will be ongoing renegotiations of relationships among students and groups from multiple cultures as each answers the question: What am I willing or able to do to fit in? What am I willing or able to do to reach out? Ultimately, within the community of the school, will each student be able to find a "safe cultural space," a place that supports the natural expression of a student's cultural identity (Collins, 1991, quoted in Fordham, 1997, p. 83)?

Fitting In

Challenges surrounding each child's finding a comfortable fit in the school environment include establishing a workable sense of self and level of power in the community, establishing and maintaining a satisfactory peer group within or across cultural lines, and negotiating satisfactorily the ongoing process of students coming to know both themselves and others in the context of students from multiple cultures. They will need to be able to "[construct] an identity that, on the one hand, does not violate one's sense of 'self,' while, on the other hand, enhancing one's sense of fit within a given context" (Fordham, 1997, p. 91).

Establishing a comfortable peer group often involves students resolving issues relating to integration and segregation. On the one hand, many majority-culture students wonder why students in cultural minorities choose to, seemingly, self-segregate. As one White student remarked: "Why do students of color feel a need to separate themselves?" On the other hand, students in the majority culture who are more attuned to social dynamics around them understand that being a student in a culture that is a minority culture in the school must be difficult. White students and students of color feel that some White students can be less than welcoming, and this leads to separation by cultural identity whether one might choose it or not.

Among minority-culture students there is also a heightened self-consciousness about the process of affiliating oneself with peers. One Latina described feeling uncomfortable that she always sat beside other Latinas in class, but, she suggests, that's only natural if they are the students who are her friends, if they are the students who have accepted her. Another dynamic emerges as some minority-culture members choose and successfully accomplish integrating into a White peer group and in doing so seem to move away from others of their same cultural affiliation. This can leave lingering scars as students progress through the grades and find themselves thinking about the choices they or others have made and the ongoing social effects of those choices.

Inherent challenges of sociocultural maneuvering can be exacerbated in disturbing ways when issues of class or wider institutional dynamics enter the mix. In a tuition-based school, some White students wrongly attach notions of financial need to students in a cultural minority. The fact that some students feel this way, however, is a measure of the challenges involved in building a true community across cultural lines. Another danger lies in the fact that students in the minority or in the majority may feel that students in the minority have become, rather than full members of the community, more a reflection of the school's commitment to maintaining a diverse student body (Fordham, 1991) or to giving majority students the opportunity to learn of others dissimilar to themselves.

Students who are in a cultural minority in a school setting, just as do all students, yearn for close friends; a pleasurable social life; and a welcoming, psychologically comfortable environment. They yearn to have many points of view from their own cultural group expressed as a natural aspect of curriculum and discussions in their classes, and they want to be freed from the burden of being seen, ever, as a "spokesperson" for their cultural group or as an "example" in relation to a sensitive issue. They yearn to have others around them who "look like me" and who share a similar cultural perspective. All of these basic desires can be difficult for students to satisfy when the majority of those around them are those with cultural backgrounds different from their own. For some students of color in this predominantly White school, the choice feels like one between "sticking out" or becoming "invisible."

Left Out

In most cases, after a period of adjustment, students in a cultural minority build a relationship to the larger school community and to a smaller group of peers that satisfies their needs throughout their years of schooling. But what happens if this is not the case? For some students, the result can be a painful sense of isolation and alienation in what constitutes much of their day. For some students who cannot build and maintain a satisfactory sense of self and belonging in the school or classroom, social isolation can be deep and prolonged. Similar to other minority-culture students in predominantly White schools, some of our students openly explain that they and their parents have chosen to have them attend an academically rigorous school over a school that might provide them a more satisfactory social life, but such an explanation provides little succor to a student who is feeling left out or lonely for many of his or her days (Horvat & Antonio, 1999). One student, whose family had immigrated to the United States from Europe, explained that after several years she still did not feel part of the school. As a result, she described herself as a citizen comfortable across the world, but someone very sad inside. One Black student described himself as feeling like "the other" most of the time, unable to let down defenses long enough to show others the kind and gentle person he really was.

Such pressures, studies have shown, can take a toll not only on students' social life, but on their academic life as well (Steele, 1992, in Nieto, 1999). Needing to use energy to build a safe space in a culturally less familiar environment means drawing energy away from other areas of a student's life. Additionally, the failure of students to connect socially results not only in individual stress but can result as well in stress on the larger student body. Socially isolated students are disillusioned, vulnerable, and at times angry students. Isolated students can, understandably, take their frustrations out on those around them. Or students in the larger community who link some students' disillusionment to a responsibility to act in ways that are more inclusive on the part of the larger group feel a sense of failure as well. Those in the larger community have, in fact, they feel, failed to create a community.

In the face of such dynamics and with the specter always looming for social failure and isolation, what are students in the cultural minority willing or able to do to establish a workable fit in the school community, and what are students in the cultural majority willing or able to do to reach out? Aside from school-initiated activities, experience suggests that each student tends to decide this for himself or herself. On a daily basis, students in the cultural majority in our school do reach out to students in cultural minorities, in class and out. And at times that reaching out has taken unusually mature and thorough forms, as when one group of students led by the head of the student government designed and oversaw a yearlong series of "racial dialogues" to help create an inviting and inclusive environment in the school. Student leaders, who came from multiple cultural backgrounds, attended workshops on leadership skills and mediation techniques, organized a series of schoolwide small-group discussions, and used those meetings to engage the student body in looking at racial and cultural issues within the community.

Research and experience suggest, however, that it is usually those in the cultural minority who do most of the accommodating in order to fit in at school. For those in the cultural majority, it is easy to move on with life as usual, and to hang back rather than reach out to welcome students with less social base in the community. But internal and external pressures to fit in lead some minority-culture students to alter the way they look, dress, speak, and think. And when this is the case, what does that mean about those students' evolving sense of identity? One danger is that "the price of a good education, a [Euro-American] education, in short, was, and still is, the denial of one's . . . cultural identity. This is the price of entry to the middle-class" (Evans, 1988, p. 185, quoted in Fordham, 1997, p. 89). What about the young Black woman who reined in her hair, taming her spirit as well, to suit the prevailing social winds? Or the young Latino who turned red when his mother greeted him in Spanish? Or Asian students or other students of color who engage in laughing at themselves in order to "gain the acceptance of white" students (S. Lee, 1996, p. 93)? Such patterns represent "one-way accommodation," and this may place an undue burden on students (Nieto, 1999, p. 74).

As adults in the lives of our students, we must be vigilant about all of these social drifts and chasms, and we must structure our classrooms to be hospitable environments for all of our students, supporting comfortable and natural interactions among all of our students and helping them build a strong social base from which to experience their days at school. We need "to understand different cultural intersections and incompatibilities, minimize the tensions, and bridge the gaps between different cultural systems" (Gay, 2000, p. 12).

HOME AGAIN

As students return home each day, they take with them the effects of their experiences at school. As the natural process of human development moves them closer to adulthood, students also show the effects of their exposure to the cultural dynamics of their school. And each day they carry home the expectations of teachers, administrators, and peers. For some students, there will be a painful sense of a growing distance between them and their home, family, friends, and neighborhood. For others, there will be a heightened interest in home and the culture of home. For still others, there will be a wish to use an emerging knowledge to enhance the lives of those they love. Other students describe a strength that has come, despite the challenges they have encountered, as the result of becoming part of their multicultural school community.

Some students of color in our predominantly White school have described a sense that they "can't go home again." Their exposure to the world of a school far from the culture and neighborhood of home has resulted in a growing distance between them and family members, friends, and the neighborhood. Siblings and friends accuse them of trying to be White because they go to a "White" school. They lose friends, they lose touch, they go a different route. One young Black woman explained that since she had elected to attend this school, she had lost touch with all of her friends from elementary school and even some of her closest relatives. Changes within herself made her feel that she and they now inhabited two different worlds.

Partly as a result of the natural maturation and questioning tied to adolescence and partly as a result of their being in a school culturally different from their neighborhood, many of these students are actively engaged in developing a deeper understanding of the culture and values of their home and the cultures and values to which they have been exposed at school. And this results in their considering which paths best suit their emerging selves. For some this means rethinking key aspects of their lives, including the religion, values, or gender roles they inherited from the culture of home. Consider this Latina's observations as she weighs competing expectations of women:

> I don't think it is possible to separate gender from culture. As a Mexican woman I'm supposed to be the passive, yielding, weak woman. My first role begins as the daughter, the wife, then the mother. I cannot escape this role. The harder I fight to become a strong woman the harder this role tries to hold me back. My own family is trying to prepare me for my role as wife and mother. When I was little I remember asking my mother to teach me how to make "papas con huevo" (potatoes and egg), and she said she would teach me because that way I would be able to feed my husband when I got married. I only asked her to teach me so I would be able to feed myself. When I get married my husband will cook for me.

Another effect of the journey back home is students' using their education to gain a growing understanding of life at home. Sometimes that can result in confusion or discomfort. "We are starting to examine our parents' beliefs on race," observed one White student. "They are much more complicated than we thought. We argue with them, we know they think we are just young. If we don't agree with our parents, who do we agree with?" One Asian-American student recalled a visit from her grandmother when she was a child: "She had such narrow eyes, I thought she was squinting. I said, 'Go like this, Grandma,' and I opened my eyes as wide as I could. She tried, unsuccessfully. I laughed at her and said, 'No, like this,' demonstrating again. She couldn't do it. I wonder if it hurt her to have her granddaughter laugh at her for having Asian eyes."

At other times that growing understanding can lead students to a deeply satisfying feeling that they have gained a greater clarity about aspects of home they had lived with, but little understood, for years, a new way of seeing those they love and the surroundings of home. Their formal education has shed more light on life at home. One White woman living in a Latino neighborhood explained after reading *The House on Mango Street* (Cisneros, 1989):

> I used to think these buildings were ugly and out of place, but now I see the beauty in them, especially in the summer, when the vines wrap around the building. I never knew many of my neighbors. Most of them are Hispanic families that don't speak much English. There are also a few old men who always sit outside the buildings and feed the squirrels. Because now I sit on the front porch swing, I smile at the passersby whether they be jogging, walking the dog, or pushing the baby cart. The more time I spend in the front, the more I feel a part of the neighborhood.

Japanese-American students have described the power of learning more about the experiences of the internment camps during World War II. For one young man, lessons in school resulted in a growing pride in his Japanese-American identity, coupled with the wish to learn more of history, and a growing interest in talking with his grandparents about aspects of their own histories. For some students, their education has given them a broader understanding of what their parents and grandparents have endured in a racist society, whether that resulted in the internment of the Japanese Americans or the treatment accorded Blacks as they hail a cab or to Latinos as they attempt to make a purchase in a department store. And some students wish to move beyond understanding to action, whether in assisting elderly grandparents to tell their story or becoming engaged in activities to address attitudes and behaviors that have harmed those they love. In these instances our students' educations have brought them closer to those at home.

BRIDGING THE WORLDS OF HOME AND SCHOOL

Students coming together in multicultural school environments do not have an easy time making "one world." Knowing more about the significance and nature of students' journeys between home and school, as well as the effects of those journeys, can help us help our students bring together the worlds of home and school as well as the disparate worlds that enter the classroom with each of our students. To do so, we need to understand the overall cultural environment of the school and, thus, something of the ways in which our students may experience that environment; understand the challenges inherent in bringing together students from widely diverging cultures and neighborhoods; and create in our classrooms a common ground for all of our students—a place where we can bring ourselves and our worlds together.

In my own predominantly White school, I know that there will be many students for whom the journey between home and school will be negligible; one world reflects an almost seamless extension of the other. For other students, the distance they travel will create challenges for them at home and at school. Once in school, some students will find many who share their cultural assumptions; others will find few who share those perspectives. Some will almost automatically feel part of a larger community; others will wish there were more classmates, faculty members, and administrators who are more like themselves. Some will attach readily to a schoolwide curriculum; others will yearn for that curriculum to reflect more of the experiences they are familiar with or the histories they still wish to discover and understand.

Each of our schools offers a distinct cultural environment in which our students' daily lives and our work with them unfold. Understanding something of the nature of that cultural environment can help us better serve the students in our classrooms. In general, is there a particular dominant cultural perspective, or are there multiple cultural perspectives reflected throughout aspects of school life? How is that cultural ethos manifest? What is the cultural makeup of the student body, faculty, staff, administration? What cultural perspectives find reflection in choices surrounding policies, hiring, curriculum, pedagogy, scheduling, and extracurricular activities? Based on those profiles, which students may find it harder to feel part of the school culture? And in our classrooms, how are we extending the cultural profile of the larger school to make the experiences in our own rooms feel inclusive?

Beyond understanding something of the cultural ambiance of the school, we need to know that our students' educations thus far about race and culture and neighborhoods affect how we come together in the class-room. Their unfamiliarity with each other, their prejudices, and some of their lessons from home may function as an initial barrier against which our efforts unfold, and prevent them from providing for each other an easy and open acceptance and trust. Many of our students come into schools distanced from each other and unaccustomed to traversing those distances. Thus we need to help them move beyond the confines of their own worlds—whichever worlds those worlds are—and the narrowness of think-ing that may accompany the familiarity of those worlds.

Further, the journey each of these students takes between home and school will shape, in part, the way they relate to the school, their class-mates, and to us, their teachers. Discovering the research of Phelan, Davidson, and Yu (1993) on the journeys between home and school has helped me begin to understand a complex series of factors unfolding in my classes as students respond to readings, discussions, and each other. Their work has helped me to understand that it is not only the nature of each child's journey, but also the combination of my students' varied daily jour-neys that will make our coming together more difficult. The nature of stu-dents' individual journeys will, in part, make the group what it is. For stu-dents who travel each day between culturally dissimilar worlds, there will be ongoing challenges involved in trying to weave together two potentially divergent worlds, as well as the challenges involved in making a home for themselves in a school that does not automatically reflect the world of home. For students for whom the journey lies between twin worlds, the challenge involves expanding their understanding and acceptance of worlds that lie beyond the confines of what has become familiar. Both groups of students are being asked to move beyond what they know, what is famil-iar, what is comfortable, and what is easy; to stretch their worlds; to expand their capacity for understanding others' values, priorities, and needs; to understand other perspectives, other lives. The challenge for us as teachers is to facilitate that movement.

In the face of significant challenges that students may experience tied in one way or another to the journey between home and school, we need to create in our classrooms a space in which students on the one hand know they can be who they are, and on the other hand can engage in activ-ities that, as a group, enlarge their own worlds and bring together their dis-parate worlds. The choices we make in curriculum, the environment we establish in our rooms, and an understanding of our students' situations can help us to do that.

Our reading lists and the focal points of our courses should acknowl-edge and respond to the multicultural nature of our classes. Writers, artists, and scholars from multiple cultures should join us on a regular basis, through their works or as our guests—in person or through films or videos. The work of scholars from across multiple cultures should fill our walls: in our students' own work, in images, and in related information.

Curriculum has the potential for bringing us together; what we study as a group creates a common focus, a common experience, and, gradually, a common background among us. That potential renders it all the more important that our curriculum reflect a culturally broad and inclusive focus, to tell us more about our own worlds and to stretch our capacities to understand the worlds of others.

Our choices as teachers should encourage students to draw on their life experiences and their facility with multiple languages in their discussions, writings, and projects. As did James Joyce, Maya Angelou, or Hugo Martinez-Serros, students should be invited to write of what they know, to contemplate and extract meaning from the most familiar aspects of their lives. Students also deserve our praise and support for their abilities in multiple languages and for the translating skills and practices they may be employing as they assist members of their family or as they work on assignments for class. In this era of the global society and global conflict, we should support a broadening rather than a diminishing of students' powers with language, whether in asking students who are bilingual to be our readers for formal presentations of bilingual poems, or, as do many published writers, to draw on multiple languages as they craft scripts, fiction, poetry, or essays. As the great writers and scholars have done, we can encourage our students to look homeward, look inward, look to what is familiar, to savor, to write about, and to build on their growing skills in one or more than one language.

We can help students understand the ways in which their knowledge and understanding of language and dialect can broaden their opportunities in the future. And out of respect for the difficulty students may be experiencing in moving back and forth between multiple languages, we can employ a variety of strategies in our teaching. We can sum up main points periodically, or place points of direction, key points, or points of summation on the board—that is, draw on the visual as well as the aural in the fast-paced flow of language in lectures, readings, or discussions. And in the context of writing workshops for all students, we can work with each student throughout the writing process, in planning, organizing, executing, proofreading, and revising their creative and analytical writing.

We need to be knowledgeable about and understanding of the survival skills necessary for some of our students in crossing neighborhood and cultural borders in our towns and cities. In the face of these challenges, students need to feel that there should be no reason to sacrifice who they are in the world of home or in the world of school. They need to be able to enter our doors bringing all that they are and all that has meaning for them, as together we help them build their futures. We can help them see themselves as emissaries moving among multiple worlds and help them to understand the power that can accrue to individuals who know how to move successfully within multiple cultures. Dartmouth College feels that such "cultural competency" skills are so important they have stressed them in campuswide activities.

We need to be alert to a sense of connectedness or isolation in our students and to reach out to those who seem adrift. As students enter what may be the culturally less familiar environment of a new school—whether through a school transfer, family move, or the natural process of proceeding through the grades toward graduation—we can help them understand the importance of remaining connected with good friends from home or their previous school as they build relationships in the setting of the new school. At times students can use writers—as well as reading and writing themselves—as friends and companions to bridge difficult times. We need to familiarize ourselves with writers from a broad spectrum of cultures. We can mention writers students might like to read, encourage them to make use of the power of their own writing to explore what they are observing or experiencing, and encourage them to share that writing with us or with others. We need to speak with a school counselor, advisor, or administrator about students whose social situation remains a concern.

Our classrooms provide an ideal environment for facilitating among students positive experiences across cultural lines, in shared study, in informal interactions, in class discussions, or in group projects. Students should know that in these classrooms they can hold on to what they value and that they can share their own knowledge to contribute to our understanding of each other and the broader world. We betray these students before us if they do not feel they can build a satisfactory connection between their lives and experiences at home and those at school, or if we do not facilitate in the world of school a coming together of students from multiple worlds.

LEAVING

One spring day each year, it is to us their teachers, as well as to those at home, that our students are saying goodbye. And then we must pause, as we have so many times before, and ask ourselves: Has the journey between this student's home and this school worked? Have each of our students' journeys been good ones, or at least sustaining and fruitful ones? Can we and they allow ourselves a last exuberant leave-taking as they move, in the first tentative steps of young adulthood, in some ways beyond both home and school?

Experience has shown us that, overwhelmingly, the journey, if not an easy one, is one the students and their parents would choose again—or choose for the next generation. We cannot say this, however, for all of our students. There are those for whom the distance between home and school is simply too great to travel in wholeness day after day. Some of those students we have lost to the streets or to other schools. Or, even though they have remained with us, we have lost them into withdrawal and isolation. We have lost students for whom international cultural trauma in war was simply too great to overcome in an urban school thousands of miles from "home." We have lost students whose own parents had rejected the color of their skin as infants, and nothing we could do could reach beyond that sense of loss. And we have lost, in a certain way, students for whom the cultural adaptation they felt they had to make was so extreme that graduation became a type of Pyrrhic victory (Fordham, 1988). Such was the case for one young Black student. As she left us, she was headed off to a predominantly White university. Only time will reveal how she will fare on the next stage of her journey between home and school.

For most students, however, even after the challenges, the struggles, and the soul-searching, there is a reasonably triumphant day, that last day with us, as they look back with satisfaction and ahead with expectation. As one young Latina observed, "Going to [this school] has made me prouder to be Mexican. I have this new-found pride for my culture. My culture is a part of me and I refuse to give that up. Whatever success I acquire when I get older won't make me forget what I've been through, where I came from, what I had to fight to achieve that success." One young Black woman explained that although she had not assimilated, just about all aspects of her life had been broadened. For one White student, leave-taking meant the end of a partnership: "I guess this is the end of our partnership. It's certainly been a pleasure, and I learned a lot. I'm off now, and thanks for everything." Or this from one young Black man: "The film on Berkeley High School [Andrews, 1994] made me become more grateful and appreciative of what I've had the privilege to do every day, which was go to an excellent learning institution where I can be myself. I'm going to miss this place. I'm going to miss this community."

CHAPTER 2

The Presence of History

On a large screen at the front of the room, a videotape about the civil rights movement carries us into the past. But as White firemen pummel with hoses young Black women in cotton dresses, I feel the tension in this classroom, our own collective histories colliding under the water hoses in front of us. When the lights are turned back on, what will we now say to each other in this multicultural classroom? History covers us with a mantle impossible to throw off. Our classes unfold beneath its shadow.

In culturally homogeneous classrooms, history may recede, taken for granted out of a sense of familiarity. In the multicultural classroom, history stands sentinel. It watches us, it covers us, it has the power to taunt and divide us. Only with effort can we make history work in our own interest, make it allow us to build to some degree, a history of our own.

"The past isn't dead. It isn't even past." Classroom dynamics among students from multiple cultures underscore the truth of Faulkner's words. The past enters the classroom with us and with our students and hovers about our explorations. Significant moments or events from the recent or distant past inform both spoken and unspoken dialogues. The presence of history, at times quiet, at times overt and dramatic, shapes not only the nature and outcome of a particular class, but the way in which a course as a whole may be experienced by students or teacher. Will the lingering effects of the past—for better or worse—move aside enough to allow us to give life to our gestures among each other in the present? Sometimes yes, sometimes no. One of the primary factors affecting cross-cultural teaching and learning is the presence and weight of history.

THREE HISTORIES, A HOST OF HISTORIES

The past enters the classroom in the form of each student's and teacher's multiple histories. Each student and teacher brings to class three distinct, related, and overlapping histories—an individual history, a family history, and a cultural history in relation to racial and cultural issues. Thus a class of 20 students reflects the potential influence and power of some 40 to 60 converging, diverging, intersecting, colliding, or competing histories, and this can result in richly complex or difficult classroom dynamics. Students' multiple histories affect who they are and what they know, as well as how they experience themselves, each other, course materials, discussions, and us, their teachers. Understanding some of those lingering effects of history can enable us to think about and oversee our classes more knowledgeably.

Each student enters the classroom with his or her own unique individual history in relation to racial or cultural issues. Memories and lessons from childhood, experiences in years or days past, have influenced the attitudes, values, and behavior each student brings to the classroom.

Surrounding each student's own history lies the history of his or her family. To what degree has the family been affected by issues of race or culture? Are they prominent issues in the family or not? What values and attitudes have gone into the countless dialogues that weave the backdrop of the student's childhood? What attitudes and beliefs, prejudices, and biases have been modeled, taught, or handed down in his or her family? What have members of the extended family experienced historically?

Beyond each family history lies for each student a cultural history with its own defining moments. Has the student come from a culture whose members have generally experienced more or less access to power? Have those in the culture in the local, national, or global context been subjected to discrimination or persecution—or been linked to its perpetration? If so, when, why, how, and to what extent?

Indeed, a web of historical threads has been woven around us in any given classroom before the first "lesson" begins. The class will unfold amid the contours of those threads—some more resilient, some more binding than others.

Consider each of the following students' multiple histories as they enter the classroom one morning.

Lakeisha, a young African-American woman, comes from a culture that has faced significant, prolonged discrimination. Her own family has been profoundly affected by an act of racial violence when a cousin was brutally murdered by White racists. As an individual she has inherited the effects of the blows of history as they have shaped both her culture and her family life. Now, buoyant and animated, curious and eager, she attends a predominantly White school where, although her cousin's death was covered in the press, few of her classmates know of him. Every day she traverses two worlds—one predominantly Black, one predominantly White.

A few seats away, a young Jewish student. Ethan's cultural history is, for him, dominated by the memories and lingering effects radiating from the horrors of the Holocaust. His own family and the families of many of his friends count among their relatives victims or survivors. His Jewish history is a central facet of his life. He studies Hebrew, he is active in his temple, it has been made clear to him that it is essential that he remember the Jewish past. Now he is attempting to understand what that history means for him as he defines his own values and positions.

A few more seats around the circle, a young German. Gisella's cultural history, in the minds of some of her classmates, includes Nazism and the Holocaust. In reality, many of her classmates know little of her cultural, familial, or individual history. Her parents have recently immigrated to the United States, constructed new lives in America, and placed their children in, in some ways, one of its best schools. For this student, a double life: memories of Germany—and especially a Germany most of her classmates have never known—and the searching for a place in this new country. She is traveling a personal journey to define herself and her direction in the face of her memories and her present life. She feels deeply a resentment of those who know little to nothing of her Germany, but whose own individual and familial and cultural histories are tied to one particular event in the history of the country where she spent much of her childhood.

Around the circle farther, a young African-American student, gently soft-spoken, often quiet. I know little of Tyrone's family history. What emerges in class pertains more to his own—one facet of which is a haunting confusion and frustration over the invisible line drawn in his city between his neighborhood, which is Black, and an adjoining neighborhood, which is Latino.

And a few seats from him, a young Mexican American. Maria's cultural history is, in the minds of many of her classmates, one overshadowed by issues surrounding immigration. She has cared for her father for much of her young life and now feels the tug of home and family as she prepares to enter her first year of college. She herself is a bright, vivacious young woman pulled one way by the power of her traditional Catholic upbringing and another by the lure of free-thinking independence.

Near her, a young White student, brisk in her observations, a light touch to her words, confident. Jessica is part Scottish, part French, but who she really is, she says, is "an American." Her family history is one that, to her, is tied to what it means to be an American. "I am an American," she says in one discussion, "I'm proud of that."

Across from her, a young African American. His uncle is serving a prison sentence. He rarely sees his mother or his father. He is living temporarily with a Latino family. Aspects of his cultural, familial, and individual histories have been marked by moments, he says, are the way they are, because he is Black.

Beside him, a young Asian-American woman. Her family has immigrated from Vietnam and settled on the North Side of Chicago. Stories and memories of fleeing in boats, life in refugee camps, eating out of tins, and of personal loss on both sides of the Pacific fill her writing.

As a teacher, I do not know these histories as these students gather before me on the first day. They have emerged as a mosaic is created, piece by piece laid into the frame of our daily meetings. Additionally, part of their complexity in a classroom is that they take shape as a blend of students' actual histories gradually revealed and the histories that classmates posit onto them out of assumptions and stereotypes. Part of the challenge of our being together will be the confusion and the sorting out of what is real and what is imagined in the history and present-day reality of each of us. But I know now that each day these histories will to some degree define the shape of our time together. Students' individual, familial, and cultural histories have in part made them who they are, singly and as a group. Their histories and my own will in part determine what does or does not occur in this class over the months we share. Further, these histories are still emerging and being created, within and around each of these students, in school and beyond. The students are in the process of discovering their own and each other's histories and of coming to terms with what those histories, singly and together, mean.

MY HISTORIES, MYSELF

One powerful effect of these multiple histories is the way in which they become aspects of the self. Students' histories are tied to identity, how they see themselves and each other. They affect what students know and the perspectives that emerge from that knowledge; they are also still emerging. These histories' intimate connection with the self means they can be tied to strong emotions. All of these factors can affect students' interactions in the classroom.

As students themselves realize, the nature of the days and decades that lie behind us shape in part who we are. As one young Asian-American student explained, who she is today, has been brought about by the nature of her past. What has happened to her, her mother, and her ancestors has affected not only her life but who she is.

Further, students' relationships to those histories affect their sense of self. Some students look back on individual, family, or cultural histories with pride and delight, others with embarrassment or shame. And in this mobile, global society, some of our students come to us with such extreme histories that remembering or forgetting them may dominate their lives.

Conversations with students suggest that how they see their histories affects how they see themselves (Robert Merrick, personal communication, December 2001). The varying ways in which students experience their histories may also have a direct bearing on the way in which they relate to ideas or to others in the classroom.

How students see themselves and their own histories is also, in part, linked to ways in which those histories are entwined with the histories of others, especially as those others' histories represent greater or lesser relationships to power or abuses of power. In cases where oppression of those in an individual's culture has been extraordinary, as has been the case for Blacks and Jews, among others, that history may become an essential part of who one is (Berman, 1994).

Beyond shaping who students are, these histories in part shape *how* students know, *what* they know, and their perspectives on a host of issues. For example, some students' knowledge of particular aspects of history is something gained only through formal education. Other students sitting next to them, however, have learned about those moments through family stories or through their own experience. For one young Latino, writer Luis Rodriguez (1993) had captured what felt like aspects of the student's own history and his family's history in the pages of *Always Running*. As a result, the student felt he had "lived it," and thus, he said, he felt more connected to this work—and understood it better—than any of his classmates.

Students with personal, experiential knowledge of certain aspects of history may question the way in which others can really "know" those same histories or the ways in which they may speak of them. For one Black student this was the case during a discussion in which a White student made a joke about "the ghetto": "I'm sorry, but what the hell does he know about the ghetto? I grew up in the ghetto on the south side of Chicago. How dare he [denigrate] me and the people in my community, struggling, for a joke."

Students' histories also influence what they know. What routes through life have students' multiple histories taken them, and what has the family or the student himself or herself deemed important to know? From the multiple histories students inherit come a host of values and perspectives.

Moreover, students' own histories and their relationship to those histories are continually emerging, in part modulated by what takes place in the classroom. As students and teachers explore a range of texts and other materials as a course unfolds, concepts or stories touching in some way on students' histories may lead them to experience a growing pride, disillusionment, or anger related to their own history and thus to a greater or lesser degree of comfort with aspects of who they are. Texts on American race relations in the past or on the Japanese-American internment camps have unquestionably had this effect on students in our course on issues of race and culture, at times straining relations in the class between Blacks and Whites, at times bringing closer together Japanese-American students intrigued by learning more of their cultural past and interesting them more deeply in the stories of their grandparents.

All of the students in the room will need to manage the complex relationships between self and history as they explore ideas and engage in classroom discussions. The fact that these multiple histories are tied so intimately to who we are and what we know means that they can breed powerful emotions. Further, their relationship to that history is in flux and may be deepened or altered depending on how their histories are perceived by their classmates.

HISTORY AND YOU AND I

Beyond affecting students' identities and the knowledge they bring into the classroom, students' multiple histories also affect how they interact with each other and with us. Their multiple histories have the power to bring students together or to divide them, or to strengthen or weaken their relationship with us, their teachers. Their histories have the power to affect their most intimate relations as well as their behavior as a group. Especially significant will be the ways in which students from the dominant culture and students from minority cultures negotiate attitudes toward each other related to feelings about the past.

Generally, a sense of shared histories—whether those histories are individual, familial, or cultural—draws students into friendships and alliances. Similarly, differences in those histories can create a distance among individuals or groups of students in class. Such social alliances and distances, in turn, can affect how students relate during class: where they sit, positions they take in discussions, and support or challenges they provide for each other as a course unfolds. And this can lead to camaraderie, awkwardness, uncertainty, frustration, or tension within the larger group. These dynamics are especially noticeable in groups where some students see themselves as members of historically oppressed groups, and others identify with the dominant culture. "Sometimes I feel like I can't connect with people of a different race or culture," one White student explained, "because I haven't been subject to the struggles and prejudices that they have."

As students themselves realize, how we see our own history is also entangled with the histories—and how we see them—of others. As students explore texts and ideas that trigger questions about histories, a host of issues tied to power and politics may emerge. Students' discussions of history will lay bare differences in lives lived close to or far away from sources of power and lives affected little or to a great extent by prejudice, discrimination, or racism, and this renders such conversations considerably more complex. In their responses to course material and their resulting interactions with each other, students find themselves negotiating the relative positions left to them by their histories. One Jewish student identified with a question, relevant to his own life in this regard, posed by a character in a short story by Bernard Malamud: "My main question to people who are so anti-Semitic is the exact same question the Jewbird asks: 'Mr. Cohen, why do you hate me so much? What did I do to you?'" (1983, p. 152).

Related to such moments is also the discrepancy in which histories or moments in history we as a nation have chosen to remember and which ones we have not. Some students in class have powerful knowledge about incidents in history not even known by other students. And this, too, can create tension among the students.

Perhaps the most difficult effect of history on students as they interact with each other in the classroom is the prejudice it leaves in its wake. As one of our White students observed one day, "Sometimes it's history that causes racism." Repeatedly, students speak and write about incidents in their individual, familial, and cultural histories that have left them feeling uneasy and prejudiced about those in other cultures. And this will be an ongoing factor for teachers as they attempt to bring students together into a cohesive group.

In addition to the lingering effects of prejudice tied to familial or cultural histories, for some students, incidents occurring during their own childhood—as part of their individual histories—leave an uneasiness about others difficult to dismantle. In the quiet and privacy of course journals, students have described a growing awareness that particular moments in their past left them prejudiced about others. For one young White student, such feelings were traced to a time in which he was repeatedly accused of being a racist; he now realizes the incident left him with a fear of Blacks. Jewish students have acknowledged finding it hard to be accepting of German students, and students with German ancestry are frustrated with students who blame them for the deeds of others tied to the Holocaust. For one young woman whose family recently immigrated from Europe, unfamiliarity with Blacks had left her afraid to walk home along city streets. And some students describe being uneasy simply with the "difference" of those who, by virtue of students' knowing few individuals across cultural lines, are unfamiliar to them. One young White woman's story of a Black friend's experience in a White-ethnic enclave of Chicago captures vividly the divide among the young forged in history: "One of my friends is black. He went to Bridgeport and went into a restaurant. They told him when he walked in the restaurant, 'We don't serve niggers.' And he said to them, 'That's cool. I don't eat niggers.' So with that smart remark they sat him at a booth. He ordered chicken and when it arrived, he stabbed it with a knife and walked out."

In class, some students, tired of navigating the cross-cultural tensions that surround them, lean on personally constructed versions of cultural or familial histories to strike out at the source of their discomfort: "If you don't like it here, why don't you go back to Africa or back to Japan or back to Puerto Rico?" or "My people made it, why can't yours?"

Students' individual histories with each other also affect the way they interact in the classroom. In classes where students have known each other in past years or in previous courses, their individual histories tied to racial or cultural issues may affect the way they interact in the new class. These histories may predispose students to gravitate to some students and pull back from others. For some students, memories of racial or cultural tensions or interactions in other settings in the school affect their reactions to each other in the new setting. In one situation, a young Black woman who was particularly politically astute and outspoken had alienated herself from a number of her Black peers by her stands on issues within the school. Another Black woman had alienated herself from other Black students through what her peers perceived was her assimilation into a group of White peers, a gesture that made some of her Black peers feel abandoned as she moved closer socially to White classmates. In another instance, a White student recalled tense cross-cultural discussions in a previous class and wondered how that would affect dynamics in the present class. For each of these students, tensions from their individual histories tied to racial or cultural issues influenced the way they related to others in their next class, whether in presentations, discussions, or their writing. Unfolding individual histories show all of our students that there are consequences for their remarks and behaviors, as the memories of previous actions follow them into the next year or the next course. As teachers, we inherit the complexity of these moments as the students enter our door.

The fact that students' histories are continuing to emerge also affects interpersonal dynamics in the classroom. What happens to them on a given afternoon or evening has the potential to complicate the cross-cultural dynamics of the group in the following days. Consider the moment recalled by a young Latino student during one class discussion. Walking home from school, he tells us, he heard a group of Whites in a car shout racial slurs and then heard the *click, click, click, click,* of the car locks as he walked by. How does that affect his return to his predominantly White school the next morning? Or consider the night when a White student, working at a fast food restaurant, was locked in a freezer by a Black man during a robbery. What about the effects of hours of televised coverage of the Los Angeles riots highlighting tensions between Black residents and Asian storekeepers, or of the ongoing violence between Israelis and Palestinians? As teachers, we must be prepared to understand, and to help students understand, the complex and sometimes contradictory emotions that may need to be navigated in such moments.

Although emerging individual histories can affect students' perspectives and behaviors at any time, one more predictable facet of the impact of emerging histories on high school students' lives is the way in which college admissions practices and affirmative action policies contribute to students' individual histories as they move through the college application process. For our students, the surface harmony and goodwill that exist across cultural and racial lines in class on an ongoing basis often develops undercurrents of confusion and tension as they check identity boxes on college applications, consult with college counselors or college representatives, and hear responses from the colleges during their senior year. According to one study, "Even if white students filled all the places created by reducing black enrollment, the overall white probability of admission would rise by only one and one-half percentage points" (Bowen & Bok, 1998, p. 36). But students themselves only experience the process through their own needs and desires. As college representatives or college counselors try to offer realistic information to students about students' chances of admission to various schools, their advice can have ripple effects beyond their own offices. Some White students experience that information—rightly or wrongly—as a suggestion that some students of color with "lesser" qualifications may be admitted before they will. Some students of color may be encouraged to highlight aspects of their identity that will augment the strength of their application; they face White classmates knowing that some colleges will favor their own applications in part because of their identity as a student of color; and they face the frustration and at times overtly expressed anger of some White students who learn that a student of color has been admitted to a college that has denied admission to them. Some students of color are left, at times, with the feeling that their own rightly won seats in freshmen classes are perceived by others as the result of a racist, unfair policy. This whole series of moments can lead to a sense of frustration, anger, unfairness, or confusion, the residue of which is brought into multicultural classrooms where students are sharing close quarters, ideas, projects, and discussions on a daily basis.

Students' multiple histories may also influence the way in which they work with us. Students' individual, familial, or cultural histories may result in an initial sense of comfort, uncertainty, or skepticism about working closely with us based on suppositions about our histories tied in part to our cultural identity.

Given the nature of moments lodged in and emerging from the multiple histories of our students, the task we have in bringing them across the deep-cut cultural lines surrounding them is formidable.

OUR HISTORIES AND THE CURRICULUM

Students' multiple histories affect how they approach materials in a course and how they are affected by them.

In some cases, students' histories predispose them to be curious about specific materials. For one young Asian-American student, the internment of his Japanese grandmother during World War II and the losses that followed in his grandmother's life left this student wanting information about the Constitution and individual rights as well as information on Japanese-American history. Students are also often excited to read works that will shed more light on histories they have begun to know through members of their families. Jewish students, for example, are often eager to read *Maus II* (1991), Spiegelman's "comic book" about the Holocaust, because they know it will help them further understand the events that made victims and survivors of grandparents and family friends.

The relationship between students' histories and course materials can also play out in the opposite direction, however. Students "tired of hearing about" particular events or histories or about circumstances not tied to their own lives may be reluctant to explore a work or may reject a work knowing no more than its focus. For some students tired of hearing about slavery or the Holocaust, just the mention of the subject elicits "Here we go again."

Students' multiple histories also affect the ways they actually experience materials and what they take from them. Students may connect deeply with a work based on connections they perceive between material and their own histories, or reject it on the basis of its lack of "fit."

For many students, the most powerful connections with material arise through finding that a work reflects in some way experiences tied to their own history, the history of their family, or the history of their culture. One Black student found this connection through reading an essay on cross-cultural relations: "The moment in this course that reaffirmed my beliefs was the *Cultural Etiquette* selection (Three Rivers, 1991). It was like someone put everything that I had experienced growing up, into a small packet." A White student whose great-grandfather had immigrated from Russia felt that Takaki's descriptions of immigrant Jews (1993) and the film *Hester Street* (Silver, 1984) were telling the story of his family.

For some students, connection with material emerges not because it reflects their own historical reality in one way or another but because it helps them understand more about lives and histories of those who are close to them. For still other students, texts, films, or discussions in class result in hearing stories similar to those they know exist in their own family histories but that are *not* being told because the family has chosen to remain silent about that aspect of their lives. Sometimes such moments in the classroom lead to students' being hopeful that they can learn more about the stories repressed in their own homes.

Although students are most often drawn to materials that speak to their own several histories, sometimes the familiar can be too close, too potent. In some cases, material explored in class makes too vivid the more hazy knowledge that students have gained about histories close to them. For one young White woman, this occurred as a classmate passed around his father's scrapbook containing pictures from the concentration camps. She found herself pulled between not wanting to see the grim images, but not wanting, either, to shut out a Jewish past. A young Black woman's response to Marlon Riggs's documentary (1987) on the origin and impact of stereotypes was so strong that she felt reluctant to draw on it in a subsequent paper and asked not to have to reference the work. Another Black student found Toni Morrison's *Beloved* (1987) too much to integrate psychologically at the time we were reading it and needed to put parts of it on hold. Latino students have sometimes found "Victor and David" (Martinez-Serros, 1988), a story of two Chicano brothers in Chicago, simply "too close to home." As a result, they have remained quiet in discussions in which they would have otherwise been key contributors. For some students, pieces that touch too close to their own histories put them, for whatever reason, in a position of knowing, thinking about, remembering, or confronting something they would rather not, and we need to respect that.

Just as many students may be drawn to—or strongly affected by— material out of historical familiarity, a lack of fit between text and a student's histories may create a wedge between the student and the material, or generate a strong reaction against the work. For one young Black woman, Arthur Schlesinger's perspectives on history in *The Disuniting of America* (1992) directly contradicted the teachings she had had on history at home:

> [Schlesinger writes about the study of history being used to help the self-esteem of people of color.] It's the other way around—to raise

your [Europeans'] self esteem. Africans built this country and waited on whites. I got the whole Eurocentric thing, but my mom counter-acted it when I got home. I never forget who I was or who my people were. I don't like this book or agree with what he's saying. People who don't know [themselves] . . . one point of view messes them up.

In the case of this young woman, the author of the text presented a world-view sharply divergent from her own, grounded in her understanding of her cultural history. Students may also be put off by texts or focal points that describe a world having nothing to do with their own.

Last, for some students, particular aspects of individual, familial, or cultural histories—and the practices tied to those histories—may have a direct bearing on the ways in which they can or cannot carry out an assign-ment. One young Asian-American student described his regret with having pressured his grandmother to speak about the grandmother's internment experiences as part of a research paper the student was writing. The stu-dent was later realizing that this was a painful period in the grandmother's history about which she had chosen not to speak. Another Asian-American student, whose family had immigrated from Southeast Asia, spoke of hat-ing a project, required a few years earlier, involving a family tree. Not only, he explains, was his family quite different from those of many of the other students, culturally it was neither appropriate nor acceptable for him to discuss the family history with his father.

Whether by virtue of their past or emerging histories, students are drawn into the works we cover in class or are distanced by them, we as teachers need to be attentive to what is occurring between each student and the material and why, in order that we may support, for each, a healthy exploration of ideas as well as vital membership in the class.

HISTORY AS WE TALK

Tied to who they are, what they know, and how they relate to specific materials in a course, students' multiple histories also come forward to affect classroom discussions.

Unavoidably, invisible lines form during discussions, creating partner-ships and divisions, support and tension. Shared aspects of histories invite alliances; diverging histories may distance students. On one day, young Black and young Jewish women experience closeness over an article on the stereotype of the "Jewish American Princess" (Beck, 1998): "I never knew Jewish women faced that," said one young Black woman. "I never knew what that [stereotype] meant. These young Jewish women [in the essay] also know what it means to be ridiculed." On other days, the young Black student who lives apart from his family spars with the young White woman who is "proud to be an American." Black students and Jewish students grow hostile with each other over the lingering effects of slavery and the Holocaust. The young German writes continually in her journal about the resentment she feels toward her classmates' attitudes about Germany, repeatedly emerging in discussions of the Holocaust.

Students' varying relationships to history, however, make for rich discussion and debate, ones that are complicated and deepened by those very histories. As we read, for example, *Maus II* (1991), I approach our first discussion with some hesitation. I know that many of the Jewish students are excited about the work. But I also know that a German student in the class has been angered by her classmates' attitudes toward Germany and has found discussions of the Holocaust particularly unsettling. As our discussion unfolds, one young Black woman says this is the first time she feels she has really understood something of the Holocaust. "When the psychiatrist says 'Boo!'" she explains, "that made it so real for me—all of the fear, all of the fear." Some of the Jewish students find the work brilliant; others are offended that such momentous history can be cast into the pictures of cats and mice in masks. One young Jewish woman says she is unable to sleep for nights after she reads it. It is horrific to her. It is a nightmare. It has brought to life her own family's and culture's suffering in a particularly personal way. In each case, one or more of the histories of these students affected how they encountered and responded to the text and the position they took during discussions. The day we discuss *Maus II*, the young German woman is absent, but I'm not sure why.

As students engage in such discussions, stories that emerge from their own histories may be brought forward and deepen our understanding of materials, issues, and each other. Stories growing out of students' own histories, the histories of those in their family, or the histories of those in their culture are often offered up, becoming stories that teach. Such stories also contribute to recognizing specific histories, and thus can provide another important function. They "enabl[e] those inside [a particular culture] to hear them acknowledged by those outside and enabl[e] those outside to hear them told by those inside" (Feinberg, 1998, p. 189).

One year, a young Latina emerged as one of our resident "storytellers." Regularly during discussions, she would announce, "I have another story to tell," and within the next few minutes her story, whether on her grandparents' experience of farm labor or on gender roles at home, would have wound its wisdom around us all.

Rich, personal stories illuminate texts, concepts, and lives, and the students know it. In one instance, an Asian-American student described how a Black student's story from childhood involving racism among White children—a racism fostered by parents—had enabled her to understand much more clearly Gordon Allport's concepts on the formation of prejudice (1958): The young Black woman had recalled, "I was at my cousins's, who live in a mixed area. They have a daughter 5 or 6 who used to play with White kids. One day the kids came to the front door instead of the back door [and said,] 'My mother told me there were niggers here, and we didn't want to run into the niggers.' They didn't know they were talking about us."

Exploring our shared history—what we share across cultural or racial lines—may initially unite us. And exploring our separate histories may produce not only understanding but tension and uneasiness. But as Freud so well understood, it is often the unique history we carry within us—not a shared history—that to a great degree shapes our attitudes and behaviors. Thus these unique histories become a powerful force in our collective lives. We may all identify with the complexities and richness of mother-child relationships in Amy Tan's *The Joy Luck Club* (1989). But until we can understand as well something of the characters' unique responses and behaviors that originate in specific aspects of Chinese history and culture and immigrant family circumstances, we will not be able to narrow the distances that separate us from them. Similarly, our students' remarks, behaviors, and interactions emerge not only from what they have in common with others in the group, but from what they have not had in common, what is theirs alone. The uniqueness of responses emerging from students' singular histories makes those responses sometimes harder for other students to understand. Supporting students' own stories as they emerge naturally in discussions, however, not only supports individual students but facilitates understanding across cultures among members of the class as a whole.

Unavoidably, conversations growing out of and related to students' histories are richly complex. Discussions about texts or concepts that touch on students' histories have the potential to generate strong emotions, to draw students together, or to move them further apart. Some students delight in such conversations even if they are complex, others are uneasy entering into such conversations, and some dread the conflict that may emerge. Some feel they cannot relate to what others are saying; others take offense at remarks in what may be sudden and unpredictable ways. For some there is the importance of sharing a story; for others, there is the importance of not sharing, of, for whatever reason, remaining quiet, holding onto silence about the past.

Further, I myself am unsure how these students will accept an exploration of moments or issues grounded in history from me, a White Southerner transplanted north, a woman whose family was biregional, and a woman whose life is what it is because of multiple types of relations between Whites and Blacks in the Jim Crow South.

Yet, as difficult as it can be at times, it is not a bad thing, the visits of all those histories. Students come away from such classes with a broader understanding of themselves and each other and their own and each other's histories, as well as the power of history in the present. For some students, the visits of history mean developing a deeper relationship with their own history. For all of the students such visits mean that those histories are coming alive, are kept alive, among us. They cannot, they will not, be lost, "disremembered," as Toni Morrison (Benson, 1987) has said. And as we wrestle with the legacies of those histories, we build a history we ourselves can share.

PEDAGOGY AND THE POWER OF HISTORY

What do all of these aspects of the power of history in the multicultural classroom mean for our choices as teachers?

A few days ago, a colleague called me into her room to see a passage written by one of her students. A White student, chagrined by Leslie Marmon Silko's observations in *Ceremony* (1977), had described the author as racist, indicating, essentially, that he wanted nothing more to do with this writer. In fact, Silko is ultimately creating a vision of unity that weaves threads from the Philippines across the desert of New Mexico to uranium mines, bomb tests, and the healing spirit of sand paintings, involving events that shatter lives and yet bring lives together. Silko's story urges us that we must learn how to be together as one people—Asians, Native Americans, and Whites.

But for this student, threats to his own values preclude his being able to make the cross-cultural leap necessary to see Silko's vision and values from the writer's own perspective as Native American.

Such was the case in one vivid instance in our class on issues of race and culture. Prompted by the urging of several young Latinas who had read the book, as well as critical attention to the work, one year I offered Luis Rodriguez's *Always Running* (1993) in a section on Latino writers. The young Latinas told me as they recommended the text, "This book tells it like it is, Ms. D." The book is graphic, violent, the story of a young man's gang life in Los Angeles and, years later, his attempt to halt the movement of his son into that same life in Chicago. But as our first discussion of the book began, in the opening comment, a White student said, "This book confirmed every stereotype I've ever had about Latinos."

In both of these moments, as one student encountered Silko's Navajo views on ranching, and another encountered the violence of young Latino gang members, these students' own histories—and the values and biases that accompany those histories—predisposed them to reject views that directly challenged their own way of thinking and their own value systems.

In the conversation on *Always Running*, the young student's opening remark rendered movement beyond that position almost impossible in a general discussion, for a number of reasons. The student had positioned herself in a mode of resistance. Her remark had immediately alienated Latino classmates who knew of both the complexity and the tragedy surrounding the phenomenon of gang life. There is no denying that the behavior recorded throughout the memoir is violent, illegal, and difficult to understand for those far removed from its context. For some of the Latino students, the life Rodriguez describes was very close to home. They feared for friends' lives and futures, and some had already attended far too many memorial services for friends who had died as part of that life. For these students, the book had spoken directly to their histories. Expecting those students, already in a cultural minority and also a numerical minority in the class, however, to provide a comprehensive context for students removed from such a context would have put an unfair and impossible burden on them. In that moment, in the midst of a discussion that had already fractured the group along cultural lines, it was equally impossible for us teachers, given the psychological tone of the class, to draw a full enough picture of these young gang members' social and political contexts to render understandable how such a life choice is made. Neither the students who did possess an understanding of the factors that can lead to such choices nor we teachers were in a position to convey effectively that complexity, in the midst of that discussion, to the student who had raised the objection. And so the conversation as a whole failed to take us closer to understanding a series of lives, choices, and issues emerging from another culture.

The following year, haunted by that moment, I took a different approach to *Always Running*. Prior to our reading the memoir, my partner screened a video clip on gang violence (Bendau, 1992; Tatge & Lasseur, 1992). It is a difficult film to watch. Young men the age of our students— as well as young mothers—speak of their Los Angeles streets as a jungle. They remember the legacies of fathers, longtime members of neighborhood gangs. They speak of a lack of belonging, a lack of power. A gun, however, one young man tells us while waving an automatic rifle, offers him power in a life he describes as "a war." After the film, students explored the reasons these young people have offered us for their choice to join a gang. Just as Rodriguez has depicted in *Always Running*, these young men suggest to us in their stories that gangs are not the problem, they are a solution. With the film as backdrop, the students were now invited into Rodriguez's memoir. The voices of the young men and women in the film took our students into the social, political, and psychological context that gives rise to their choice to become members of gangs. This time, White students and Latino students were broadly engaged in conversation about the memoir.

With images from the video still fresh, our students were now able to travel with Rodriguez through his life on the streets, witness him turn to writing as a way out, and then face the loss of his son as the son, years later and half a country away, repeats the choice of his father to turn to gang life. Because this time the students entered the memoir aware of the context of these young people's choices, they were able to understand, even though they did not accept as "right," the choice of these young people. Aided by the video, students whose individual or family histories precluded their having knowledge of these social factors were able to move into this memoir and allow themselves to try to experience it through the eyes and lives of those who live it; the memoir and the lives within it were now less alien, less provocative, less easy to dismiss. Students whose individual and family histories meant that the types of moments in the film were all too familiar were moved to draw on those histories, share their experiences, and broaden our understanding of the film. Unlike the year before, when the White student simultaneously opened and in some ways, closed, a potentially rich discussion of issues surrounding gang life, this time our discussion was full and multifaceted, both sympathetic to the feelings of entrapment of young people who see no other options, as well as thoughtfully skeptical or critical of those who choose a violent path in the face of that entrapment.

By the end of this discussion, because it was not foreclosed prematurely, we were able to gain insight into a series of cultural issues that are not only compelling in their own right, but that also, in part because of our diverging histories, have the potential to divide us in the classroom.

What such moments suggest to me is the following: As teachers, we need to recognize the power of history in our classroom. We need to acknowledge and discuss its power and complexity with our students. We need to make curricular choices that allow students to find their own and others' historical perspectives in course materials and to vary those perspectives as a course unfolds. We need to help students understand the ways in which our histories may affect our relationship to the materials we encounter and the conversations we have with each other. And we need to support the students in their struggles to understand their own and one another's multiple histories. In this way, we can use history, often a factor that can pull us apart, to help bring us together.

Respecting the power of history in the multicultural classroom, I favor attempting to move students into an author's or scholar's world through establishing a context for the students, guiding them across the cultural divide. And from within the perspective of the author's culture—albeit as a visitor—we can begin to explore the perspective that will flow from that writer's position. This can be done with a related film or with an introduction to the writer's life, experiences, or point of view. Invited in that manner into a writer's or scholar's point of view, students themselves often take on, as a challenge, wanting to understand that perspective. Then, as they enter the text, they are assembling the pieces of the writer's perspective along with the author.

Coming too rapidly to perspectives—grounded in histories—that are contrary to students' own or that are confrontational may leave students feeling threatened by the challenge that those perspectives provide, not only to their own long-held assumptions but to those of family and friends who have shaped those perspectives. In those instances, "healthy" psychological defenses become mobilized to disarm the threat, and as part of that disarmament, students will reject the writer and his or her view. The more I have worked with the cross-cultural teaching of literature, the more I have come to rely upon gradually helping students move step by step from perspectives grounded in one history or culture to perspectives grounded in another. To do so, I try to take them into aspects of history and culture before a given author speaks directly to them, to create a context, an invitation, to preempt the threat that may render them defensive and, out of that protective posture, to shut out, reject, and lose the value of this voice.

In teaching *Always Running,* the second choice of pedagogy worked because "education" preceded that moment in which a student's defenses were triggered by information that overwhelmed on some level her view of the world, information that was too far removed from her own reality to understand, or too threatening to allow for a psychological equipoise suitable for engaging in an open discussion. Once students' defenses are mobilized, it is much more difficult for students' or teachers' efforts to move beyond that natural psychological barrier to allow education to take place. Understanding the nature and role of students' diverging histories in mobilizing their defenses as they approach materials or as they engage in discussions can enable us to make pedagogical choices that will allow our students to remain open to an exploration of diverse points of view long enough to hear them, think about them, discuss them, and make a more informed judgment about them.

At the beginning of a course or a class now, my students and I talk of histories. We bring the presence of history into the open. And we talk of how hard it is, partly because of our different histories, to encounter points of view unlike our own or to engage in cross-cultural discussions. Our conversations about the power of diverging histories set up a different expectation in the students: This is hard, I will try to do it. Building on this expectation, we can enable students to take on the challenge of wanting to understand something complex and to understand it not in the context of their own world (and therefore as a potential threat), but in the context of this writer's world. Then values in Luis Rodriguez's world of young gang members or Leslie Marmon Silko's world of the Navajos can be viewed and understood not as a personal threat but, in the context of the writers' own worlds, as a form of survival.

CONCLUSION

At times I am overwhelmed by the complexity and effects of submerged or emerging histories in the multicultural classroom. The power of history to affect individual students and the group, as well as the work we had envisioned for any one day, is significant. Sometimes, for me, the weight of history or the tensions emerging from histories that collide in the classroom are almost insupportable. But then I'm privileged to see a moment when history comes alive for students in the best sense of that word. Or I am deeply moved by a moment when students are trying so hard to move beyond aspects of history none of us would choose to repeat.

Can we escape the power of our multiple histories in a classroom? Would we want to?

In the midst of creating our own histories and the history of a class, we are visited in the classroom by other histories close and distant. But caught in the swirl of merging or colliding histories, I am reminded of artists who have gazed on the past, ancient and recent. They, as well as these students, help me to understand the visits of history.

Writers as distant and different as Sophocles (1977) and Toni Morrison (1987) knew that the presence of history is a persistent force across cultures and eras. Whether giving us stories of ancient Greek kings or 19th-century American slaves, they knew that the histories of individuals are intertwined with the histories of families and the histories of cultures. They knew also that there is something compelling about those histories visiting us, invited or uninvited, quietly, stealthily, violently, intruding as we go about our lives. And they knew that history affects who we are, what we know and do not know, how we connect with others and the spaces around us, how we talk with each other, how we approach and learn about our lives and our world in the present. They knew we are ambivalent about it, split in our desire between wanting to forget and needing to remember. They knew that histories' visits leave us with revelation, pain, and mystery. All of this may be played out in a classroom of students from multiple cultures.

These writers suggest that we cannot escape history. So do the students who gather before us from the multiple cultures that make up the United States today. For one young Asian-American student, our being able to be together, coming as we do from such different histories, was, in her mind, tied to discovering aspects of history—or experiences—that we share.

As the bell rings on each new class, in order to help the students, I must be knowledgeable and open about the limitations or advantages allotted me by virtue of my own several histories as well as knowledgeable and open about the power of the histories each of these students asserts or endures, and the way those histories may support or derail the best intentions for a class. But knowing that history will come and will remain among us, we can experience it as a rich dimension of our time together.

CHAPTER 3

The Role of Racial or Cultural Identity

When you know somebody's race, what do you know? Virtually nothing. You add to it all the stereotypical information and the baggage, but you don't know anything about that person just because you know race.
— Toni Morrison

To say that ethnic identity is socially constructed is not to say that it is somehow unreal, to deny the complexities of our own positionality, to claim that these are not differences that make a difference.
— Henry Louis Gates, Jr.

When it comes down to it, race does and doesn't matter.
— a White high school student

A young Latina craves reading Latino/a authors as she moves toward adulthood. A young Black woman says in a group discussion that she wishes she were White. Other students don't know how to respond. A White student asks of his Black classmates during a class discussion: "What do I call you?" A young Asian-American woman rues the fact that there are so few students who "look like me." All of these instances reflect students engaging in aspects of developing or understanding racial or cultural identities in a multicultural school community.

Partly the natural result of maturation and partly the result of pervasive consciousness and divisiveness tied to racial and cultural identity in this nation, as students from multiple cultures gather in schools, they wrestle unavoidably with "Who am I?," "Who are you?," and "Who are we in relation to each other?" Sometimes those questions are posed openly in conversations. Sometimes they emerge more subtly, or sometimes they remain unspoken, their presence felt amid the countless exchanges among classmates and teacher in the multicultural classroom.

58

Although adults may not be so quick to say it, our students know that "race does and doesn't matter." Our students bring into schools the effects of living in a racialized society. Although many critics of multiculturalism reject any emphasis on racial or cultural identity and in fact see its growing importance as a threat to national unity, those identities are already powerful factors in our students' lives when they enter schools and classrooms, and they can affect in deep and lingering ways what unfolds there. Another factor involved in the complexity of cross-cultural teaching and learning is the role of racial or cultural identity.

Students' attitudes and behaviors toward each other are tied to the effects of living in a society in which children gradually come to understand not only themselves and their own racial or cultural identity, but come to understand themselves in the context of "the other," and the questions, distances, and judgments that may arrive with that knowledge. As Beverly Tatum has so richly explained in *"Why Are All the Black Kids Sitting Together in the Cafeteria?"* (1997), many of the dynamics we observe in schools and classrooms are tied to the process by which students develop racial identities in a culture that has, throughout its history, placed an emphasis on racial identity.

Aspects of racial and cultural identities can become, at times, central for our students and for us as teachers, from the time we call roll until they leave us. They influence how students perceive themselves and how they perceive and interact with others—those within their own culture and those in other cultures. And they influence how our students experience and respond to the materials or the pedagogies through which we engage them.

MY NAME, MYSELF?

One series of issues tied to racial or cultural identity that emerges in the multicultural classroom surrounds the nature of names. One of the most basic, most emblematic aspects of our identity is our name. Many of the students who enter our classrooms carry significant aspects of their identities and their histories in their names. Their names may reflect aspects of familial or cultural pasts and values. Some of our students' names tell stories, some speak of belonging, some—in the minds of students—speak of neighborhoods. Students' names may speak of continuity or breaks with cultural pasts.

Classroom dynamics surrounding this aspect of identity include the importance of both given and family names. For some students, the origin and meaning of their given names represent deep ties to parents when mothers or fathers have selected with great care names associated with values or history embedded in the family's culture. But for students from cultures not broadly represented in a given classroom or from cultures with which other students are less familiar, the beauty and meaning of a name may be dimmed in the student's own eyes—at least temporarily—by the effect of its unfamiliarity among students whose own names are more familiar. Such moments prompt some students to wonder with envy or resentment: Why isn't my name more like the names of my classmates or friends?

While some students carry names deeply embedded in aspects of their culture, other students have inherited names changed to fit the needs of parents or grandparents wending their way through the challenges of immigration. "Our name used to be Epstein," explained a young Jewish student in one discussion. "My grandfather changed it. He thought it would be better for us when we came to this country." Students then inherit a clear symbol of one form of disconnection with part of their own familial and cultural past, and the stories linked to the moments surrounding the decision to change the family name are indices of values stressed by the immigrating family.

Students enter our classrooms with varying relationships to this aspect of their identity, and the origin and meaning of their given and family names may lead to moments of rich and complex personal explorations, as when one cluster of students shared stories of the situations that had prompted each of their families to change the family name. They may also lead to moments of awkwardness or humiliation. Writers Sandra Cisneros (1989), Hugo Martinez-Serros (1988), and Frank Chin (1991) each describe, in their fiction, incidents in which the use of the names of children of color by teachers or peers have altered the way the children experience them. So, too, potentially, in the lives of our students. In the context of institutions in which children come together from multiple cultures, a student's name may become a source of embarrassment or pride. For one young Black woman, the powerful and poetic meaning of her name was lost as its sound among some of her White peers cast it as "ghetto," a designation she felt the name had now placed on her as well. Mispronunciation, comments, or ridicule by teacher or classmates, a tittering among other students when the name is called—all can contribute to a sense of unease on the part of the student in relation to this aspect of his or her essential self. In one poignant series of moments, a young Black student spoke for the first time openly and with great pride about the Swahili origin and meaning of his name, given by his father and tied to the father's wishes for his son's journey through life. What had moved him to speak of his own name was hearing a Japanese-American guest panelist speak of rejecting one of her names—tied similarly to family and cultural history—out of the embarrassment it caused her around Whites.

WHO AM I?: EMERGING RACIAL AND CULTURAL IDENTITIES

Students almost by definition reflect identities that are emerging and in flux. Beyond the names by which they identify themselves, our students are exploring and trying on identities even as they are constructing them. Racial identity development theorists suggest that in a society where racial and cultural identity has significance, part of the process of constructing an identity includes the construction of a racial or cultural identity (Helms, 1990, 1995; Tatum, 1997) that develops alongside other psychosocial aspects of the self. That process occurs in stages and can affect at any given time the way an individual feels about his or her own identity and culture as well as the identity and culture of others. Because of the historically unequal distribution of power in this nation, that process will unfold differently for Whites and for persons of color.

The roughly identifiable stages that constitute the development of a racial or cultural identity have been described in racial and cultural identity development models. Originally developed in relation to Blacks and to Whites (Helms, 1990, 1995), more recent research has led to describing racial and cultural identity development in relation to Latinos (Casas & Pytluk, 1995), Asian Americans (Sodowsky, Kwan, & Pannu, 1995), and biracial individuals (Kerwin & Ponterotto, 1995). Another model focuses more generally on the development of ethnic identity in adolescents (Casas & Pytluk, 1995; Phinney, 1993).

Although racial identity development theory has long been familiar to academics and to professionals in counseling fields, Beverly Tatum, then dean and professor of psychology at Mount Holyoke College, understood the ways in which aspects of emerging racial identities are relevant to dynamics in schools and classrooms. Closely attentive to her own students' observations and writings, Tatum realized that a knowledge of racial identity development could be helpful to educators and to students themselves in understanding broadly experienced culturally related phenomena in schools. Her resulting writing bridged the gap between research and theory and the classroom. Beginning with a seminal article in the *Harvard Educational Review* (1992) and later through her widely acclaimed book *"Why Are All the Black Kids Sitting Together in the Cafeteria?"* (1997), Tatum showed that understanding aspects of racial identity development can help students and adults who work with them understand more about themselves and their interactions with each other, and therefore, potentially, approach more thoughtfully the ways in which they work and play together.

Countless classroom moments reveal glimpses of students developing and coming to terms with their own and each other's racial or cultural identities. What is clear in multicultural classrooms is that our students are moving between degrees of comfort and discomfort with their own identity and their own identity intertwined with the identity of others. Some students express a curiosity about what it would be like to have a different racial identity; other students reveal moments clearly tied to contemplation of the meaning of racial or cultural identity. Developing a racial or cultural identity prompts enough thought that one White student suggested it requires a special kind of energy, energy that could be used in other ways. Our students' awareness of their own or each other's emerging racial or cultural identity is apparent in their interactions, their discussions, and their writing.

Emerging Identities: White Students

Consistent with identity development models describing White identity development (Helms, 1995; Tatum, 1992, 1997), many White students in multicultural schools are moving from a position in which they lack awareness of Whiteness tied to race, lack the knowledge of privilege that attends being White, and lack an understanding of Whiteness as it may be seen by others, to a reconceived notion of Whiteness.

Initially White students may downplay race as it involves themselves or others. Our White students frequently see themselves as having no cultural identity. Such perception is grounded in seeing Whiteness—in a predominantly White culture or institution—as "normal" and individuals of color as "different." They also may not "see" the racial identity of others. As one young White student observed, "I never think of my friend as black." This particular relation to Whiteness and to the racial identity of others results in several issues for White students. Such a position obscures White students' sense of their own culture as it is experienced by those in other cultures, especially those in cultures of color. And it prevents them from understanding the privilege that has attended being White in a race-conscious, White-dominant society.

Classroom discussions or incidents related to race and culture, however, may move White students in the direction of seeing Whiteness through the eyes of others, especially students of color, and this begins to move them toward a new relationship to their sense of self and to their sense of others. One of our White students recalled a moment when that had happened for her: "I never thought of [the Black boys in the pool where I was a lifeguard] as a color, and I was shocked to find that people looked at me as a color. It was a rude awakening." As White students' awareness of Whiteness deepens, they may experience discomfort or guilt over Whiteness or a fear or resentment of people of color. Our White students have regularly expressed a sense of "White guilt" or a guilt tied to the advantages of being White, even feeling "trapped" in being White. They also express feeling "sick of feeling guilty." Other White students, responding to a sense of discomfort over Whiteness, express resentment toward, or a feeling of having to prove themselves to, classmates of color.

As White students' consciousness of their identity deepens, they also begin to gain some idea of the power of Whiteness in a predominantly White culture. One of our White students suggested that without doing anything, Whites have what they need from the beginning. Another White student explained that she had experienced a simultaneous awareness of her own privilege and the lack of privilege accorded to others on the basis of race. This was vividly clear in a moment she described after spending several hours waiting in line at the county courthouse: "I was standing with a number of people of color and we got talking. I knew that I had 'gotten off' my traffic violation and none of them had. I knew that that was about [racial bias in] the criminal justice system in this country. And I don't know what to do about it."

Once White students do become more aware of Whiteness as it has often been seen or experienced by those in cultures of color, as well as the nature and effects of White privilege, they must come to terms with that awareness. For some, this new awareness results in a reconception of the self in one's society—no small step for adolescents already spending considerable time and psychic energy focused on unsettling questions of identity. For Whites, therefore, schoolroom discussions or interactions may move them in subtle or dramatic ways from a sense of "racelessness" to a knowledge of "being raced," and the societal benefits that may or may not accrue with that identity.

By the end of their high school years, many of our White students remain wedded to unexamined dimensions of Whiteness, especially Whiteness as seen through the lenses of those from cultures of color. Others are wrestling with the management of White guilt, the privileges associated with Whiteness, or with a resentment toward those in other cultures whom they blame for their own sense of discomfort. Still others, as they begin to understand their Whiteness and its fuller meanings, have involved themselves in addressing directly issues of injustice tied to racial or cultural identity. They have become what Tatum refers to as "allies" (1997, p. 108). In one instance, White students and students of color organized a club to explore issues related to race and culture in their own lives and in the school community. Becoming part of a coalition of students from multiple cultures, White students in the group had not only internalized a reconception of Whiteness, they had become, with their classmates of color, instruments of change, leaders involved in thoughtful community action in their school.

Emerging Identities: Students of Color and Biracial Students

Students of color, too, experience a shift in the way they regard themselves and others as they construct a racial or cultural identity (Helms, 1995; Tatum, 1992, 1997), and that movement takes them generally toward dismantling the effects of racism as it affects how they experience themselves and, related to that, from lesser to greater confidence in embracing racial or cultural identity.

Consistent with racial or cultural identity development theory for people of color, some of our students of color have described having, at one point, a sustained identification with the dominant culture. Some Latino and Black students have described seeing themselves for extended periods of time as "White" or have articulated wishes to change the color of their skin to white.

One or more experiences with racism, however, often move students of color into a deepening sense of identity. Some of those moments are powerful enough to remain prominent in our students' memories for many years. One young biracial woman, prompted by a question on a college application essay, recalled a series of such moments. Her first-grade year, spent in the South, yielded experiences, she said, that she would spend many years trying to forget. Told by White children at school that she could not join them in play because she did not look like she fit in, she spent many hours alone. Eventually she made her own place to play, in her room at home.

One young Asian American explained, "It's hard to realize you are different from others. Being a minority I think that one's [outlook] on life changes every second, feeling outraged at one moment, but complacent the next. Growing up in a society where one wants to fit in, it is hard to take a step back and realize that you are different from the rest."

As students of color come to embrace their racial identity more fully, they may move into a period of wanting to surround themselves with overt signs of of their own culture and to remove themselves from those in the dominant culture. In the classroom, for many of our students this is reflected in taking particular pleasure in studying the history and literature of their own culture, in deepening relationships with peers and adults in their own culture, and in distancing themselves from peers and adults in the dominant culture. Our students have also taken on positions in the school that give them an opportunity to take public stands on racial or cultural issues about which they feel strongly.

By their later years in high school, many of our students of color describe looking at themselves and others from a position of maturity, comfort, and pride in relation to their own identity. They are able to look back onto tumultuous times when they were deeply involved in exploring aspects of who they were and forward through the lens of one at ease with oneself. One young Black woman wrote that, just like Frank Chin's character Donald Duk (1991), she had come to realize she could appreciate both her own culture and the culture of others. She had moved from preferring almost exclusive association with those in her own culture to appreciating ties across cultural lines. Excluding those from other cultures, she decided, meant losing an opportunity for significant friendships.

By the time they leave us, many of our students of color have approached discussions of critical issues of race and culture from a sophisticated metaperspective. One young Latina's explanation of the significance of culture and identity, for example, suggested that, deprived of having others acknowledge their cultural heritage, individuals become colorless, incomplete, a fragment of who they really are. Students have moved to the lectern in classrooms and in assemblies to educate their classmates about their cultures, speaking out as the young educators they already are, speaking to their classmates and beyond them, to the world that awaits them.

Although some of our students see themselves as developing one particular cultural identity, students whose identities are tied to two or more cultures, or even two or more countries, experience identity development influenced by their ties to multiple cultures or, in the case of students who have immigration as part of their own or their family's history, multiple cultures based in multiple countries. Consistent with identity development models for biracial students (Kerwin & Ponterotto, 1995; Tatum, 1997), our students whose identities are emerging from more than one cultural base have described feeling pulled in several directions tied to multiple cultures that are part of their identity. Or they express puzzlement, anger, or resentment at the fact that those around them may expect them to identify in such a way as to exclude an essential part of their background and sense of self. Such pressures are clear when college applications request information about students' ethnic identity or college counselors mince no words in explaining which identity on the college application will generate the best chance for admission. Such was the case for one Japanese-Irish student: "I feel guilty sometimes when I pick either being Japanese or Irish, because I'm hiding a part of me. Doing college applications can be very stressful, especially the part where it asks for your ethnicity. What do I put?" We have also seen students taking delight in the richness afforded them by their connections to more than one culture. This same student explained, "Coming from two different races gives me an advantage in society. I can either claim I'm Japanese or Irish because I'm exactly half and half."

Descriptive of many of our students' experiences is Phinney's (Casas &

Pytluk, 1995; Phinney, 1993; Tatum, 1997) generic ethnic identity development model for adolescents. Consistent with Phinney's observations, we see students in each of the stages described on the path toward solidifying an ethnic identity: students who, for one reason or another, evidence little interest in ethnic identity; students who appear to be in the midst of considerable struggle involving ethnic identity; and students who describe a sense of who they are with clarity and assurance.

Moments that reflect students' thinking about aspects of their racial or cultural identity reveal in a host of ways the reality, the significance, and the complexity of the process by which students construct youthful identities in a racialized society. They also suggest that racial identity development theory and models may help students and those of us who work with them to understand what our students may be experiencing, how the process of racial identity development may affect our shared experience in the classroom, and how we as teachers can respond in knowledgeable and sensitive ways in the face of that aspect of our students' development.

EXTENSIONS OF MYSELF:
WHAT DO ASPECTS OF MY LIFE SAY ABOUT ME?

Beyond the challenges involved in developing a comfortable sense of who they are, our students' observations reveal that they are also exploring the ways in which specific aspects of their lives further define who they are. In their own or others' eyes, how do aspects of their lives—homes, neighborhoods, friends, values, styles, or relationships to specific issues—that may be tied, by themselves or others, to a specific culture relate to who they are?

For some students, their homes and neighborhoods feel like extensions of themselves. For one young Latina, her neighborhood and its images had become part of her sense of self. Impressions and memories—whether of gunshots or holidays—had taught her about life and enabled her to find out who she is.

Other students, however, feel that connections to neighborhoods sometimes shroud who they are. Consider the words of one young woman who identifies as part Indian, part Black:

> I remember one day I was coming home on the bus and began to open my door. A man who was standing at the bus stop happened to see me and asked, "Do people actually live in that building?" I replied with a polite smile and a nod and continued to walk into the building. In the back of my mind all I could think was, "If only he knew." But it's not only the building I live in, it's the neighborhood,

too. When people ask me where I live and I reply, you can see a quick change of facial expression, the kind where they try to make it look like nothing is wrong with that, but I know deep down inside they are probably thinking bad thoughts—gangs, murders and drug-dealers. [One of writer Sandra Cisneros's characters (1989)] doesn't want anybody to judge her or her people by the stereotypes, by the statistics, and by the news. [I too] wish people would stop judging the book by its covers.

White students, too, express interest or concern over the manner in which a house or a neighborhood casts light on their identity: Does their home or neighborhood suggest, in fact, who they think they are, or not?

WHO ARE WE IN RELATION TO EACH OTHER?

In addition to trying to understand themselves, our students are also trying to understand each other in relation to racial or cultural identities. Beyond "Who am I?," students are wondering "Who are you?" and "Who are we in relation to each other?" In the daily activities of a school or classroom, students are repeatedly experiencing themselves being reflected back to themselves through the eyes, words, and gestures of those around them. These interactions are additional ways through which our students are constructing their identities (Taylor, 1994). All of us discover and develop our identities not solely on our own but in response to and in concert with those around us. This process includes our looking at, speaking with, and interacting with each other. It includes our looking out at others and seeing ourselves as "the other." It includes issues surrounding how we wish to identify ourselves and one another; meeting one another's expectations; bearing up under the weight of the effects of prejudice, discrimination, and racism; and finding a comfortable social fit, in school and beyond.

For some students, seeing themselves through others' eyes represents a type of awakening. They are fascinated with discovering new dimensions of themselves revealed in classroom discussions or in literature, and such moments can lead students to clarifying aspects of their sense of self or broadening their knowledge of themselves.

In other moments, seeing oneself through others' eyes leads to confusion and discomfort. Students know that the larger American society has chosen to elevate certain cultural identities at the expense of others. As a result, when students come together in classrooms, the process of seeing themselves through each other's eyes can lead to disquieting comparisons. What is reflected back to them about their own identity may offend them, as when a White student is made aware of the racist nature of a comment or gesture. Or it may make them feel demeaned, as when White students decry affirmative action programs, implying in the process that "less qualified" students of color are taking "their" spots on college admission lists, or that "too many Asian students" are being admitted for the process to be fair.

Students, however, are all involved in their own process of discovering where they stand in relation to those from their own culture and to those from other cultures—German to Jew, Black to White, Black to Black, White to Latino, Asian to White. And there will be countless interpersonal dramas played out in our classrooms as students come to terms both with their own and others' developing sense of cultural identity. Some of those moments will be poignant and filled with a growing and healthy awareness of each other on the part of these young adults. Some moments will be illuminating for individuals and for those around them. And some moments will be disruptive or disturbing.

What Do I Call Myself?

One set of issues surrounding identity for students as they interact with each other involves the ever-evolving identifiers we employ to speak of ourselves and each other.

Many of our students are actively engaged in exploring how they see themselves and how they are, or wish to be, seen by others. For many students, selecting a designation for self-identifying is anything but automatic, and questions surrounding this issue emerge regularly in hallways, meetings, and classrooms as students attempt to broaden avenues of communication with each other across cultural lines. Students may struggle, for example, with whether they see themselves as "American'"; whether they self-identify as a "hyphenated American," for example, Asian-American; and how they see themselves within larger cultural designations: Do they consider themselves, for example, "Black" or "African-American"?

Some students speak of nestling into one designation or another based on their relationship to others whose opinions matter to them, or on their knowledge of politics, history, or family lineage.

Some students readily embrace the multifaceted identity suggested by hyphenated designations, while a "hyphenated identity" is troublesome or inaccurate to others. "I am an American," said one young student of European descent in a discussion focusing on aspects of American history and American character, "and so are all the people in this room. It's destructive to break ourselves down into categories such as 'African-

American, Asian-American.'" Because this young woman comes from a northern European background, she is considered by some as the "norm" in this country and has—in the words of Mary Waters (1998)—"optional ethnicity," not an option for students from many other cultural backgrounds. Across from her, a politically astute young Black student objected to her observation: "Yes, I'm an American, but my experiences have been vastly different from yours. I see myself as 'Black.' In many ways, I *don't* choose to see myself as an 'American.'" One young Black woman explained, "I'm Jamaican. Don't call me 'African-American.'" For one young Asian-American student, a hyphenated designation, she explained, only served to draw attention to her "difference" from those in the dominant culture, with whom she was most comfortable identifying. For other students, a hyphenated designation represents a frightening suggestion—shared by Arthur Schlesinger (1992)—that we as a nation are dissolving into separate "tribes," threatening national unity. For one young White student whose family included an interracial relationship several generations past, the idea of hyphenated identity violated all that she defined as "America."

In the process of self-identifying, students may also choose for one reason or another to tuck away one or more aspects of their cultural identities. Students may self-identify exclusively as "human" or as "American." Biracial students speak of adopting one identity rather than another, or publicly acknowledge different identities in different settings. For one student, this became apparent as he self-identified differently in class discussions than he did in one-to-one discussions outside of class.

Or biracial students may be hurled by the behaviors and attitudes of others into a feeling of having "no identity" by virtue of their mixed identity. For one light-skinned student of biracial parents, personal discomfort arose in his daily life at school from Black classmates' objections that he was too light to be Black and from White classmates letting him know he was too dark to be White. Rejections by both students of color and White students made it more difficult initially for this student to develop a sense of belonging in the school and left him frustrated and self-doubting.

What our students have repeatedly made clear to us, however, is the importance of being able to define themselves. Many of our students are acutely aware that many of the labels attached to them have been created by those in other cultures. They also know they are often misidentified by others, not only by their classmates, but by their teachers, and this is unsettling to them. Students, just as do most adults, do not want to be defined by others. They want to define themselves, no matter that that designation may shift with time or place or circumstance. And they want that identity to be respected.

What Do We Call Each Other?

In addition to challenges surrounding the ways in which students self-identify, students are confused about what to call each other. This uncertainty regularly surfaces in classroom discussions and can lead to awkwardness, discomfort, and tensions among students. Why is this an issue?

The labels used for designating cultural identity are generally not understood, not easy to understand, are constantly changing, and vary according to a number of factors. About any one cultural designation, there may be no clear consensus. Self-labeling and the labeling of others varies within a given cultural group and across cultural groups, evolves through time, and varies across regions. How individuals self-label or label others may depend on their stage of racial or cultural identity development; experiences and values; political affinities; or regional affiliation. A few examples indicate the complexity of the issue: Some Blacks self-identify as "African American," others as "Black." Native Americans may refer to themselves as "Native American" in one region of the country and as "Indian" in another. Politically active Latinos may prefer "Latino" to "Hispanic" because of negative associations with the Spanish conquest of Latin America. Most Asians in the United States prefer the politically neutral term "Asian American," based in geography, to "Oriental," a term tied to historically negative Asian-American stereotypes. Most individuals prefer for themselves a designation tied to a specific country, such as, "Korean," "Dominican," or "Salvadorian," to more general labels such as "Asian American" or "Latino." "People of color" is preferable to "minority" for some, since the term "minority" is often used in instances in which it is not an accurate descriptor and is applied inconsistently to population groups.

The labels by which we identify ourselves and each other reflect personal and intimate aspects of ourselves and are tied to our everyday communication with each other. They are linked to our sense of self—how we see ourselves and how others see us—and how we see others. They are an often unstated but not insignificant facet of communication between individuals within or across cultural groups. We and our students may wonder: How should I refer to you? How would I like you to refer to me? even if it is not stated. The fact that such questions often go unstated leads to less understanding, more confusion, and more tentativeness, and this hampers engagement in comfortable cross-cultural conversation and collaboration. "I've gone to this school for fourteen years," said one Jewish-American student about the power of labels, "and I still don't know whether or not to say 'black' or 'African American' or even 'colored.' Of all the things that we address in the class [on racial and cultural issues], this bothers me the

most, simple communication. I don't feel comfortable to say anything."
Further, some students know—but others do not—that "mistakes" or inac-
curacy in designations of each other can have immediate and lingering
repercussions.

Uncertainty about what to call each other is associated, in part, with
a lack of experience. The ripple effects of racism have resulted in issues of
language and identity being difficult, awkward, or painful to talk about, so
we avoid doing so.

The issue of what we call ourselves and each other is also significant
because it is commonly encountered. As teachers we need to be sensitive
about the issue as it relates to our relationships with students and as it
affects the way students relate to each other. Questions surrounding how
individuals identify themselves and others emerge not only in our classrooms, but in social settings, in workplaces, and in the writing of texts.
Thus, to help students understand the complexities of this aspect of identity—that is, its role and impact in communication—is to help them understand an issue that will accompany them well beyond our schoolrooms.

Labels of identification are powerful. They are tied to a sense of self,
communication, and relationships; they are tied to politics, to history, and
to power. They are tied to "who will decide who I am—I myself or someone else?" They carry weight, they can offend, they can strain and damage
relationships and communication. And they can help facilitate them.

The Expectations of Others: How Should I Be Who I Am?

Beyond deciding on ways to identify themselves and each other, our students are also struggling with meeting the expectations of others related to
their racial or cultural identity. Many students regularly express feeling
pressured to meet powerful stated or unstated expectations on the part of
those within or outside their own culture. And they describe being judged
and accepted or rejected on a regular basis by those who deem that they
have fulfilled or failed to fulfill particular notions of a specific cultural
identity.

Such pressures lead to students' feeling the need to prove themselves
within already shifting boundaries of definition. They're not sure what it
means to be who they are, and yet "failing" to meet expectations tied to
that identity can lead to self-questioning, self-doubt, and even self-loathing.

At times, students report, even as they are trying to be who they are,
others think otherwise. Such was the case for one young biracial woman:
"I have been asked, 'Can I touch your hair?' 'What race are you?' Then I
tell them I'm American Indian and Black. Then they question me, 'Are you
sure that you are not Puerto Rican or Mexican?' And I'm just amused

because I just told them the answer. They ask me again as if I told them the wrong thing or because that was not what they wanted to hear."

Students of color, especially, face peer pressure repeatedly from members of their own culture about the degree to which they are, for example, "acting Latino" or "acting White." Images of "Oreos," "bananas," "apples," and "coconuts"—of being one "color" on the outside and "White" on the inside—hang over their choices. Are they "black," "yellow," "red," or "brown" enough, or are they somehow a "sellout," catering too much to the dominant White culture, and therefore "White" on the inside? Or students attempting to meet the cultural expectations of peers and teachers at school may find it difficult to also meet parental expectations tied to parents' notions of choices appropriate and consistent with a particular cultural identity. "It's extra difficult to be Mexican American," explained one young Latina about such pressures, "because you have to be twice as perfect. In the Anglo culture you have to work harder to be accepted because you have darker hair, eyes, and skin. In the Mexican culture you have to be sure to remember your roots or they will call you a 'sellout.'" Or as one young White woman wrote, "Some may consider me a sellout, but there are times that I wish I were another race. Walking around [one of the local public schools] during school hours I walk with my head down, and my face burning—hoping not to be noticed, but I feel that I stick out like a sore thumb. Often I feel ashamed for feeling this way."

Some students of color experience pressure *not* to embrace their racial or cultural identity. Not naive to interpersonal or institutional dynamics in predominantly White settings, students of color may perceive that they have a greater chance of success by downplaying their racial or cultural identity. Such a choice can become a double-edged sword or represent "a Pyrrhic victory" (Fordham, 1988) for students. Although making assimilationist gestures can be "advantageous" for the student in specific instances, those "advantages" may come at a significant psychic and social cost. The student is caught simultaneously between the process of developing and solidifying a racial or cultural identity, and responding to pressures toward "racelessness" (Fordham, 1988, 1991), that is, denying that same identity. Such pressures may emanate in some ways from students' own needs in a particular setting, or, more generally, from the subtle or overt ways in which those in institutions—adults or peers—emphasize certain choices, values, and behaviors over others. Students who submerge aspects of their racial or cultural identity may enjoy specific pragmatic advantages, but such a choice may also pull them further and further from their own cultural moorings, including ties with home, family, neighborhood, language, and customs. One young Black woman captured the significant strains of such pulls in a poem she published in the school literary magazine.

In some settings, as in predominantly White private schools, some students of color may find themselves experiencing the pressure to be "raceless," that is, to act in ways that minimize their own racial or cultural identity, at the same time that, on some level, they are expected to be "raced" as "proof" of the "diversity" of the institution, and these pressures occur at a time when they are involved in establishing a mature identity tied in part to race or culture (Fordham, 1991). Such pressures for students have raised serious concerns among families and educators (Fordham, 1988, 1991; Tatum, 1997).

In part because of such pressures, students may also engage in "code-shifting" (McDermott, 1977, p. 17, quoted in Nieto, 1999, pp. 43–44), adopting different personal styles to fit the needs of specific settings. In discussions related to cultural issues, students of color often speak of being one self at home and in their own neighborhood, and another self at school. For one of our students, this took the form of changing clothes before and after school. Many students, especially students of color in predominantly White schools, have found code-shifting a useful or necessary choice. But such a choice can carry the weight of an undue burden.

Other students may create an "oppositional identity" (Fordham & Ogbu, 1986; Tatum, 1997, pp. 60–65), an identity that meets the expectations of those who matter to them, but that places them in an oppositional relationship to values perceived to be values tied to another culture. For example, some students, in attempting to create an identity satisfactory to peers (and therefore to themselves), may create an identity that opposes their fitting in in particular settings or that opposes the academic expectations of the school, since to some students, that means "acting White." For one of our Black students, avoiding such pressures meant turning his back on friends of many years and wondering whether new friends would be there for him. Such choices reflect multiple pressures on students and can affect both their social lives and their academic achievement.

Thus the pressures of meeting the expectations of others related to cultural identity may have a direct bearing on the choices students make and the ways they interact in the classroom. What many students yearn for, they tell us, is the freedom to be who they are, as tentative and still-emerging as that self may be. But as long as they feel pressures to meet the expectations of others with regard to their racial or cultural identity, we will see the effects of those pressures in school and in the classroom.

The Weight of Prejudice

Especially significant is the role and power of prejudice, stereotypes, discrimination, and racism tied to racial or cultural identities in these students' young lives. Students of color and White students carry the burden of dealing with identities constructed not by themselves but by others, based on myth, falsehoods, inaccurate generalizations, ignorance, and intolerance. In multicultural schools and classrooms, misinformed, ignorant, and cruel words and actions have the power to affect students' lives and sense of self on a daily basis.

As our students' discussions and writing make clear, the effects of prejudice and racism on their emerging sense of self are one of the cruelest results of their growing up in a nation where many adults have decided that an unequal status exists among its multiple cultures. Cruel judgment based on racial or cultural identity results in our students' being insulted and humiliated. It results in tears and isolation. It even invades their dreams. Here one young Black woman explains such a moment:

> I had an awkward dream that was so stupid, bizarre, and scary at the same time. I was downstairs all alone downloading something [on the computer] and as it was downloading slowly, this joker clown popped up on the screen and started screaming, "Hurry up, you nigger!" I ran away and tried running up the stairs but I couldn't move. I was crying so hard and I saw myself running and I was a little girl. This was so strange but what the hell is that supposed to mean? No one has ever said that word to my face so this really bothered me.

Such assaults on their sense of self can leave students frightened, angry, less confident, and feeling invisible, neither seen nor known. It can leave them needing to "prove" themselves acceptable. It can leave them hurt and self-doubting. One young biracial woman noted, "[White] people are too afraid to pass by a person of color. Sometimes I think it's funny; other times it confuses me, because if only that person looked past the color of my skin, they would know that I couldn't harm a fly." A young Black man recalled this moment: "The other day, I was walking down Belmont towards the [El] with a friend of mine. As we passed [a White man], he shouted out, 'I can't stand 'em . . . every last nigger.' I have experienced this before, and therefore knew my options and the consequences. So I walked away shaking my head, thinking about how ignorant that man was." White students, too, can experience such moments: "Today [one of the Black students] said a friend of his calls White people 'devils.' A young Chinese-American student recalled experiencing fear tied to his identity on a family trip: "On my trip we passed by a town called Orange City in Florida. My father commented that a KKK rally was going on there. I realized these people are responsible for lynchings of blacks and really hate me without knowing me. I saw all white people in the cars. This instant was when I was really petrified of whites. I grew up with whites but to know that they could just hit our car and like that I would be dead and they would have their kicks . . ."

Knowing that they have been and will again be subjected to such judgments, students tell us they know they have to be prepared to mount a response, and they themselves will have to decide what that response will be: will they walk away; will they try to prove others wrong; will they let the action or remark, as one young Black student said, "bother me or mature me?" Or will it, as another Black student said, "make me a warrior?" It is, they tell us, an ongoing and tiring struggle, one, some of our students say, they are not always up to. But they feel they need to know their options and how to choose a response. Another young Black man explained:

> As a young black male, if I walk into a room, I'm going to prepare myself to show them I'm not what they think I am: young, ignorant, and a gang banger. I'm not going to be a "dumb nigger"—no brains, all my life wear my hat back, all my money comes from drugs, and I'm gonna be dead by 26. My momma's raising me to be different. You have to do this so you don't get called a "dumb nigger." I can't change my skin color. You can't let society do it to you.

Such pressures have effects far beyond the social, as well. Students using energy to fend off the slings of prejudice have less energy to devote to their studies (Steele, 1997; Steele & Aronson, 1995).

In our schools and classrooms, to what degree will our students be able to define themselves—and to what degree will they feel defined by others, especially in ways that are destructive and bear no relation to their actual selves? And within our sphere of influence, what are we as teachers prepared to do to make experiences in our schools and in our classrooms as safe and as productive for our students as we would want them to be for our own children?

WHERE DO I FIT?

Beyond developing and coming to understand a sense of self, many of our students are also wrestling with where they "fit" in a society and in an era in which cultural and racial identities have been given considerable weight. Just as do their journeys between home and school, students' pressures and uncertainties surrounding identity prompt students to think broadly about fitting in, within school and beyond, in the larger society. Since our students receive a host of messages from the larger world that we don't all fit together easily—hate crimes, racial profiling, limited television roles for persons of color, and the like—they are left with having to discover where they *can* find a comfortable social fit. For some students this appears to occur quite naturally. They create or join a comfortable peer group within or across cultural lines. For some, however, that fit is not automatic or easy to find. They may opt to mix with those from other cultures, and be rebuffed by those in the other cultures or by those within their own culture who resent their choosing movement out of the circle of peers within their own culture. They may opt to remain with those within their own culture and be criticized for separating themselves from those in other cultures. Many students of color rightly feel that in these matters they face a double bind: assimilate and be criticized for not holding onto their cultural identity, or hold onto their cultural identity and risk "sticking out," becoming "invisible," or being left outside the mainstream. And if they do not find a comfortable social fit at school, they risk feeling marginal, isolated, and lonely. In the face of these pressures, students tend to gravitate toward social groups where they feel most comfortable, and that is usually with those most like themselves. For this reason, they feel most comfortable in schools where there are a reasonable number of students who, as one student said, "look like me." Even the choice by students to affiliate with those who are most similar, however, results in criticism by those who favor greater blending of students across cultural lines in the school community.

Consider the following situations shared with us by our students. Many Jewish students have had experiences tied to prejudice, bigotry, and exclusion based on cultural identity, and that leads them to "identify with" students of color whose cultures have also experienced cultural oppression. Yet Jewish students are often seen by students of color as "White" and therefore enjoying the privileges that attend Whiteness (West, 1993). Asian-American students have spoken of identifying with and assimilating into the dominant White culture and its institutions of power and privilege and of finding it alien to self-identify as a person of color, while Whites around them regard them as "other." One young woman described her emerging identity as a Latina in a predominantly White society. Skin color, language, goals, and tastes left her dangling between two cultures. Eventually she gave up trying to belong and focused on seeking a happiness she could live with herself.

Questions surrounding racial or cultural identity as it affects social belonging may be more complex for students who are adopted or those coming from biracial backgrounds. How does the child self-identify? How has the family self-identified? How has the family handled identity issues with the child? Does the child favor, for any number of reasons, identification with one culture or another, or equally embrace more than one? How do other students identify their classmate? One young biracial woman wrote an allegory early in her high school years entitled "Oreo." In the story, her narrator is "in the middle." Groups of Black students and White students exert so much pressure on her to "choose a group" that she goes home in tears and withdraws from her new school to return to school in "Normal, Illinois."

Finding for themselves an appropriate cultural fit means that students are faced with yet another set of confusing pressures that complicates the process whereby they construct and maintain their youthful identities.

MUST WE EMPHASIZE RACIAL OR CULTURAL IDENTITY?

But perhaps we must ask ourselves: Why all of this emphasis on racial or cultural identity? And why does all of this matter to the teacher in a classroom of students from multiple cultures? Haven't we as a nation spent decades boasting that the national agenda on civil rights has righted much of what plagued past centuries characterized by racism and segregation by racial identity?

If, in fact, our national efforts had been successful, maybe it would not matter. But as Beverly Tatum (2001) answered one group of parents in Chicago who posed that question: "[Race] should be irrelevant but it's not, and because it's not, we should talk about it." As it is, our students, our faculties, and our administrations are divided by aspects of race and culture, and thus it matters in the classroom. Where students are in relation to their own identity and culture and the identity and cultures of students around them will affect to some degree how they relate potentially to every other individual in the room—including us, their teachers.

Moments tied to racial or cultural identities may be as simple as choosing where to sit or as ugly as a slur intended to hurt, hurled under the breath. Seating patterns that reflect students' seeking support in the culturally mixed environment of the classroom replicate, at times, the self-segregating tendencies observed in the larger public areas of the school, with students of color clustered together and White students clustered together.

Aspects of racial or cultural identities also result in alliances and tensions as students discover among their classmates others with similar views or those with views opposing their own, troubling to them, or offensive to them. In one recent class in our course on racial and cultural issues, several young Black women in similar stages of exploring their identities formed a natural bond throughout the course—supporting each other; delighting in one another's responses; reflecting similar stances on issues affecting themselves, other Blacks, or Whites. A number of White students found their alliance intimidating and indicated privately that they felt inhibited in expressing their own views, so powerfully did they experience the alliance of the three affable and voluble young Black women.

All of these issues surrounding personal identity are compounded by the fact that adolescent identities are in flux. As students are solidifying their sense of self and developing a racial or cultural identity, they move back and forth among key stages in that process. This means that in working with students, teachers can observe, for example, that a White student moving from a stage in which he or she has little sense of Whiteness to a stage of coming to terms with White privilege and White racism may experience significant disjuncture with his or her previous sense of self. Or a Black student at one time animatedly attached to a White teacher may move toward exclusive association with Black students and teachers and overt rejection of White students and teachers as a stage in solidifying her own identity as a young Black woman. The resulting shifts in alliances and rejections among friends, classmates, and teachers, though natural in the context of racial or cultural identity development, are not necessarily easy to understand or to accept, especially by those unfamiliar with this facet of identity development.

Students' relationships to their identities also affect, in part, the way in which they approach, explore, and respond to course materials and activities. What students bring to and take from readings, films, and speakers; dynamics that emerge during class discussions; and the richness of students' thoughts revealed in the privacy of papers or course journals all further suggest the importance of this facet of their developing selves.

The "hidden curriculum"—what may be conveyed inadvertently—or the "subjective curriculum"—how students relate personally to curriculum as it relates to their individual racial or cultural identities—can be powerful. To what extent will students be able to "identify with" or connect with a reading, a project, a course? Will that connection be one that excites and involves students? Will the work or the ideas being discussed hit too close to home for students to feel comfortable discussing them? Will a particular text or ideas emerging in discussions elicit such discomfort related to racial or cultural identity that they trigger not only a strong emotional response, but also a rejection of the material and a discussion of it, or withdrawal altogether from the process? Will students discover, in their work, ways of thinking or role models who have gone before them who open up ways to be who they are, ways to be who they want to be? For one White student, several novels by writers of color in our course on racial and cultural issues offered insight into her own search for identity. She later wrote: "Reading about various characters has provided a wealth of ways to find one's identity, and ways to accept it. It is important to know that there is not just one way to find an identity, because often it is a lifelong struggle. This is comforting, especially to adolescents, who are at the peak of struggling to find an identity they can call their own."

One young Asian American, distrusting that "her/story" would be told in a history course, took to the lectern and filled in the class on aspects of Asian-American history, focusing primarily on early immigration issues and ending with playing an audiotape of an Asian-American musical group whose lyrics probe discrimination against female Asian Americans. What her actions said in part was: "This history and these issues are a significant part of who I am, and this is what I am thinking about in relation to my own culture and to the dominant culture." Our students search for themselves in materials—for material they can identify with. And they seek to find meaning related to who they are or who they yearn to be, in discussions, readings, and projects.

A Native American student hungering to read more of Native American history or literature may approach with anticipation and eagerness the works of Native American novelists or scholars. For a White student reluctant to acknowledge White privilege and "sick of hearing about racism," those same texts may ignite visible resistance that affects the way the class as a whole experiences the text.

To what extent will a White student be willing or able to engage in a text by a confrontational author of color? To what extent will a student of color be willing or able to engage in the work of a "major" writer or thinker whose assumptions are clearly belittling to those in the student's own culture—as is the case with many canonical texts by well-known White writers?

The nature of students' responses to materials—and this is tied to racial or cultural identity—is significant not just because those responses are associated with freedom of expression on the part of students, scholars, or artists, or because, in the minds of some, they smack of "political correctness," but for the pragmatic reason that natural, thoughtful, and emotional responses to texts shape the way a classroom experience will unfold. Sometimes those responses can result in group dynamics difficult for both the students and the teacher to manage. Those responses can also trigger moments of breathtaking beauty—an illumination of what's possible among students in a classroom.

WHAT DOES THIS MEAN FOR THE TEACHER?

Complicating these dynamics further is the fact that many of these issues surrounding racial or cultural identity apply as well to the teacher who will be with these students for a significant length of time during a vulnerable and impressionable period in the students' lives. Especially in multicultural settings, the overall tone of a given milieu or a specific situation or moment in the teacher's professional or private life may—and indeed should—prompt the teacher to raise within himself or herself questions similar to those his or her students may be posing: What is my cultural identity? What is my relationship to that identity? What issues are unresolved for me in relation to that identity? How will aspects of that identity affect what I teach and how I teach it? How do I feel about and how will I interact with each of the children before me, relative to my own cultural identity, background, education, values, and biases?

Understanding multiple aspects of racial or cultural identity—our own as well as our students'—as they emerge in the multicultural classroom can help us understand and respond to complex aspects of our own and our students' attitudes and behaviors, and ultimately create a more meaningful classroom experience.

OUR CLASSROOMS AS A PLACE FOR WHO WE ARE

Given the very real challenges facing our students as they mature in this multicultural society, we need to establish a climate of respect in our classrooms where emerging identities can thrive and the challenges related to racial or cultural identities can be understood, recognized, and addressed in the day-to-day life of the classroom. Establishing a climate of respect includes drawing on useful theories, recognizing the power of curriculum and pedagogy, and responding to individuals and the group as students develop their sense of self in the times we share.

Drawing on Useful Theories

Stumbling onto Tatum's article on the use of racial identity theory in her Mount Holyoke classroom (1992) revolutionized the way I view dynamics in my classes. Information on racial identity development has helped me become aware of the complex process by which students may be developing a sense of who they are in this multicultural society. It has helped me see and understand some of the attitudes, choices, and moments that surround us in the classroom in a useful context and to help students do the same.

Knowing how helpful the theory was to me, I now share that information in various ways with my students. In our course that focuses directly on issues of race or culture, we spend one class examining racial identity development theory, working with a cluster of models—for Blacks, Whites, Asians, Latinos, biracial individuals, and ethnic adolescents. Students choose any one model that interests them to work with, summarize the stages involved in that model, and note the stages they think may be particularly interesting or challenging. In any work with racial identity development theory, I make sure I draw on a full range of models so that no students feel left out or pressured to work with models inconsistent with the way they view themselves. I also caution students that such theories or models can easily be misused in insensitive or racist ways. Individuals may resent being "categorized" according to a theory or model. A particular racial identity development model may be incorrectly employed based on an erroneous assumption about an individual's identity. And assuming that individuals can be categorized according to these models can resemble prejudice or racism: prejudging an individual based on a supposition about a racial identity.

A class discussion of the theory and the ways in which it may be useful in helping us understand our own attitudes and behaviors or the attitudes and behaviors of others follows. Applying the theory to young characters' interactions in a work of short fiction such as R. A. Sasaki's "First Love" (1993) gives students one tool for thinking about and understanding moments in their own lives. About one such class, a young Black woman wrote later, "The [topic in this course] that really made me happy was Tatum's (1997) description of whiteness and blackness. She hit on everything. I almost cried. I had basically gone through every one of those stages. I never knew anyone could know *exactly* what I was going through."

In other courses, as issues surrounding identity arise, I explain generally to the students that in a society that has emphasized racial identity, some researchers believe that each of us develops a racial identity over time. Where we are in developing that identity can affect how we feel about our own identity and culture as well as the identity and culture of others.

Many of our students—White students, students of color, and biracial students—have found that knowing the theory of racial identity development is helpful in and of itself. Students' understanding of racial or cultural identity development can also carry longer-term advantages: "Adolescents who have explored and understand the meaning of ethnicity in their lives are more likely to demonstrate better adjustment than those who have not" (Nieto, 1996, p. 262).

Useful though this theory is, however, it cannot explain all of the moments in front of us. Sometimes students of one racial or cultural identity sit together not because of an evolving sense of self, but because, studies show, we tend to gravitate toward those like us in building friendships.

And moments of disconnection around us may emerge not through the search for self, but as the result of overtly expressed racism. Further, acceptance of the fact that we each develop a racial identity embeds the phenomenon of identity based on race further into the national consciousness and perpetuates distinctions among us by race, neither of which may be optimal. Dismantling divisions among students may be our goal, but the reality of life in our classrooms is one in which racial or cultural identities play a role.

An understanding of theory (Nieto, 1996; Tatum, 1997) has also been useful to me in helping students address the confusion surrounding the language we use to identify ourselves and each other. Challenges tied to this aspect of identity emerge as we get to know each other in the classroom and as we strive to build meaningful conversations across cultural lines.

Classroom experiences as well as research suggest a number of ways of helping our students with this aspect of their lives. We can recognize the uncertainty and the effects of that uncertainty tied to the process of identification among students: that students want to know how to address each other; they want to know more about how and why individuals identify themselves in specific ways related to race or culture; and they may be uncertain about how they wish to self-identify or be identified by their classmates. We can recognize that students' sense of themselves is in flux and shifts over time.

In general, I make use of the following guidelines in my own interactions and share them with my students: 1) We cannot easily know how an individual self-identifies and should never presume to know. Issues surrounding cultural identity are too complex and multifaceted to do so. 2) We should understand the importance of cultural identity for individuals and respect individuals' need to self-identify. 3) We should use designations that individuals themselves prefer. 4) We should use the most specific term rather than the more general term, for example, "Salvadorian" rather than "Latino" (Nieto, 1996; Tatum, 1997). 5) We should be aware that the way in which we use labels of cultural identity has the power to enhance or damage relationships.

In the course on issues of race and culture, as I introduce one or more authors from a particular cultural background, I include information on how some writers or critics from that group feel about particular designations. Amy Ling, for example, provides a clear overview of this issue in her article "Teaching Asian American Literature" (n.d.), a piece I draw on in introducing a segment on Asian-American writers.

Establishing a climate of inquiry and respect facilitates students' asking of each other the questions that can help them understand how their classmates wish to be identified. In our race- and culture-conscious society, such understanding helps students to be more comfortable with each other and to move toward less awkward and more natural conversation.

The Role of Curriculum and Pedagogy

Recognizing and respecting students' uncertainty relating to identity can allow us to provide them with opportunities to explore those issues, through aspects of course design, through addressing questions that emerge in the natural flow of our being together, or through addressing questions generated by readings or discussions.

Texts, films, discussions, and writings offer students rich opportunities for exploring multiple aspects of identity, on their own or with classmates. Major works of literature as well as collections of shorter works offer stories of emerging selves, of inclusion and exclusion, of expectations, or of finding a fit in society. *Black Boy* by Richard Wright (1945), *This Migrant Earth* by Rolando Hinojosa (1987), *Bless Me, Ultima* by Rodolfo Anaya (1972), *House Made of Dawn* by N. Scott Momaday (1989), *Sula* by Toni Morrison (1973), *Donald Duk* by Frank Chin (1991), *The Joy Luck Club* by Amy Tan (1989), and *My Name Is Asher Lev* by Chaim Potok (1972) all offer meditations on constructing the self. A superb series of anthologies, *Growing up . . . Asian American/Black/Chicano/Native American/Jewish* (Hong, 1993; David, 1992; Lopez, 1995; Riley, 1993; Adler, 1997), as well as individual anthologies—*Half and Half* (O'Hearn, 1998), *Identity Lessons* (Gillan & Gillan, 1999b), *Unsettling America* (Gillan & Gillan, 1994), *Coming of Age in America* (Frosch, 1994), *Growing Up Ethnic in America* (Gillan & Gillan, 1999a), *Growing up Latino: Memoirs and Stories* (Augenbraum & Stavans, 1993), and *Post Gibran: Anthology of New Arab American Writing* (Akash & Mattawa, 2000)—simultaneously enable students to build reading backgrounds across cultural lines and to explore multiple aspects of identity. Gish Jen's "What Means Switch" from *Growing up Asian American* (Hong, 1993), a short story I teach in the freshman course on genres, portrays two children—one Japanese and one Chinese—in a wealthy suburb of New York trying to figure out how to regard each other at the same time they are developing a sense of themselves. The story delights and intrigues students considering issues of identity in their own lives.

Good films and texts often generate discussions among students about cultural identity, and from those discussions comes more understanding. One of the most powerful discussions in our class on issues of race and culture emerged in response to *The House on Mango Street* (1989), as Cisneros's young female character Esperanza recalls moments when a nun in her school shamed her about where she lived or when her needs for a home outgrew the succession of disappointing houses of her childhood and led her to seek a "home of her own" that would be a more apt expression of who she was and who she wanted to be. The lyrical text prompted a classwide discussion on homes and neighborhoods and who we are.

Such classroom discussions enable students to tell their own stories and to hear the stories of others. In that way they are educated more broadly about aspects of identity in a racialized society. Discussions allow students to learn ways to handle challenges related to identity and to know such challenges are widespread. Such conversations can help students feel less alone in what they may be experiencing. They can also help students understand the need both for finding a comfortable peer group and for developing skills that may help them to cross cultural borders as they mature in this multicultural society. Through such conversations we teachers learn not only of our students but also of the ways in which the institution itself is being experienced by students—the degree to which students feel they can or cannot be who they really are in their days at school.

Further, issues of identity, whether emerging from students' own questions, offered by well-known writers or filmmakers, or shared in classroom discussions, make rich ground for original writing, and thus provide students with opportunities to research, describe, or analyze this crucial process of becoming and, along the way, learn more about themselves or others.

Cognizant of the ways in which students' identities may influence how they experience and respond to materials and discussions, I attempt to provide materials emerging not only from multiple cultures but from multiple perspectives within those cultures, and to vary the intensity of the focus and the materials. During discussions, I try to create an atmosphere supportive of students' wide-ranging responses to materials and to pedagogical choices and an understanding that students will have varying degrees of knowledge and comfort in discussing issues tied to self and others. Both active participation and quiet contemplation are welcomed responses.

I remain attentive to the ways in which students cluster themselves in the room and whether or not they appear comfortable in the larger group. I pay attention to the ways in which materials and discussions draw together or strain students' relationships with each other. At times, such dynamics become a focal part of our discussions. In other instances, I may seek out one or more students to help them understand what may be unfolding. In these instances, drawing on or reminding students about racial identity theory may help students understand some of what they are thinking, feeling, or observing.

In the face of the complex relationship between racial or cultural identity and our students' experiences in school, we should not enter the multicultural classroom naively. The reality of identity challenges facing our students should encourage us to provide them with opportunities to explore such issues as part of their education. We need to enable each of our students to find themselves in the works we teach, and we need to understand that what we read and how we talk about what we read may have a wide range of effects on the students in front of us related to who they, and we, are. As these effects emerge, we need to be ready to understand them and to address them with our students. We need to know that curriculum and the way we approach it may well trigger difficult moments. We need to be ready at any moment to intervene in conversation that leans too hard on any student's identity, and to ensure that conversations are conducted in the spirit of respect and exploration. We need to help students understand the impact of their observations on those who do not share their perspective. We need to support students' fleshing out differences of opinions in a constructive manner. We need to enable them to understand further their own position through seeing its impact on others, as well as helping them come to understand alternative ways of viewing culturally influenced points of view.

Supporting Individuals and the Group

Beyond drawing on theories and making use of curriculum and pedagogy, creating a climate of respect for emerging identities in the classroom means responding to needs of individuals and the group.

Part of that responsiveness includes respecting the uniqueness and role of names in our students' lives. I remember the words of a former student who, chagrined by those who refused even to try to understand or pronounce correctly her name, had said: "If you can't take the time to get to know my name, how can you get to know me?" With her words still echoing, I take an interest in students' names. I ascertain how they wish their names to be pronounced. The beauty or meaning of a name often becomes part of the earliest conversations individual students and I share. And as we all grow to know each other, I support students' speaking of the origin and meaning of names as part of classroom discussions or writings exploring texts and films, as well as our own and each other's lives.

As students explore who they are in the natural evolution of our time together, I support them in that process. I make available bibliographies and a room library of titles from multiple cultures to support an emerging need on the part of students to explore more deeply the literature and history of their own culture. I understand the need in students to seek out peers in their own culture. Simultaneously, I support the fact that students of color in a predominantly White school may need to seek out a group of peers within their own culture in formal as well as informal ways, through clubs or discussion groups. I realize and accept that I myself and their White classmates may be rejected or excluded as part of that process. I support individual students who may be experiencing challenges involving their sense of self in a multicultural community. Through conversations with students, I help them explore ways to move beyond the confusion or disillusionment that can accompany our journey toward creating and understanding the self, especially through their relationship to writing or reading. And with all of my students, I try to facilitate, on an ongoing basis, rich communication and experiences with each other across cultural lines.

I am aware of the pressures experienced by students as they attempt to meet the expectations of those around them. I try to remain alert to any students exhibiting signs of stress tied to feeling a need to meet multiple expectations and, if necessary, find appropriate help for them, whether through conversations with a member of their family or through administrative or counseling support within the school.

I support students' drawing on the power of their identity, history, and language to read, to write, to speak, and to take stands, to use who they are to inform their work so that no students feel they have to become "raceless," to shift who they are at the beginning or end of the day, or to make choices that serve others but not themselves. I want all of my students to know that our relationship to success resides within who we are as individuals and is not limited by the narrower expectations that some individuals may have of us. And, it is crucial to me that all of my students know that they "fit" in this classroom.

In addressing students' needs, I also acknowledge that students' racial and cultural identities serve not only to ground them, but also, in part, to divide them. Our students need us to be their allies and to be there to help them in such moments. We need to make our rooms and our hallways safe zones, where students are knowledgeable about the damaging power of prejudice and discrimination, and value, instead, gestures of inclusion. We need to intervene immediately at moments in which students may be cruel with each other. In a constructive manner, we can examine such moments with the students involved. We can offer them, perhaps, new and multiple ways of seeing such moments. We can help students understand what that type of behavior does to someone else, and what it may do to themselves. We can look at prejudice and discrimination in the context of our learning, and contemplate together the effects of our choices as present and future decisionmakers in this country.

CONCLUSION

Teachers reside—and conduct their classes—within a vortex of contradictory contemporary attitudes and behaviors related to race and culture. Mirroring to some degree the observations of Toni Morrison and Henry Louis Gates, Jr., as well as the observation by one of my students, that frame the beginning of this chapter, our students know that racial and cultural identity both does and does not matter. Ignoring the fact that racial and cultural identity can and often does matter, however, "forecloses adult discourse," as Morrison herself has suggested (1993, p. 10), as well as forecloses acknowledging and addressing a significant aspect of our students' lives. On the other hand, discussions focusing on racial or cultural identities unfold next to any attempts on the part of the nation or the school or the teacher to dismantle artificial divisions based on race or culture. Further, in addressing directly divisions emerging from racial or cultural identities, whether through curriculum or pedagogy, the teacher participates in validating and perpetuating the language if not the fact of those divisions.

What it seems important to know, in the midst of this complex and ever-changing social landscape, is that a host of factors related to racial and cultural identity comes into play in our multicultural classrooms. Students are coming into their mature identities in a society in which racial and cultural identities continue to matter. And this complicates our students' coming of age and their interactions with their peers and with us, in school and out. The challenges our students face in constructing identities in this multicultural society become part of the fabric of life in our classrooms. Whether through the relative clarity and openness of questions and dialogues or through countless more subtle exchanges—in whispers, gestures, or glances—our students are attempting to understand more about themselves and each other. Issues of racial or cultural identity affect how students experience themselves, those around them, and us, their teachers. They also affect how students relate to the day-to-day activities we construct in the classroom.

And so each of us must ask ourselves: Do I understand something of the complexity of the issues surrounding emerging identities among these students in front of me and in my own life? Am I alert to multiple ways in which students' confusion, attitudes, or behaviors surrounding racial or cultural identity may affect moments in the classroom? Am I being attentive to the importance and significance of names? Are the choices I make on a daily basis—whether in formal or informal communication or in designing curriculum and pedagogy—ones that facilitate growth on the part of individuals and the group? Will I be able to manage and to help my students manage the powerful and sometimes awkward or painful moments that may arise spontaneously in class discussions or classroom interactions in part related to facets of emerging racial or cultural identities? Am I facilitating these students' growth in cross-cultural communication, understanding, knowledge, and relations? Are my choices in the classroom ones that support these young adults in their steps toward mature selfhood and all of the shimmering complexities involved in that solitary journey?

As teachers in classrooms of students from multiple cultures, we need to be cognizant of all of these aspects of identity. Such knowledge will help us think more fully about what we teach, what we do not teach, and how we teach it. It will help us more fully understand dynamics unfolding in front of us and within us; how students respond to readings, projects, or discussions; and how they engage or do not engage with each other or with us. Ultimately, our understanding these dynamics will influence whether or not we and our students develop a caring and successful working relationship during our time together. And it will influence the degree to which we are able to support each of these students in their exploration of the world and on their journeys toward adulthood.

To invite our students into the process of learning and support their movement toward adulthood, we need to construct our courses, design our reading lists, and make choices regarding pedagogy in ways that acknowledge the complexity of identity and identity development in a multicultural society. The materials we choose should mirror and challenge, as well as allow students to explore, aspects of their developing selves. In that way our courses will further invite our students into the joy of learning that matters in our lives, wherever they are in the ongoing process of discovering and shaping their identity.

Acknowledging and supporting our students' emerging selves as well as addressing the challenges that may be tied to that experience is appropriate in the multicultural classroom because our society has created a milieu in which racial or cultural identity becomes a factor in students' lives and in their education. Such choices in no way convert education into therapy or intrude into the business of parents. Rather, if we acknowledge who our students are, we must acknowledge the multiple identity challenges heaped on them in this society that they carry with them into our classrooms. Knowledge about and thoughtful approaches to that complex area of students' development can help them feel less alone and confused, within themselves and by those around them, as they go about the tasks of learning.

Our students want to feel confident and comfortable with who they are. They also yearn for recognition and connection. They want their classmates and their teachers to know, accept, and respect them. They do not want to be misunderstood, rejected, or excluded. For our students, understanding multiple dimensions of their own and each other's racial or cultural identities is tied to that need and, therefore, to our work in teaching them.

CHAPTER 4

Multifaceted Discussions

Picture an overhead projector in the middle of a classroom. On a large white screen at the front of the room is a pen-and-ink sketch of a woman. Although all of us in the room are examining the same image, as we begin to describe what we see, what becomes clear is that some of us see the craggy profile of an old hag while others see a dashing young woman. Those who see the hag have a difficult time seeing the young woman, and those who see the young woman have a difficult time seeing the hag, even with classmates attempting to guide them. Most students acknowledge that they find it difficult, if not impossible, to see both women simultaneously. The optical illusion I refer to may be a familiar one, but the process of viewing and analyzing the image as a class illustrates vividly significant components of discussions in multicultural classrooms, ones that make such conversations as necessary, important, and compelling as they are difficult.

Now consider the following series of moments in a course on racial and cultural issues. For juxtaposing perspectives on the study of history, students have read chapters from Ronald Takaki's *A Different Mirror* (1993) and Arthur Schlesinger's *The Disuniting of America* (1992). Within minutes of our approaching the opening chapters of Schlesinger, students have engaged in a particularly passionate discussion of what it means to be an American. White, Black, Asian-American, Latino, Russian, and Middle Eastern students divide over the use and meaning of cultural labels; the value of ethnic neighborhoods divides Whites students, who question self-segregation by ethnic identity, and Latinos, who suggest that such neighborhoods evolve because the dominant culture has excluded whole groups of individuals in the first place; and one White student suggests that those who don't like America could go back where they came from. The quiet narratives of Ronald Takaki or Arthur Schlesinger have anything but a quiet effect in our multicultural classroom.

We see things differently. It's hard to see things the way others do, even with help, and it is especially difficult, perhaps impossible, to see the same thing, in two ways simultaneously. Each of us brings to bear on the issues in front of us the influences of our culture, histories, and identity, as well as our values and priorities. It is precisely such multiple perspectives and layers, emanating from the diverse lives and experiences represented among our students, that make conversations across cultural lines so important and so interesting, but at the same time render a series of challenges, for our students and for us as teachers.

WANTING TO KNOW/AFRAID TO TALK

Once students become part of a multicultural school community, they take their places in classrooms next to students they may know well and students they may not know at all. This familiarity or lack of it may be more profound in multicultural schools, since students next to each other may come from unfamiliar neighborhoods and unfamiliar cultures. Classrooms are spaces in which students' lives are constructed and shared on a daily basis, but in multicultural classrooms, students are less likely to know one another's worlds or even how to talk with them about them.

Our students want to know each other, they wonder about each other's lives, and they want to feel comfortable with one another in the classroom. But most students are afraid to ask of one another the questions that would help them to do that. As one White student explained, "Some of my friends are black, some are Latino, some are Asian, some are Native American. I always want to ask them things about their families or cultures, but that's still a line that's scary to cross. I have crossed it a few times, but it always makes me nervous that I'll say the wrong thing." Additionally, many students have been raised not to acknowledge racial or cultural difference. Toni Morrison has rued, "The habit of ignoring race is understood to be a graceful, even generous, liberal gesture" (1993, pp. 9–10). Further, there may be few opportunities for students to engage in serious conversations with each other about significant issues.

The unfamiliarity students feel with each other across cultural lines, their wish to know more about each other, as well as their uncertainty about how to do so, mean that students need opportunities to talk with each other. But they cannot by themselves construct an environment in which such moments are possible.

And so we must help them to do that. We need to give them the forums, the practice, the support, and the guidance they need to learn to speak with each other about issues that concern them.

Such conversations help students understand more about each other and multiple perspectives on important issues, and to understand just how hard it is sometimes for us to talk with each other about matters that concern us. They also prompt students to think about their attitudes and actions. But conversations across cultural lines are not always easy to engage in, especially when they involve issues close to students' lives as individuals and as a group.

CONVERSATIONS, LANGUAGE, AND CULTURE

Language itself creates significant challenges in cross-cultural discussions.

One of the reasons students remain tentative in talking with each other across cultural lines is the uncertainty they feel in addressing each other. The same complexity and confusion surrounding the ways students identify themselves and each other render their conversations more complicated. As we explored in Chapter 3, students do not know what to call each other, and this contributes to their uncertainty about how to engage in meaningful conversations. Thus, helping students know how to address each other can help them move toward more comfortable conversations.

Beyond questions surrounding the language we use to identify ourselves and each other, our students have concerns about what language is permissible—and in what circumstances—as they discuss issues related to race or culture. Students are aware that certain words are potent, but various uses of words over the years have led to more confusion surrounding their place in conversation. Racial designations or racial slurs are among those words. One young Black woman described in her journal in the course on issues of race and culture how strong emotions within her raised questions about one such word: "I hate [the word *Negro*]. It makes me cringe. I think I need to know some more background on where that word came from. Maybe if I knew that, I would find a reason for this intense hatred."

Few words carry more power or engender more confusion for students than the "n-word," *nigger*. Many students know that this word has more power than most to hurt and inflame. Recent aspects of popular culture also mean that the word has entered the vocabulary of songs popular among the young. Many White students, often divorced enough from the word's historical context, come to believe that the word, being used as it is among popular songwriters, must be an acceptable word for them to use, too. They may also hear friends of color use the word in a jocular or affectionate context with each other. Most Blacks, however, remain deeply offended by the use of the word on the part of Whites. Not understanding the ground rules for the use of the word leads some students into destructive moments with each other. Students discover that the word contains enough potency to significantly damage relations with friends and acquaintances.

Given the real power of words in our lives, when students engage in classroom conversations with each other across cultural lines, they need mutually agreed upon guidelines that will enable them to converse with each other without insulting their classmates or destroying communication. If, for example, students are reading literature in which the word *nigger* is used, as is the case with a number of frequently required texts such as Harper Lee's novel *To Kill a Mockingbird* (1960) or Richard Wright's auto-biography *Black Boy* (1945), how will students engage in conversation about the book? Will they use the word or not, or use an abbreviation? And what are the effects of any one of those choices? Will they read the word if they are reading segments of the text aloud? If so, who will do the reading—the teacher? a White student? a Black student? a student from another culture? And what will be the effect of that choice? More general-ly, if students are discussing aspects of culture, history, identity, or lan-guage, will they use the word or not? And how will either choice be han-dled? One White student wrote, trying to figure it out:

> While a good [number] of students agreed that it was okay to use the word [nigger] in historical or educational context, [one young Black woman] still strongly disagreed. The very word, she said, made her feel like crying and she hated to even read it aloud. I had never known anyone to feel so strongly, so I held her opinion in high regard. The rest of the class did not necessarily do the same. At first, I disagreed with her and thought that we should still be able to say it in context in class. But then I realized that if the word offends even one person, we should at least try to refrain from using it.

Such questions are not limited to the role words will play in our stu-dents' use of language. A White professor at a community college in Louisville, Kentucky, felt he had lost his job for discussing with his students the power of the word *nigger* to offend, in an introductory course on inter-personal communication. A Black student took complaints about the use of the word in class to Rev. Louis Coleman, founder of the Justice Resource Center. Later the professor was asked not to return, although the reason is disputed (Colin, 1999).

Questions surrounding language also contribute to the frustration stu-dents feel in trying to articulate their ideas about sensitive subjects. Since most students lack experience in engaging in conversations across cultural lines about significant issues close to their lives, they have little clarity about how their words or concepts may affect classmates from cultural backgrounds different from their own. Some students tend to be tentative, searching, cautious, and reserved in asking questions and raising points;

others, more bold. But, unavoidably, in the flow of a conversation about sensitive topics, students are going to make observations that are troubling to their classmates.

Many statements in cross-cultural conversations will be contested by classmates who bring different life experiences to the moment or who experience statements differently from students making the points. Then the speakers are faced with reconsidering the statement: explaining "that's not what I meant" and trying to reword the statement; growing frustrated and yielding the floor; or feeling caught in a moment in which they actually did say what they meant, but are now realizing the consequences of articulating the idea, on others. This facet of communication can leave students—speakers or listeners—embarrassed, hurt, frustrated, angry, or confused. Such moments can cause students to withdraw from the conversation, or they can alter the flow of the conversation altogether. As students gain practice in engaging in cross-cultural conversations, however, they become more aware of the way they are being perceived by others and of the ways in which they have to work at expressing themselves more precisely. At times, students' frustration about communicating effectively with each other suggests an almost poetical but unrealistic yearning: "If only I could say it right, all these confusions and tensions would go away."

One of the brightest lights in all of this confusion, however, is the power of language, ultimately, to bring us closer together. Repeatedly we have watched students grow closer over the course of a semester through the power of sharing their words. As students encounter one text or concept after another and work with them in group discussions, they begin to develop a shared vocabulary, a common language. Their growing fluency with a common language allows them to deepen conversation, to lessen confusion and tension, and to find delight not only with the increasing sense of control they are gaining over difficult ideas and subjects, but with the greater ease they are beginning to experience in communicating with each other.

THE RICHNESS AND CHALLENGES OF MULTIPLE PERSPECTIVES

Multiple perspectives, central to groups of students from diverse backgrounds, provide both opportunities for learning as well as challenges to successful communication. At the heart of most conversations across cultural lines are multiple perspectives, and the advantages of conversations involving multiple perspectives on specific issues are obvious.

Discussion of complex ideas from multiple perspectives is often what makes education, at any age, so compelling. Most students enjoy expressing their own opinions and hearing the opinions of their classmates. Consistent with the appeal of critical thinking, many students prefer the openness of exploring multiple ideas to the rigidity of a prescribed way of evaluating a text, a phenomenon, or a concept. Students like hearing different responses to the same question, even if they don't agree with some of those responses. "I never realized how many people have the same questions I do and yet feel completely different about the topic," wrote one White student in her journal for the course on issues of race and culture. For another White student, moments that revealed the most divergent perspectives became the most interesting: "There were several times in class when I could practically feel two sides of an issue repel each other. These times were the most significant to me." Because such conversations often stretch the edges of what students know, as those conversations unfold, students may hear information for the first time.

Discussions involving students from multiple cultures also help students think more broadly about issues and prepare them for conversing and interacting across cultural lines in the multicultural and global society they are inheriting. Discussions involving multiple perspectives increase students' awareness of themselves and others. For one young Black woman, conversations in the class on issues of race and culture meant that for the first time she felt as self-conscious as she thought Whites must often feel when they speak and do not want to seem prejudiced. And at times conversations grounded in multiple perspectives enable students to see that even those they felt "could never understand," do.

These conversations are not easy to engage in, though. Our students know it, and we know it. Students find it challenging to say precisely what they mean and to respond to comments their observations may elicit. In the course of these conversations, students hear points of view that are hard to hear or that they do not want to hear, opinions that may go against what they have been taught by figures of authority throughout their lives. They hear opinions that they do not agree with, and that pertain to their common practices or gestures. They hear opinions about what they and others should and should not say and do.

But sometimes sound learning involves a degree of discomfort. "To some extent," bell hooks reminds us, "we all know that whenever we address in the classroom subjects that students are passionate about there is always a possibility of confrontation, forceful expression of ideas, or even conflict" (1994, p. 39). Walter Feinberg counsels that the best teaching in a "liberal, multicultural society" helps students understand the effect of their words on others, the different ways they might be interpreted: "The way to teach students to engage in public discourse is not to require them to mute their own unique cultural voice but to teach them how to have that voice heard by others who may not agree with it" (1998, p. 225).

Some students like to talk a lot. Others would rather learn by listening, writing, or reflecting. Some students need help to be heard; others need help not to dominate the discussion.

Further, the cultural identity alone of a given speaker affects how material will be offered and will be received by an audience. The effects of information offered about a particular culture by a cultural insider will potentially be different than the effects of information coming from a cultural outsider. Many students are acutely aware of the tendency in schools to cater to perspectives of those in the dominant culture at the expense of those from minority cultures; thus, perceptions about minorities from the outsider voices of the dominant culture can easily produce skepticism, frustration, or anger among students in the cultural minority. This was the clearly the case one morning as a White guest speaker inflamed Black students through his use of statistics on the incarceration of Black men. Later in the day, in a discussion in their American Literature class, Black students expressed their rage over the White speaker, to them seemingly cavalier and insulting with his statistics. The central concern of the speaker was lost as the power of the White outsider perspective overshadowed for young Blacks in the audience what should have been the more powerful message: the real danger facing the Black male in contemporary American society.

Further, class discussions, even when they are focused and well overseen by a conscientious teacher, always contain an element of the unpredictable. Teachers can never eliminate the possibility or the effects, on individuals or the group, of the loose cannon. A student's eagerness, naivete, ignorance, frustration, or cruelty may lead him or her to make a remark that has the capacity to deeply wound a classmate. Unavoidably this threatens not only the unfolding conversation but, potentially, a student's sense of self, the psychological tone of the class, students' relationships with each other, and students' relationships with the teacher upon whom they depend to keep a classroom safe.

Beyond the multiple perspectives that actually emerge in classroom discussions lie perspectives that never, in fact, enter discussions but that affect in one way or another the tenor or substance of those discussions. Cross–cultural discussions about racial or cultural issues are multilayered as well as multifaceted. Multiple discussions exist simultaneously—discussions that do take place in class; discussions that are wished for but do not occur, leaving a sense of yearning or frustration in their wake; observations submerged beneath the surface that never emerge or that emerge in the privacy of journals and are thus never broadly heard or known; those submerged whose power nonetheless has the capacity to affect what is openly said; those that carry over into the spaces outside the classroom, broadening the effects of the conversation that has already unfolded; or those that do not—as students develop a sense of holding onto something evanescent that has left them somehow changed but that can never exist in quite the same way beyond that moment in time. In one instance in a particularly quiet class of students, a reading aloud in class of an essay by activist women of color (Three Rivers, 1991) triggered weekend arguments and conversations that students brought forward into class conversations on Monday morning. The intensity of the ensuing debate raised the level of vitality, openness, and candor in discussions for the duration of the course.

Students engaged in cross-cultural conversations are not only learning from those conversations, they are practicing how to do them. They are learning how hard such conversations are to conduct, and at times how hard it is not only to be understood but to understand others with whom they share their classes and their school.

Our students know that there are significant differences between themselves and their classmates based on history, cultural affiliation, values, priorities, and life experiences, and that this will at times affect their ability to understand and relate to each other in a group discussion. One effect of this aspect of these conversations is to create both alliances and distances among classmates. Students who find that they share opinions on key issues are often drawn together, while students who find it difficult or impossible to understand each other may grow more distant. If the opinions held by one member of the class are shared by no one else, the resulting isolation can jeopardize the student's connection to the class or to the course as a whole. "In class it gets tiring having to hold your own and having absolutely no one to support you," wrote one young Black woman about an earlier discussion. "Voicing opinions when they don't agree with the [opinions of the] majority, falls on deaf ears, so why waste breath?"

Some of those interpersonal effects are brief and quickly forgotten; others linger and affect future classroom dynamics and conversations. Over time, however, classmates who share meaningful conversations on a regular basis generally progress from feelings of awkwardness and uncertainty with each other to developing a shared set of experiences that brings them closer together. And this is a process quite moving to be part of.

THE EMOTIONAL LIFE OF DISCUSSIONS

The closeness students feel with issues tied to their interests, passions, identities, histories, and cultures means that cross-cultural conversations about significant issues can grow emotionally laden. This factor, too, renders them complex.

Many issues tied to race or culture tap deeply into students' own relationships to history, to culture, and to identity, and this means that conversations on significant issues can quickly become personal. This in turn increases the level of emotion and vulnerability for all involved. Emotions can also run high when students voice strongly held opposing viewpoints. Debating those perspectives can produce a competition of values, assumptions, and histories that can affect students in deeply personal ways. Students may leave such conversations confused and frustrated, if not angry or hurt. When students' emotions are engaged, there is also less control for students and teacher. And this can lead to more anxiety and uncertainty among students and teachers: The conversation unfolds on an emotional edge involving both public and private emotions, and therefore the process becomes more unpredictable. Too much or too little emotion may result in withdrawal from the conversation on the part of individual students or in widespread discomfort in the group.

In addition to the excitement and intellectual challenge often generated by complex and multifaceted conversations, discussions across cultural lines can evoke a series of specific emotions challenging for individuals or the group to accommodate. Chief among those emotions are fear, anger, and guilt. Such strong feelings, in turn, can trigger defensiveness.

Students describe numerous fears tied to cross-cultural conversations. Many students fear offending their classmates—peers within their own cultural group or those in other cultural groups. They fear how they will be seen by others as a result of the points that they make—or do not make— or the questions they raise. They fear how others will respond or react. They fear rejection, accusations, and confrontation. They also, at times, fear what they hear or learn. For one young White woman, such uneasiness extended to conversations beyond those conducted in our own class. Describing her responses to student conversations about those in other cultures in the film *School Colors* (Andrews, 1994), she wrote, "I heard points of view that were new to [me], and these opinions scared me." Although some uneasiness and fear may be expected in discussions, too much uneasiness may lead to students withdrawing from the conversation or to the conversation breaking down altogether. Or, as some of our students note, to a lack of progress in being able to use good conversations for fostering growth and understanding.

Conversations across cultural lines may also trigger anger, and that anger can be provoked by others, by specific material, or by the process of the conversation. Students may be angered by the attitudes, words, or actions of classmates or teacher. They may be angered by material that presents a point of view with which they strongly disagree. Or, if the material reflects a criticism they feel applies to their own attitudes or behaviors, they may experience the point of view as an accusation, and this can generate an angry response.

Anger may also be triggered by the process by which the conversation is unfolding. Students need to know that someone is in charge in a classroom and that they can depend on that person to keep a healthy focus and direction to the conversation as well as a sense of order and safety for each of the students. Perceiving that a discussion itself has gotten out of hand makes students uncomfortable and at times angry, especially if they feel that one or more students are not being protected from the words or gestures of another. Students want to know that they will not be singled out in discussions or their experiences used as examples in ways that can make them uncomfortable before a group of their peers. They want protection from disrespect, cruelty, racism itself, and accusations of racism. Their own sense of uneasiness and insecurity means that they want teachers to intervene in a difficult conversation in a timely and responsible manner and steer it in a way that allows each of them to hold on to a sense of self while continuing to further the discussion. One difficulty for the teacher lies in discerning when an "uncomfortable" conversation is in fact a healthy sharing of contradictory viewpoints that should be allowed to develop further, and when the conversation has veered into an area that in some way threatens the well-being of an individual or the group.

Conversations such as these may also set off feelings of guilt. As conversations focus on violent, unjust, or painful aspects of history or human behavior, or as classmates relate stories of their own or their families' or friends' lives, other students may, rightly or not, feel implicated in the attitudes or behaviors being reflected in the observations. While some students confidently maintain their separation from injustices with which they had nothing to do—because they occurred either in the past or in moments removed from their own lives—other students personalize the implications of stories and feel a sharp and lingering vulnerability. And in some moments, attitudes and behaviors that are tied to students *are* being criticized. At such times students may experience intense discomfort with themselves, with their own cultural identity—indeed, with their own body and skin.

Multicultural conversations can also trigger defensiveness. Although challenges to students' own opinions often provide healthy moments of growth, material that overwhelms a student's ability to absorb and work with specific concepts may set off strong defenses. Students' defenses are mobilized when words, ideas, images, or behaviors coming from texts, films, presenters, or classmates threaten their sense of self or worldview. Once students' defenses are engaged, they may want to discredit or reject the source of the material that has so troubled them or withdraw from the conversation altogether.

Some students themselves recognize the pattern that leads to defensiveness in classroom conversations as well as its effects. This was clear in one young Black woman's observations about responses to a reading on cultural etiquette (Three Rivers, 1991). "Discussion of the book upset me," she wrote, "because it showed how when something sounds different from what one thinks, then defenses automatically go up and criticism [of the source] always follows." She later urged her classmates to take the time to listen to one another's points of view and in that way to learn something. Barker-Hackett and Mio agree with this student's instincts to help classmates understand their defensiveness: "If people become more aware of their tendenc[y] to . . . become defensive . . . , they gain more control and can choose to do something else. Instead of being afraid or uncomfortable, they can take the opportunity to learn something new" (2000, p. 124).

Moments of strong emotion are sometimes unavoidable in conversations about issues close to students' lives, and such moments affect students differently. For some students, complex and emotional discussions are satisfying. Some students feel energized by debate characterized by strongly held opposing viewpoints. For others, such conversations can become uncomfortable. And this can result in anger or tears, withdrawal from the conversation, or a wish to leave the room. In these instances, too, the teacher must be sensitive and observant enough to sense what is unfolding and offer guidance in a timely and constructive manner. "Instead of trying to find a quick solution or trying to make the [individuals] feel more at ease and comfortable," what may be most helpful is encouraging individuals and the group to try to understand the responses (Barker-Hackett & Mio, 2000, p. 122).

Emotions tied to these discussions can be deepened if a student has few to no classmates who share his or her perspective. And as we adults know too painfully, we cannot always compensate for the needs young people have for approval, acceptance, and inclusion by their peers, no matter how much we ourselves support or encourage them.

Complex cross-cultural conversations can also become too emotional or too personal. Teachers need to maintain a zone of safety for each student and the group. Teachers are not therapists, and the schoolroom is not a therapist's office. We need to maintain a clear distinction between discussions that involve a healthy sharing of multiple points of view on significant issues, and conversation that veers into focal points or levels of disclosure inappropriate in a classroom setting.

Regardless of students' reactions as a conversation unfolds, how they look back on it later may not be so clear. Some students look back on complex or difficult conversations as particularly memorable and instructive: The discomfort of the moment led to important levels of understanding about a key point or issue. But this is not always the case. Difficult cross-cultural conversations can lead students to shy away from such experiences in the future.

Given the emotional nature of issues that arise in the multicultural classroom, we must be vigilant about the ways in which each student is experiencing our classroom conversations.

And we need to help our students understand the origins as well as the effects of strong emotions and responses that may be evoked by cross-cultural conversations.

THE SELF AT THE CENTER:
JOURNEYING TOWARD A MULTICULTURAL PERSPECTIVE

At the center of these potentially fast-paced and intense conversations is each individual student in the classroom, and the complexity of the experience for any given individual is another factor that makes these discussions challenging for students and teachers. Simultaneously, students need to respond to materials and each other, as well as manage the multiple perspectives emerging around them, their own perspective and emotions, and the interaction of their peers. In multicultural discussions students are being asked to take a journey from the relative narrowness, familiarity, and comfort of a monocultural perspective to the relative breadth, complexity, and uncertainty that can accompany a multicultural perspective. Along the way, students may face challenges to their sense of self and their sense of the world, and they may experience a less familiar process of education.

Students' socialization generally includes the transmission of family culture and attending perspectives, values, and assumptions, reinforced throughout childhood. In some cases that socialization includes the pressure to educate others about aspects of the family's culture and to remain within that culture as they look toward dating, the future, and marriage. Students also tend to see and describe themselves as fair-minded and just; they tend not to see themselves as prejudiced or racist. Most of us, our students included, however, have no idea how bound we are to and by our own assumptions or how those assumptions appear to others. We also tend to seek confirmation of the self, our experiences, and our sense of history.

Cross-cultural conversations, however, require students to see their perhaps unquestioned assumptions through others' eyes and points of view, and this means that such conversations can be experienced by students as a challenge to their sense of self. If the comments of other students reinforce their own thinking, they may feel excited and motivated to move deeper into the conversation, but challenges to their points of view mean that not only their own points of view but the points of view of those clos-est to them—family and friends who have influenced them—may be com-ing into question. Students have to absorb both what might be new infor-mation and the challenge to what has been familiar in their thinking, as well as the challenge to those who may have fostered their perspectives in the first place. Challenges to the images we have of ourselves can yield dis-comfort, disorientation, and disillusionment. We can absorb such chal-lenges and integrate them, or we can reject the message, the messenger, or the process that has brought us these challenges and discomfort. For any of us to acknowledge the rightness of an opposing view takes strength and flexibility of mind. These factors mean that students are simultaneously constructing who they are, coming to terms with who they are, and hear-ing and managing observations that may challenge who they are. And this is taking place in the company of others.

If students can manage the challenges to their sense of self, however, they can and often do move toward a sensitivity to multiple perspectives across cultural lines and a comfort with opposing viewpoints. During the course of a conversation or over the course of a school term, many students move from a position of defensiveness, denial, or rejection of opposing viewpoints into a position that enables them to understand the merits of contradictory viewpoints. This position may offer them not only an overview of an issue, but a meta-awareness, a metacognition about their own position and knowledge.

In multicultural conversations about significant issues, students may also be engaging in a process of education less familiar to them. In many courses, a teacher explains concepts to be understood, memorized, and repeated, on tests or in writings, by students. In courses dealing with issues tied in one way or another to race or culture, multicultural conversations about issues close to students' lives, however, can cause students to call into question ideas tied to self, family, religion, neighborhood, culture, or coun-try. Students need to try to understand and tolerate multiple, sometimes opposing viewpoints, some of which directly challenge their own values and assumptions; and they need to tolerate the personal and emotional nature of such discussions. In most courses, students and teacher look together toward an additional focal point—an equation, an epoch, a paint-ing. In these cross-cultural conversations, however, as students respond to materials, they often raise questions about particular cultural perspectives, and as they do so, they may look at each other, to each other, to supply the answers, and this can make for exciting or difficult moments. Such moments may delight students as they share experiences and wisdom in their answers, or may make students self-conscious or resentful over the expectation that they must explain aspects of life in one culture to a person in another culture. Discussions of significant issues are also often left unresolved, unended. And most students have little practice with engaging in such conversations. All of these factors mean that students need to tolerate a high degree of uncertainty and ambiguity in the process of learning.

While students are engaging in new learning, they may experience pressure to "unlearn" what has constituted familiar thinking. Students may feel some of the ground beneath them crumble as conversations call into question assumptions and perspectives that have informed their life throughout childhood. This, in turn, means that students are being asked to move off of their grounding in particular issues, off of their center, onto new ground. This emotional and intellectual decentering can be, as it implies, destabilizing. Education is often associated with building a more solid base; this process often involves disassembling part of what we know. What should we hold on to and defend? What should we modify or let go of? Throughout this process students are being jolted out of a sense of security, however "false" it may have been. This is potentially an uncomfortable moment for any learner, but it can be especially so when it occurs in a classroom of one's peers, peers from whom one also often wishes to gain acceptance, respect, support, or understanding.

The way in which individual students manage this process depends not only on each individual's experience but on other factors as well. How comfortable are students with their own identities and histories? How comfortable are students with other students in the class and with the teacher? What is the cultural identity and background of the teacher? What is the level of didacticism used by the teacher? What perspective is being presented in material or in questions or observations by students? Are materials and observations subtle or direct or confrontational in their message?

The naturally occurring pressure on individual identity and values as well as the confusions and uncertainty that emerge during these discussions mean that students must be able to absorb and respond to challenges to their sense of self while preserving the integrity of an emerging self. Teachers must be able to facilitate students' growth and protect against individual and group fragmentation. Teachers must help students establish and remain faithful to the intellectual focus. And they must modulate the levels of stress, anxiety, and wounds that are a natural aspect of discussions involving multiple perspectives on significant issues.

In some ways, to grow comfortable with participating in multifaceted cross-cultural discussions and with developing multicultural perspectives on complex issues means traveling beyond the socialization and grounding each of us has had in our homes and cultures. It means taking a long journey toward a sense of equilibrium involving a comfort with one's own self and views, being able to examine and respond thoughtfully to opposing views emanating from other perspectives, and being able to build cross-cultural relationships based on knowledge and understanding. Such growth does not necessarily take place in a single class, a course, or a year. Some will make the journey to meta-awareness and metacognition; others will reject the perspectives that challenge their own and the process that supports that investigation. It is perhaps a lifelong journey, asking students to develop a multicultural perspective. We can, however, support them in this process in ways that potentially give them skills beneficial for the rest of their lives.

SUPPORTING CROSS-CULTURAL CONVERSATIONS

As students engage in cross-cultural conversations, they need to have confidence that we are there to look out for each of them and for the group as a whole.

What years of overseeing such conversations have made clear is that our students want to be able to discuss significant topics with each other, to voice their opinions, to be heard, to be respected, and to learn from each other. They want their classmates to be respectful of each other in speaking and in listening.

Students want their classmates to think before they speak, but to speak from the heart. They want them to balance honesty with sensitivity—to be truthful, but to be cognizant of the way their words and actions may affect others. One young White woman in our course on issues of race and culture explained that while any discussion of race and culture may make individuals uneasy, we must respect others' feelings and temper honesty with sensitivity, not because of "political correctness," but because such choices facilitate conversation, and conversations on these topics are important.

Our students want to know that each of their voices can be heard. They want to know that no one voice or group of voices will overwhelm another. And they want their classmates to be good listeners—-to be able to listen to what may be unfamiliar or difficult points of view and to keep an open mind. Further, in conversations that involve issues close to our lives, seemingly inconsequential individual gestures, attitudes, and behaviors can take on more significance. The sidelong glance, laughter, whispering, inattention, leaving the room for any reason—can all create an impression of disrespect or rejection.

Students also want the freedom and the privacy not to have to engage in such discussions. Some students' shyness or their reluctance to share their ideas in a large-group discussion precludes their feeling comfortable engaging in conversations that are controversial, multisided, or emotional. They need the space and freedom to learn in a way that accommodates their needs. They may want solely to listen or to work with such issues through other means, including the privacy of a paper, course journal, or project. Experience has shown us that students who wish to learn primarily by listening or writing, rather than by participating in discussions, take away from these conversations every bit as much as do those who may emerge as discussion leaders, bold and self-confident day to day.

As texts, films, and conversations entail confronting racially or culturally sensitive material, students find support in guidelines for the use of language, and a type of discussion decorum, most usefully when they themselves have helped debate and structure those guidelines. In response to that need, in our course on issues of race and culture, as we approach material that contains sensitive language or is likely to trigger conversation about such language, we provide background on the language and initiate a discussion about the language itself prior to the students' encountering it—the history and effects of such language, and the reasons for its lingering power. We let the students as a group suggest ways of handling such language. Doing so preempts awkwardness and lessens the chance of someone stumbling into insensitivity or cruelty linked to such language. And we give thought to selecting who will read aloud sensitive passages, knowing such choices can have potent effects: Will the student asked feel put on the spot? Feel uncomfortable? Treat the moment in ways bound to offend? Asked about such choices, students often suggest using volunteer readers, but our own judgment needs to be exerted as well. We are also aware that the meaning and impact of words will differ depending on whether author and reader are insiders or outsiders relative to the cultural context of the words in question. Black authors using the word *nigger* or Jewish authors using the word *kike* will affect students differently than will authors outside of those cultures, as will whether a Black student or White student, Jewish or non-Jewish student reads aloud those same words.

Students also appreciate support throughout these conversations to maintain a respectful focus and tone and to manage the complexity of colliding perspectives. As our own students encounter what may be a disorienting array of points of view, we help them understand more about the process of communicating across cultural lines, and the multiple perspectives such conversations involve. We let them know that their opinions on difficult subjects have been influenced—but not determined—by their lives thus far, their histories, and their cultural identities, and that they are still evolving. Sometimes raising such awareness can also lower the risk of the maverick remark that can devastate individuals or corrupt further attempts at conversation.

Because cross-cultural conversations can become emotionally intense, the class and course as a whole profit from our varying the nature of the works and ideas under consideration, as well as the pace involved in addressing material. In our course dealing directly with issues of race and culture, we alternate shorter texts by contemporary historians or by thinkers such as Malcolm X, which may be unstintingly direct in their messages, with related longer works of literature that by nature tend to communicate through suggestion, metaphor, artistic order, and beauty. Varying the pace and material in this way allows students to digest what they are being exposed to and to remobilize their emotional and intellectual resources to absorb new material, to regroup within and among themselves.

As students engage in these conversations, they also need to know that we are aware of the challenges to their sense of self. We can help them understand what may be taking place within themselves and around them, and why such conversations can have such powerful effects on themselves and others. We can help students understand the ways in which multiple perspectives challenge our sense of who we are and what we value. We can help them understand that to attempt to view issues from a position different from our own, or from what we have inherited, or from multiple perspectives, may take time and may feel uncomfortable. Some students bring flexibility and resiliency to such a forum; others can be considerably more rigid or more vulnerable. If we are to continue to engage them in the process of learning, however, we need to let them know that the process is hard, and support them wherever they are. We can assure them that this process is a valuable one, that they are gaining skills that will serve them, potentially, for the rest of their lives, in the workplace and in their personal relationships. Students need and deserve our compassion as they expand their ways of seeing and knowing.

Our students want help with what they cannot understand. They want support when they feel alone, confused, or threatened by ideas, attitudes, or gestures that unsettle their sense of self, their sense of their world, or their sense of those around them. They are depending on us to guide them and to be in charge: to support a robust but healthy exploration of ideas from multiple points of view. One young Black woman in the course on racial and cultural issues described what worked for her: "There seems to be a relaxed atmosphere in the room while we conduct our discussions, and there is also a set boundary we know we can't cross."

In supporting these complex conversations in our course on issues of race and culture, we try to help students understand and respect the difficulty of the process and the long way this requires us to travel. We offer them reassurance: It is a rich but sometimes difficult process to learn from our own and one another's histories, identities, and experiences; to hear multiple voices and stories; to stretch in ways that allow us to know ourselves, each other, and significant issues through a broader lens. We let them talk. We listen. We try to help them understand why difficult moments occur and to give them practice with responding in useful ways (Adams, Bell, & Griffin, p. 78). We try to help them conduct their dialogues in a space between open and closed; between curiosity, idealism, and eagerness, and a level of involvement or withdrawal that makes conversation impossible. If there is too much intellectual or emotional challenge, we will lose our students; if there is too little, there will be little growth. We want to keep all of our students engaged. Our own experience in overseeing these dialogues has led us to conclusions consistent with Palmer's description of a useful and supportive classroom environment: "Bounded and open . . . hospitable and 'charged.' . . . [It] should invite the voice of the individual and the voice of the group, . . . honor the 'little' stories of the students and the 'big' stories of the disciplines, . . . support solitude and . . . community, . . . welcome silence and speech" (1998, pp. 74–77).

For one young Asian-American student such an environment enabled him to ask the questions he wanted to ask, grow closer to his classmates, and learn from their ideas:

> This has been a class based on discussion, and I have been the most interested in the comments of others. I think I have gotten to know the members of the class better, and I feel closer to them. I value each of their comments, no matter how much they conflict with my own. Class would have been so boring if everyone had the same views, there would be no differences. I know lots of classes where I've gone into class with a set opinion, only to change it due to a well thought out statement by a classmate. If anything, my knowledge has been expanded a hundred-fold. I've learned things about different races and cultures that I was either too embarrassed or too shy to ask about.

Students gain skills in cross-cultural discussions only through practice, through learning under our guidance how to use language to facilitate understanding and how to avoid language that defeats the goal of communication. They need to hear themselves and each other and, through the give-and-take of conversation, learn what works and does not work in cross-cultural conversations. If we value developing in our students an understanding of cross-cultural communication, we need to make conversations across cultural lines a priority in our time together and to assist our students each step of the way as they engage in them.

CONCLUSION

To create a trusting environment for cross-cultural conversations is to support young thinkers in a significant exploration of their world. As students talk with each other in our presence, they are also learning more about how to engage in such conversations. They are finding out how to do them by doing them. They are also beginning to understand such discussions—their multiple facets, layers, origins, effects, challenges, and rewards. And, some quiet learners among us may never feel quite comfortable joining these broader exchanges. But experience has shown that once we in the classroom become accustomed to hearing, in lively debate, the multiple voices and points of view that surround us in schools today, we are left forever changed. Our students know and we know that every voice matters. And when a single voice is gone, we miss it. We miss each student's perspective—unique and searching and complex that it is—as it enables us to see more, to learn more, and to think more broadly about the world around us.

CHAPTER 5

Authority Shared and Shifting

In a key scene in Frank Chin's novel *Donald Duk*, 12-year-old Donald confronts his history teacher in the midst of a slide lecture on Chinese-American history. "Mr. Meanwright," he says, "what you just said about the Chinese is not true. . . . You are . . . sir, Mr. Meanwright, not correct . . ." (1991, p. 150), and, armed with a stack of books fresh from the library, the young Chinese-American student proceeds to prove his point in front of a hushed class.

In the novel, driven by a need to confront his own identity and past, young Donald Duk begins to research the history of Chinese Americans. What he discovers along the way fills in, for him, the untold story of his people and raises questions about how history is written—who tells the story, why that is the case, and what the results are. His teacher is well intentioned and well educated and offers his students a perspective shaped by the history department at the University of California at Berkeley. What occurs in class, however, is a collision between a submerged history, freshly discovered, in the hands of a passionate and perceptive young student, and a history traditionally offered in American schools and textbooks.

The result of that collision is a naturally occurring transfer of authority from its traditional locus with the teacher and the author of a standard text, to the statement of a 12-year-old grounded in an alternate version of history. The teacher knows this has occurred. And the class knows it. In this fictional case, young Donald ultimately feels triumphant about publicly righting the telling of his history; Mr. Meanwright is unsettled, left stammering that Donald has caught him "unprepared"; and the class, although initially uneasy, is offered a fuller perspective on Chinese-American history and character.

Although the scene is fictional and represents for Chin the challenge necessary to better the study of Chinese-American history in American schools, at the heart of the scene is a host of questions relating to authority in the multicultural classroom, especially those questions tied to the authority of the teacher, the authority of competing views of history, and the authority of a student. Questions raised by Chin's fictional scene approximate, perhaps more than the author could realize, actual questions surrounding the nature of authority as teachers and students come together from multiple cultures.

Exploration of significant issues in multicultural classrooms invites a more complex way of thinking about authority in a classroom. Exploration of these issues is best served not by the traditional structure of authority resting solely in the hands of the teacher, but in an authority shared and shifting among teacher, scholars or artists on the subject, and students.

Similar to that moment when young Donald confronts his history teacher in San Francisco, in an open discussion, across cultural lines, of issues linked in some way to racial or cultural histories or identities, there will be a host of moments when the source of authority will shift away from the teacher to other voices of authority, including those of the students themselves. In such moments, the teacher will share his or her authority with others, and to the degree that that authority has been vested almost solely in the teacher, the authority of the teacher will be lessened and the authority of others, including that of the students, made manifest. Indeed, there will be many moments when authority undisputedly rests in the hands of a student. Simultaneously, the source of authority may shift from ones that are more public, published, or widely assumed—lectures, texts, or films—to less familiar or more private and personal sources of authority—alternate views on the issues or individual testimonies and recollections growing out of a particular identity or lifetime of experiences.

Why is this so? And what are the effects on teachers and students of this shared and mobile base of authority?

AUTHORITY AND DISCUSSIONS

Issues tied in some way to race or culture are by nature complex and multisided. Wisdom about them is found in multiple complementary or competing perspectives by noted thinkers or artists. To explore them in any depth requires examining not one but a number of thinkers on a given issue. Wisdom about the issues is also found in the voices of students, because in countless instances, life experiences growing out of racial or cultural identities yield a profound kind of understanding about those issues. The fact that indisputable authority on issues may reside within the students themselves makes these discussions somewhat unique, and that uniqueness has to do with bases of knowing.

In discussions of issues tied to race or culture, the authority of the teacher—what he or she has gained by years of study, as well as through experience—is often matched or surpassed in power by the authority of a given student—what that student has gained by virtue of living a particular life, especially as it relates to experiences tied to his or her racial or cultural identity. In discussions involving students from multiple cultures, the self-described personal racial or cultural identity of individuals in the group often becomes a particularly salient factor. Points of view shared on the issues are often shaped by experiences related to those identities. For one Asian-American student, this was clearly the case one day as a Black student and a White student discussed Arthur Schlesinger's *The Disuniting of America* (1992). Here he describes the moment in a journal entry: "A black student was arguing with a white student. The black student argued that he couldn't be proud to be living in this country because of how his people are being treated. The argument became very heated. I think the reason why the black student became so angry was because he knew from experience and from being a black man in the U.S. that he was right." Personal experiences tied to racial or cultural identities and the wisdom that comes from those experiences become a powerful source of knowledge in discussions, at times overshadowing other sources of information on the same issue. In our experience, observations growing out of personal experiences can become an exceptionally valuable source of learning in the classroom.

Further, where personal identity and experience are among determinants for knowledge and understanding, even accounting for the power of empathy, the *limit* to any one individual's knowledge and understanding—his or her authority—is also apparent. This is true for teachers and for students.

For one White student this became particularly clear as he recalled, in a journal entry, a presentation he had prepared for class:

> After reading what [Michael Dyson] wrote [in "The Plight of Black Men" (1998)], thinking it over and presenting to the rest of the class, I knew exactly how little I actually knew. To seem so confident in speaking about something I did not, and will not, understand was difficult. I can read what he has to say, empathize with it, but never truly understand it. Understanding comes from experience, and I will not ever experience the same things and injustices that he, or any other black or obviously minority person, experienced. From this, I was able to empathize more with other people and groups. Whether I agree with them or not, they have different understandings than I do, and thus do things differently and react to situations differently. It is hard to do, hard to watch a situation I don't agree with, occur, but there are reasons behind it which I can't take away and can't necessarily understand, and that is important to know.

Thus, theoretically, both teachers and students bring to a given discussion both a substantial storehouse of knowledge and authority as well as a clear limitation to that knowledge and authority. And as information brought to a discussion includes information tied to particular identities and experiences, authority will shift among members of the discussion group—teachers and students alike.

As a result of these factors, it becomes important to acknowledge and draw on multiple sources of knowledge in exploring issues linked in some way to race or culture—significant thinkers on the issues and the wisdom of the students themselves. In doing so, the authority of the teacher will be shared with others and shift among the teacher, authorities represented in the course syllabus, invited guests, and the students themselves. This shared and shifting locus of authority is a naturally occurring and healthy phenomenon that can result in a fuller and more satisfying learning experience. But it can also leave students and teachers uneasy. To understand this more fully, let us glance for a moment at a few broader observations about authority in the classroom.

AUTHORITY AND VOICE IN THE CLASSROOM

Authority in the classroom reflects a number of distinct features.

Generally, a marked age difference exists between the traditional figure of authority in the classroom—the teacher—and those over whom this figure "has authority"—the students. The teacher's charges may be exquisitely vulnerable or openly disinterested in acknowledging the power of any authority. Students' relationships to themselves, to each other, and to the authority figure are constantly evolving.

Educational authority is also multifaceted. Teachers must be both "*in* authority," that is, able to facilitate the conditions through which learning can take place, and "*an* authority," knowledgeable in a particular subject matter as well as in matters of teaching and learning (Neiman, 1986, p. 64). Further, true authority emerges from the "consent" of those over whom authority operates, and without "respect," that authority "dissolves" (Nyberg & Farber, 1986, pp. 8–10). The way in which teachers manage authority in a classroom has a direct and powerful effect over what does and does not go on there, for any given individual or for an entire class. Additionally, when teachers exercise authority, they also model it for their students; they are engaged, consciously or not, in teaching about authority though the exercise of authority. In fact, teachers "have a special obligation to teach *about* authority while they act *as* authorities in supervising education" (Nyberg & Farber, p. 11, 1986). And because their authority is being exercised in a forum for learning, teachers should also be able to foresee and even facilitate the end of their own authority. Teachers must help their students understand "how and when to resist and challenge" the teacher's own authority, and teachers must be able to understand, accept, and support that moment when it occurs in a healthy fashion. One effect of that moment, however, is that "to question authority successfully is, in a way, to *become* authority" (Donald Kennedy, quoted in Nyberg & Farber, 1986, pp. 9–11). Thus, healthy classroom dynamics reveal both the exercise of authority and the relinquishing of authority, the passing on of authority from one individual to another.

Authority practiced in a classroom is complex in additional ways as well. The way authority is both exercised and experienced may be influenced by culture. Some individuals conceive of authority as "earned," while others see authority as conferred by "role." In discussing issues of authority for Black students, Delpit says that many people of color understand authority to be earned. If a teacher sees her authority as vested in her by virtue of her role, and her authority remains unearned in the eyes of students for whom earning that sense of authority is a prerequisite for respecting that authority, there may be difficulties between teacher and student (1995, pp. 35–36). A Chinese-American student, however, taught in the home that the role of teacher presumes authority, may have quite different expectations, not only in relation to the fact of the authority of a teacher, but in relation to the way in which that authority will be exerted. "Chinese culture emphasizes submission to authority. The parent is the authority in the home, as is the teacher in the school" (Zhou, 1997, p. 195). Thus, teachers should be circumspect about the nature and role of authority they adopt in the classroom and the ways in which it may be experienced by individual students as well as the class as a whole.

Authority in a classroom is also tied to ways of knowing. The authority associated with knowledge of subject matter or pedagogy, that is, teacher being "*an* authority" (Neiman, 1986), is a form of authority that can easily shift if teachers respect, as part of classroom life and discussions, the authority of knowledge tied to experience. Both teachers and students bring into the classroom a storehouse of knowledge tied to life experiences and affiliations, an "authority of experience" (hooks, 1994, p. 89). As that authority is shared in the classroom in the form of responses, stories, or anecdotes from students' own lives, it can take on a particularly powerful and effective role in communication and in the dissemination and analysis of ideas and concepts.

Because the teacher and all of the students come into the classroom bearing this "authority of experience," acknowledging and supporting that authority and form of knowing can also support the power of each individual's voice—the teacher's voice and each student's voice. The notion of student voice as it relates to authority in schools and classrooms is one that has deep roots in dialogues about multicultural education. This is especially the case as the notion of voice is examined in relation to the historically unequal access of individuals in various cultures to power in the United States. One of the privileges accorded Whites as members of the dominant group is that of being heard. Whites "have had the power to control discourse . . . to silence or interpret other people's voices and cultures" (Howard, 1999, pp. 61–62). This phenomenon can affect voices in the classroom if some students' voices are or appear to be privileged at the expense of others or if some students' voices are silenced by virtue of their membership in a marginalized group.

While many White students may have grown accustomed to having their voices heard, this is not the case for students of color in educational settings. In their studies of high school students, Davidson and Fordham have focused on the silenced voices of Mexican and African-American students, respectively. As Davidson says in describing Marbella, a bright, energetic young woman whose family had immigrated from Mexico, "Marbella often falls silent in integrated settings, not speaking unless spoken to" (1997, p. 28). Or as Fordham explains about successful young African-American women at a public high school in Washington, D.C., "[They] have learned not to speak, not to be visible" (1997, p. 97). About one such student, Fordham writes, "Her invisibility, her silence . . . enabled her to become the 'successful' student she was in high school" (p. 87). Without the support of those in authority in schools and without properly managed forums for discussions, including our own classrooms, many such voices have been silenced.

Not all educators, however, are sanguine about the role or power of "the authority of experience." Diana Fuss, author of *Essentially Speaking: Feminism, Nature and Difference,* maintains that students use such information to assert authority over others or to shut down the voices of others (1989).

But our own work in multicultural classrooms suggests that experience provides a significant way of knowing, and that it gives a legitimate form of authority to each of us in the classroom. Supporting the sharing of that knowledge can enhance our understanding of each other and of significant issues. Valuing knowledge gained through both study and experience, and valuing the contributions of both teacher and students, is well suited to dynamics involving authority in multicultural classrooms.

CHALLENGES FOR STUDENTS

Although being confronted with numerous authorities on the same issue can lead to broader thinking and can be intellectually stimulating, such a process can throw students into visible discomfort. In instances when authority is shared by multiple convincing thinkers, for the students a key challenge becomes: Who or what is right? Whom do I trust? Whom do I turn to?

In the face of numerous compelling and opposing points of view on an issue, the challenge to the students to draw their own conclusions can be beset by significant confusion. Moreover, as in the case with the history texts that young Donald presents to his teacher in Chin's novel (1991), some of the most important thinkers on these issues are those whose work challenges long-held or long-taught versions of history or literary greatness. The ideas they offer may challenge the ideas students have held for years.

Consider the use of James Cone's work on the lives of Martin Luther King, Jr. and Malcolm X. In our course on racial and cultural issues, students explore side by side the leadership styles and directions taken by Dr. King and Malcolm X throughout their lives. Although some students may have become almost overfamiliarized with the work of Dr. King, especially his famous speeches and philosophy of nonviolence, many students have less understanding of the life and speeches of Malcolm X. White students, in particular, often come to and respond initially to his speeches with reservation, if not discomfort or denunciation. As students study the childhoods and eventual stands of each leader, however, their initial understanding of each man is made much more complex and nuanced. This is especially the case as students ponder specific twists of each leader's life. Dr. King, raised in the segregated South, became a proponent of integration, and turned to nonviolent resistance to address racism. Malcolm X, raised in integrated schools, favored separatism, and advocated "any means necessary" to end racism. Dr. King saw a "dream" in America; Malcolm X, a "nightmare." In their later years, however, both began to move toward and adopt aspects of each other's stands (Cone, 1991). As students learn facts they had not known about the two leaders, they find their original ideas concerning the two men being challenged. They must integrate new ways of thinking about them and, out of a growing number of perspectives, draw their own conclusions. Similarly, for example, students exposed to some six to eight viewpoints on affirmative action must eventually develop their own position.

Such moments may propel young thinkers into something resembling Sartre's notion of the "terrible freedom," a "freedom from all authority"

("Jean-Paul Sartre—Biography," 2002): "Man is in consequence forlorn, for he cannot find anything to depend upon" (Sartre, 1956, p. 295). Students may be frightened by an awareness of the freedom they actually possess. In the face of multiple competing viewpoints, students have freedom to move among multiple perspectives to develop their own points of view, and that can be unsettling for some. One reason for this is the fact that many students have "already been trained to view themselves as not the ones in authority, not the ones with legitimacy . . . students get scared that [the teacher is no longer] the captain working with them, but . . . just another crew member—and not a reliable one at that" (hooks, 1994, p. 144). Such moments lack the familiarity, clarity, and relative simplicity that comes from a single voice of authority located with the teacher, the form of authority most frequently operating in a classroom.

This invitation to consider multiple points of view on issues that relate in some way to cultural history or identity, each of which has a certain authority, can overwhelm for another reason. Many such issues exert more than a passing intellectual hold on the students. Issues related to racial or cultural histories or identities can affect students today and in the future in very real ways, and the students' ability to process relevant information and make well-informed decisions about the issues can have real consequences in their own and others' lives. And they are aware of this. Often, a nagging discomfort with unresolved feelings about specific issues follows students out of the classroom into the remainder of their day. This is clearly the case, for example, for our high school seniors, White students and students of color, as they follow the evolution of affirmative action policies or other policies tied to racial or cultural identity in university admission practices.

Admitting and examining multiple authorities on ideas or issues poses another challenge for students: It raises questions directly about authority itself, especially who is or can be an authority on a given subject. This is especially evident in instances surrounding authority as outsider versus authority as insider. Who is the author of a given story or history and what does that mean—from what background and set of biases does this story emerge, and how does that affect the telling? Who has the right to tell my story, my history? What is the virtue of the outsider as authority or the virtue of the insider as authority? Consider the following example: Traditional accounts of American history have most often emerged from the perspective of White Americans. When Arthur Schlesinger offers a meditation on the uses of history, he decries the thrust toward what he calls "compensatory" history to balance the treatment of American history in American schools (1992, pp. 49, 96–99). For one of our young Black students, however, Schlesinger's own observation smacked too much of the "outsider" perspective. "I have a history," the young woman noted in the midst of one discussion, "it's not 'compensatory.'" For this young woman, Schlesinger remained unable to see beyond the edges of his own prejudiced assumptions. If anything, her comment reminds us, the same "celebratory" approach to history Schlesinger condemns in relation to more recent approaches to the history of people of color could be applied to decades of White historians telling the story of American history from the standpoint of those "celebrating" *their* culture or viewpoint (p. 97), a history through which the fates of people of color were often trampled or ignored. Schlesinger is the insider commenting on the history of White America, but an outsider commenting on the history of people of color, and many of our students understand the difference of that perspective and its effects.

Involvement with multiple voices of authority also raises, in very real ways, larger central questions relating to authority. Author Frank Chin's novel (1991) gives students one set of answers, but those answers in themselves usher in a new set of questions. Donald Duk, Chin's young Chinese-American student who attends a private school in San Francisco, discovers that his own research in a city library produces more reliable information about Chinese-American work on the transcontinental railroad than that being offered by his well-educated history teacher using a history text written by one of the teacher's own professors at the University of California at Berkeley. The young student presents that information to the teacher in front of the class. Other students in Donald's class are faced with two opposing glimpses of Chinese-American history. The novel also probes the moments during which history gets written: Who has the power to do that, why, and what story that results in. As our own students in Chicago explore the meaning of the novel, they, too, are left wondering: Who tells the story of history? Why? Is there a "true" version of any history? Which version of history are we to trust? And beyond that to: How does one know the truth about any given moment or story? Such questions lead our own students not only into sophisticated questions of epistemology—how do we know or trust what we know?—but also into an interest in knowing more about the sources and reliability of information that surrounds us in this information age. Such philosophical questions can be exhilarating to pursue, but they can also leave students, just as they do adults, with more questions than answers.

Further, as a shift of authority unfolds, the traditional structure in a classroom also shifts, and this movement poses its own set of challenges. Once traditionally accepted sources of authority are thrown into question, including those of the teacher, a respected scholar, or a published work, students lose the security of familiar guideposts in a classroom. If authority shifts visibly from teacher to student, or if the authority of one text can be challenged or debunked by equally convincing opposing texts, a traditional order and basis for understanding in the classroom has shifted, and students may become uncertain about the ground rules accompanying this shift. This can easily produce uneasiness and confusion. Students' uneasiness or insecurity with the shared or shifting authority may in turn result in their taking out their discomfort or frustration on classmates or teacher.

CHALLENGES FOR TEACHERS

For teachers, the initial challenge in working with multiple authorities on issues related in one way or another to race or culture lies in choosing which voices of authority will enter the forum: what scholars, writers, or artists will—and will not—be studied? Who will—and will not—be the guest speakers? Any one teacher's opinion on which voices seem the most humane or essential or radical will most likely not be shared by another. Any attempt at the most balanced approach will emerge unavoidably from the biases of the individual teacher. And since these issues by their nature hinge in many instances on politics, values, background, and point of view, any choice can be considered "political," suspect, or controversial. In Nyberg and Farber's discussion of authority in education, this is a given: "The nature of schooling is a product of decision, but whose? Ultimately, and in the deepest sense, the answer is a matter of politics, and political judgment" (1986, p. 12). For example, does one include, in a course on racial and cultural issues, material from *The Bell Curve* (Herrnstein & Murray, 1996) because of its impact—in one way or another—on the national debate about the measurement of intelligence, especially in a nation so enamored of standardized testing? Or does one refuse to legitimize the argument in the book by opting to keep it off a course reading list? And at what point does a course intended to promote a healthy exploration of significant texts and issues veer into an abuse of the power and authority of a teacher, that is, into indoctrination? Schoolteachers, after all, hold a "platform that others do not enjoy and that is easy to abuse. They should be careful to avoid using that platform to advance strictly or discriminatory private agendas" (Feinberg, 1998, p. 224).

Additional challenges will be found in the course of overseeing the play of multiple authorities and their effect on students. This is especially the case when multiple voices of authority are contradictory, when voices of authority are confrontative, or when authoritative points of view challenge students' most basic assumptions.

For teachers unaccustomed or uncomfortable with admitting the limits to their knowledge or with sharing their authority, a shared and shifting base of authority can produce an immediate and lingering uneasiness. And once the wisdom and authority of students grounded in their experiences enter the conversation, the shift in authority *will* take place. Teachers who deny it risk appearing foolish in the eyes of their students, who perceive readily where a convincing form of authority lies in specific moments. But teachers who deny the opportunity for students to draw on, share, and learn from these powerful bases of knowledge—located among the students themselves—also eliminate from the dialogue some of the most valuable and potent information on the issues. Minimally, in working with these issues in an atmosphere of open enquiry, teachers must be able to move steadily between serving as the primary source of authority on a given issue and relinquishing that role when the locus of authority shifts naturally to other members of the group.

Teachers must also be able to distinguish between authority associated with intellectual influence, being "*an* authority," and authority associated with the power to set guidelines in other areas of the classroom experience, being "*in* authority" (Neiman, 1986). A shift in authority related to subject matter means that teachers must be even more adept at knowing when and how to resume or exert authority for purposes of classroom leadership: moderating discussions, clarifying points, maintaining an appropriate tone of inquiry, protecting vulnerable young thinkers, and protecting against fragmentation of the group. That is, teachers must be able to move back and forth between holding on to their authority to offer a focus, structure, clarity, guidance, support, stability, and reassurance while sharing their authority on subject matter.

Teachers must accept the fact that their true authority—the authority vested in them not only by years of study and experience but also by their students' respect—will be strengthened not by their adamant hold over it, but by their willingness to acknowledge its limitations and to relinquish it to others, including those who, albeit years younger, in key moments reveal a natural and indisputable authority of their own.

SAVORING A SHARED AUTHORITY

Despite these challenges, the advantages of accommodating a shared authority in multicultural conversations are significant, both for students and for teachers. For the class as a whole, the shift of authority provides a democratization of teaching and learning. A wide range of authorities complement each other as teacher and students together pursue a greater, broader, more profound, and more realistic understanding of complex issues. Moreover, since so much of working with issues tied in some way to race or culture is, ultimately, about finding satisfactory ways of sharing power and opportunity, to deny or thwart a shared authority in learning about these issues is to establish an inherent contradiction between the substance of the learning and the process. In 1987, Sleeter and Grant noted that while much work had been done on the curriculum associated with multicultural education, little had been done in forging a new and appropriate pedagogy. Since then, however, bell hooks, Lisa Delpit, Sonia Nieto, James Banks, Vivian Gussin Paley, Geneva Gay, Gloria Ladson-Billings, Christine Sleeter, and others have offered significant ways of thinking about pedagogy in the multicultural classroom. To support a shared form of authority in the exploration of issues tied in one way or another to race or culture is consistent with many of their findings and observations, and promotes a synchronicity between the meaning of many of the issues themselves and the way in which they are explored.

Supporting the dispersal of authority across a broader range of voices, whether acknowledged authorities or the experiential voices of students, also moves toward righting the historically lopsided dispersal of voices of authority in the integrated, multicultural American classroom. Most integrated American classrooms have traditionally been dominated by White voices: White teachers, literature and texts by White writers, disciplines offered through a White lens. This has had the multiple effects of reinforcing the authority of the dominant culture and leaving little room for voices of color to be heard, for students of color to see their own experiences associated with voices of authority, or for all students to become acquainted with authorities of color. One extreme example of this is the book *Black Like Me* (Griffin, 1961), which won acclaim in some circles for offering an understanding of what it meant to be Black in the segregated South. The author was a White man who dyed himself black. The book is still used in some schools. Such practices and materials have done little to encourage students of color to see themselves or others of color as persons of authority on any subject, or for White students to see individuals of color as voices of authority.

In addition, traditionally accepted sources of authority have been found lacking in adequately addressing perspectives or realities of people of color. History books, course reading lists, films, and children's books have all been shown historically to reflect incomplete or inaccurate portrayals of the American experience. And supposedly relatively neutral sources of information—the news or textbooks—have been shown to be riddled with deep-seated biases. Many of our students, as well as scholars, are aware that it is the outsider perspective that has dominated the telling of stories of those in minority cultures.

For students of color, models of authority used in the classroom have often been cultural outsiders, and in many instances students of color have felt such outsiders to be lacking authority in telling their stories and history. Such was the case for the young Black woman who raised significant questions about the work of historian Arthur Schlesinger (1992). As she explained in one discussion, she does not believe that her history is "compensatory" or that to tell her history is to use history as "a weapon," as Schlesinger suggests. Her people were there, she explains; they were part of American history then and should be part of its telling now.

For this young woman, Schlesinger's outsider perspective in this instance is simply not accurate. What Schlesinger deems compensatory is in fact to her no more compensatory than his history would be to him. Both are elements of the history of America. The long tradition of more objective outsider, esteemed in relation to writers such as Alexis de Tocqueville, has an honest challenge placed before it by this young woman's questions: From the inside, you would see things differently. Many of our students today raise significant questions about authority and perspective. And the nature of their questions means that their questions have every bit as much weight for me as do some of Schlesinger's assumptions. Further, to gain some glimpse of what students of color have faced for years in classrooms in relation to outsider authority, one has only to use material by respected authors of color—for example, famous speeches by Malcolm X—to see how uncomfortable and resistant students in the dominant culture can become in relation to authorities offering perspectives from outside White culture.

As with Frank Chin's character Donald Duk, the young Black woman who questions Schlesinger's perspective recognizes that she has been failed by authorities outside her culture. And so she seeks a fuller telling of her story.

Many young people have reason to distrust such "authorities." They have reason to seek authors and authorities who will more fully and adequately tell their story.

Thus, even while Dewey promoted the active participation and engagement of all students (1916/1966, p. 339), available texts and pedagogical practices have historically done little to acknowledge authorities of color, link voices of color with authority, or facilitate students of color being able to relate personally to views of those in authority. Such practices, along with the natural questioning of adolescents, have spawned an active and reasonable distrust of received authority among students, especially among students of color. For all of these reasons, White students and students of color may well call into question traditional sources of authority and be well served by—as well as powerfully affected by—the broadening of legitimate authority in the classroom.

In an excellent discussion of insider versus outsider perspectives in telling the stories of individuals and groups, Walter Feinberg reminds us that one result of oppression is that many perspectives have been ignored or invalidated, and that this leaves us with inaccurate views. Such silencing "has important psychological and spiritual consequences. People are unable to recognize themselves in stories that are about them and hence come to feel alienated from their own culture in its external presentation." All of us must be able to tell our own stories (1998, p. 196).

Further, it is particularly important for this to take place in schools, since hearing stories from insider perspectives enables all groups to gain a "reconstructed understanding" of the stories that have been told by out-siders. Supporting the voices of scholars from multiple cultures as well as the voices of our students broadens students' understanding of their world, one another, and crucial issues; enables both insider and outsider voices to be heard; and leads to a "fuller understanding of [multiple] cultural forms" (Feinberg, 1998, pp. 196, 199–200).

For students, another advantage of exposure to multiple sources of authority is that the notion of a single "truth" about complex issues crum-bles in the face of multiple, varied, complementary or competing perspec-tives. In such moments, the notion of "the truth," often touted by propo-nents of "the great books" or by critics of multiculturalism, becomes a moot point, since it is readily apparent to those in the classroom that there is a host of truths emerging directly in front of them. This yields for stu-dents a fuller understanding of issues and experiences.

And in the face of multiple truths emanating from multiple sources of authority, the burden of analysis, of ultimately deciding how to think about a particular issue, rests solidly with individual students. Despite the confusion this may generate, such moments demand from students an active engage-ment with competing viewpoints if they are to draw conclusions. Students must be active learners who take part in shaping their own systems of belief.

Having to confront questions about the nature of authority itself, although discomforting at times, also heightens students' awareness of the importance of background, point of view, bias, and assumptions in the shaping of a work or statement and in the way that work or statement may affect others. As one White student noted, "Throughout the semester we have been discussing point of view and credibility. In Schlesinger's readings (1992), *Donald Duk* (Chin, 1991) and *Cultural Etiquette* (Three Rivers, 1991), we questioned 'truth.' It was not until reading *[Cultural Etiquette]* that I realized fully the notion of point of view." Students also begin to understand how those same elements are at play in their own statements, observations, or conversations.

Welcoming into the dialogue the authority that emerges from students' experiences means that students can hear firsthand about the very real effects of significant issues on people they know and care about. Life stories emerging from the varied identities and experiences represented in the class confirm the complex and potent nature of the issues under exploration. Students' stories of mothers or sisters or themselves being followed, because of their racial or cultural identity, in department stores, or of friends being harassed by the police, make clear what these issues mean in students' own lives. In one poetical rendering of such moments, a young Latino described oppression as a press on the spirit, making one's life harder and crushing one's soul.

Students also stand to gain a sense of power and even joy as they realize that their ability to reflect on experiences and convey them clearly—that is, to author them—can give meaning, coherence, and form to those experiences. Students have the opportunity to make their experiences matter, to address their concerns in a constructive manner, and to take an active role in raising the awareness of others. They can come to see one another as thinkers and as unique sources of powerful and useful information. That is, they can come to see both themselves and one another as valid sources of authority. To broadly support students' authoring their own ideas guards against the silencing of any voices in the classroom—the voices of students of color or the voices of White students. Dispersal of authority supports adolescents' natural and healthy questioning of authority as they themselves move toward and experiment with positions of authority.

Author Sandra Cisneros remembers clearly her initial relationship with schools, and then that rather spectacular moment—and what it led to—when she discovered her own authority:

INTERVIEWER: There is a little interlude [in *The House on Mango Street*] where the child runs into one of the nuns who teaches at her school and the nun points up to a window and asks, "Do you live there?"

CISNEROS: I used to be ashamed to take anyone into that room, to my house, because if they saw that house they would equate the house with me and my value. And I know that house didn't define me; they just saw the outside. They couldn't see what was inside. I wrote a poem that was a precursor, or perhaps the same story—about an apartment, a flat, . . . and *House on Mango Street* began that night, that same night. It was an incredible moment. It all began at that same time. I can't tell you whether the poems came first or the stories; they all came like a deluge. It had been as if all of a sudden I realized, "Oh my God! Here's something that my classmates can't

write about, and I'm going to tell you because I'm the authority on
this—I can tell you."

At that moment I ceased to be ashamed because I realized that I
knew something that they could never learn at the universities. It was
all of a sudden that I realized something that I knew that I was the
authority on. . . . The neighbors, the people I saw, the poverty that
the women had gone through—you can't learn that in a class. I could
walk in that neighborhood, and I knew how to walk in that neighborhood, and they didn't. So to me it began there, and that's when I
intentionally started writing about all the things in my culture that
were different from them—the poems that are these city voices—the
first part of *Wicked Wicked Ways*—and the stories in *House on
Mango Street*. I think it's ironic that at the moment when I was practically leaving an institution of learning, I began realizing in which
ways institutions had failed me. It was that moment in Iowa [at the
Iowa Writers' Workshop] when I realized my difference from the
other classmates as far as our class differences, our cultural differences, my color difference—all of which I had acknowledged but I
couldn't articulate as such until that moment in that seminar class: I
began intentionally addressing the issues and using the voice that I'm
now known for; I began searching out writers who were writing the
types of stories that I wanted to read; I began, in essence, trying to
piece together those parts of my education that my education had
missed, to fill the void so to speak.

Or, as one of our own students, a young White woman, said after a
particularly complex series of discussions, "I knew I had found my voice
and now all I had to do was learn how to make it louder than a whisper."

For teachers, satisfaction comes from enabling students to begin to
understand the complexities of issues emanating from the past or the present and from introducing students to multiple valuable thinkers at work on
significant aspects of our lives. It comes from having the strength and
courage to share our own authority. And it comes from being able to establish the conditions of learning in which the authority of the next generation
of thinkers can be born and nurtured.

SHARING AUTHORITY IN THE CLASSROOM

All of our students enter our classrooms with wisdom and interests emerging from their varied and distinct experiences in homes, neighborhoods,
and communities, and they come to us hungry with questions. Providing
opportunities for students to draw on their wisdom, their interests, and

their questions can enrich our classes and nurture a sense of emerging authority in our students.

Picture the following moments in a variety of courses, all of which grow out of and foster an emerging authority in students from multiple cultures: In a course on classic and contemporary fiction, a Jewish student offers the class a multimedia PowerPoint presentation on the effects of the Holocaust on the visual arts, an extension of studying a short story growing out of that same period. Together, students tack up as hall displays scripts and poems written as part of their comparative study of drama and poetry in a course on genres. Scripts detailing the challenges of immigration move between the language of the character's home and the language of the new land. Poetry resonates with issues emerging from identities straddling two cultures in the United States. Students simultaneously studying American history and American literature engage in social action on issues of their choice in the city of Chicago as an extension of the values and commitments of activists and writers they are examining throughout the American experience; later they present their findings on the connections between issues explored by historians and writers and real life in the neighborhoods around them, as well as additional ways those issues might be addressed. As part of that involvement, students from a Latino neighborhood work side by side with students from other neighborhoods to protest the presence of a coal-burning plant in the neighborhood. A young scholar-athlete triggers and leads a discussion in class on the effects of discrimination on women in sports. At the end of our course on issues of race and culture, one student notes in his journal that the most valuable aspect of the course for him was hearing the perspectives of classmates from multiple cultures in classroom discussions.

Classrooms that reflect a shared and shifting authority reveal a vital, involved group of students who take an active role in their learning and who broaden the tone, focus, and outcome of their classes. Respecting the authority of our students and supporting our students' respect of a shared base of knowledge resident within and among themselves, in classroom interactions, discussions, writings, and projects, can foster such engagement.

As part of our classroom partnership and our dialogues, our students should know that all of our ideas—teacher's and students'—can be examined in the spirit of open inquiry. Our students should also be able to trust that as their teachers, our authority will be steady and reliable in providing guidance and support, directions and limits.

To help our students expand their thinking and test their emerging ideas, further their powers of analysis and develop crucial skills in cross-cultural communication, we need to build reading lists and course focal points that assure multiple cultural perspectives and multiple perspectives on the same issues, and to support students' sharing their own diverse per-spectives through discussions. We should provide for our students both insider and outsider perspectives, and acquaint them with the work of indi-viduals in authority across a broad spectrum of cultures. Writers, artists, and scholars of color as models of authority should occupy a central place in our courses.

Essential to our work should be helping each of our students to dis-cover, develop, and use their own distinct voice in speaking and writing. Students should "author" their ideas for an actual audience on a regular basis, through articulating their ideas in discussions and presentations and through clarifying those ideas as they respond to their classmates' ques-tions. They should write about issues and aspects of life that have meaning for them and share that writing with their classmates, in formal and infor-mal readings, in small groups and in larger groups, and in displays and publications within and beyond the classroom.

Fostering a shared and shifting authority means that our students are expected and trusted to assume a significant role in animating and shaping the vitality of the classes we share. In doing so, they can come to develop and to trust a sound authority of their own. As teachers, we can take pride in helping students become strong and articulate spokespersons for significant issues, spokespersons who bring to the forum an ability to examine ideas from multiple cultural perspectives, and thus reflect key qualities so broadly needed today in the leadership circles of our towns, cities, and nations.

CONCLUSION

The multicultural classroom presents teachers and students with the oppor-tunities, the challenges, and the rewards of working with multiple sources of authority. Additionally, our increasingly multicultural and global socie-ty demands that all of us gain the capacity to consider, understand, toler-ate, develop, and act on information involving multiple authorities and per-spectives. Understanding and supporting a legitimate shared and shifting nature of authority in the multicultural classroom can assist us in working effectively with our students. Assisting our students in developing their own sense of authority as well as helping them develop the capacity to work with multiple sources of authority can, in turn, better equip them for their futures. Frank Chin's 12-year-old Donald Duk embodies one role model for the multicultural classroom. We need to be prepared to under-stand and to serve his needs.

CHAPTER 6

Anatomy of a Failure: The Impact of Curriculum/ The Power of Pedagogy

This is a story of regret. In attempting to work with racial and cultural issues as they relate to curriculum and pedagogy, I have made many mistakes. This is the story of one of those mistakes. This is also a story of looking back over the years, into the past, at a choice gone bad, but I do so because I think it raises questions that should not be disregarded in the multicultural classroom.

*   *   *

Even for Chicago, the May morning dawns cold. The small touring bus snakes south on Lake Shore Drive in rush-hour traffic. Within the next three hours these 15 students in a course on Chicago writers will bring alive, as tour guides, the literary life of their city.

In Hyde Park, the bus circles off the outer drive and pulls alongside Gwendolyn Brooks's high-rise. Braced against cold winds off of Lake Michigan, we follow our tour guides for this stop, two young Black women. Beneath Ms. Brooks's own home, we hear of her distinguished career as well as verses chronicling moments in her family life and her desires as a child to leave the "front yard" and explore a darker side of human experience. At Edgar Lee Masters's former home, the present owner joins us unexpectedly and regales us with lore about the writer and his house. A few blocks later, a young White woman recalls, through the words of Upton Sinclair, the hardships of Lithuanian immigrants trying to survive in the jungle of the stockyards, now largely abandoned. A young Latina takes us to Hull House and pays tribute to the work of Jane Addams. And in Washington Park, through passages by James T. Farrell offered by two young Black men, we follow the route of the city's Irish and

African-American young caught up in the racial tensions of 1919, only weeks after White boys have, in reality, pulled a Black child from his bike and beaten him into a coma on a nearby street. We pause in front of one of the city's oldest skyscrapers to hear Carl Sandburg's early poems about these then-new and mystifying structures. On Division Street, in the heart of the city's "Polish Triangle," two young White women share with us the tough and gentle voice of Nelson Algren and his portrait of a boy in search of his mother, a boy who, like so many of Algren's characters, will be left to fend for himself on these city streets. Last, we enter a darkened blues bar—closed except to us—where three young White students take the stage and celebrate the poetry of African-American poet Sterling Plumpp, accompanied by the wailing saxophone of Von Freeman, the subject of Plumpp's poetry.

With each stop I feel a thrill—the language of these authors heard at the sites of some of their most famous works. By noon, we emerge from the blue-neon-tinged darkness of the bar into the brightness of midday, and head back to school. I look over the students, laughing, pensive, and I know they have created magic this morning, in this city of writers, "city of big shoulders," and a city some have called the most segregated in the nation. I know, too, pensive like some of them, that we have shared other moments in this course on Chicago writers that were not magical—that tore at us as a group and made me question some of my most fundamental gestures in teaching. At the heart of education today, especially in classes of students from multiple cultures, lie questions about how knowledge is built: what comes together in that process, what supports the healthy building of knowledge, and what impinges upon it.

CARL SANDBURG AND THE MULTICULTURAL CLASSROOM

On a wintry afternoon several months before our literary tour of Chicago, we have begun to examine the poetry of Carl Sandburg, Illinois poet laureate and one of the most famous voices associated with the city. A young White student leads us in a seminar presentation. His thesis: that Sandburg's socialist views permeate his poetry in his support of the worker. In preparation for the seminar, I have asked the class to read a cluster of poems the night before, and after the student has led the class deftly through a discussion of "Chicago," "Halsted Street Car," poetry on child labor, and on women who have lost the ability to dream, he turns to a pair of poems on Black workers, startling even in their titles: "Nigger" and "Singing Nigger." Hesitantly, the student refers to the poems in a way that places Sandburg's descriptions of Black workers into a framework about stereotypes, and thus makes them more approachable. By the end of his presentation, his work with the poet has been full and informed.

As we begin to absorb the impact of these two particular poems, several Black students speak up. The poems have deeply offended them. One young woman has spoken with her mother about them when she encountered them the night before. Another asks, "What I want to know is: Was 'nigger' *ever* okay?" As tensions mount, a young White woman explains that she feels that students know the images of the Black workers are not real, that the poems are obviously from another era and will not have the effect, now, of reinforcing racist thinking. If anything, she suggests, they show what Blacks have had to contend with. As tensions in the group deepen, I attempt to provide further historical background for the two poems: We are coming to them some 80 years after they were written, "Nigger" in 1916 and "Singing Nigger" in 1918. They come from a different time. And although they are disturbing, they are tied to a significant aspect of Sandburg's life and work: He was deeply involved in issues involving racial equality, especially for Blacks on the city's South Side, and in fact was honored with an award by the NAACP for his work on civil rights. One young Black woman counters that that makes little difference in the face of the reality of these poems today—their messages and their meaning and their impact. As the class comes to a close, we part with tension in the room palpable.

That afternoon and the next day, I'm deeply troubled by the way the class has unfolded, especially with my having placed those particular poems before the students with no initial context—when they were asked to read a sampling of Sandburg's poetry the night before—and my having decided to use them at all. When I reread the poems, I wonder how I could have erred to such an extent. What was I thinking in including those two particular pieces? To examine that series of moments and perhaps to learn from them, we need to understand something of the way knowledge is constructed in the classroom within the contexts of culture and power.

KNOWLEDGE CONSTRUCTION IN THE CLASSROOM

In any classroom, at least three existing bodies of knowledge will merge in the process of students building new knowledge: the knowledge embodied in the curriculum; the knowledge reflected within the teacher and his or her choices regarding curriculum and pedagogy; and the knowledge represented within and among the students.

Unlike the "banking" model of education described and rejected by Paulo Freire (1971)—that is, a teacher "depositing" knowledge into learners—classes like the one in which this series of moments occurred unfold in a give-and-take flow of ideas. But beneath the apparent open dialogues between teacher and students lie layers and layers of culturally based assumptions and forms of power.

Further, the knowledge that is brought to the classroom and the knowledge being constructed in the classroom are composed of both subjective and objective elements. Our experiences, histories, and identities influence the way we view and understand the world. They affect how we perceive, interpret, and construct information (Banks, 1996; Ovando & Gourd, 1996).

In the case of the series of moments surrounding the study of Carl Sandburg, subjective and objective forms of knowing came together and collided from the worlds of the poet, the teacher, and the students. Let us examine for a moment the nature of what Sandburg knew and placed into his poems, what the teacher knew and brought to her teaching, what the students knew and brought to their learning, and how those bases of knowledge affected what happened in the classroom that afternoon.

A POET'S PERSPECTIVE

Carl Sandburg's consciousness about race began in the small Midwestern town of Galesburg, Illinois, where the poet was born to Swedish immigrants of modest means. The Galesburg of Sandburg's childhood—from 1878 to 1902—offered the young boy the legacy and spirit of Abe Lincoln as well as the shouts of a lynch mob outside the local jail. By the 1850s, one-sixth of the town's population was Swedish immigrants, along with many Irish Catholics, a few Chinese and Italians, some Japanese students, and many Blacks, since Galesburg had been a haven along the Underground Railroad (Niven, 1991). Swedes, Italians, Jews, and Blacks passed each other on village sidewalks. And children coming to terms both with language and with each other, learned young the lingo of stereotypes and epithets. Sandburg describes in his autobiography what he heard around him: "A Jew was a 'sheeny.' The Irish were 'micks.' A Swede was a 'snorky.' A Yankee was a 'skinflint.' The Germans were 'Dutch.' The Italians were 'dagoes.' A Negro was a 'nigger' or a 'smoke.' I heard Irish boys say of themselves, 'Us micks' and Negroes speak of themselves as 'Us niggers'" (1953, p. 281).

At home and about town, however, young Sandburg lived his own life on the side of tolerance, fairness, and justice. He recalls the dignity of a wiper for the railways taking his Friday night walks to meetings, and the stump-legged Black man who created his own society amidst the detritus of the rail yards. On one occasion he watched with boyhood curiosity a town mob call for the lynching of a Black man who had accidentally killed a White man in a barroom fight. After the sheriff had provided for the safe removal of the prisoner, "The crazy show was over. We drifted away into the night. Some of us glad it turned out as it did, others sad and disappointed" (Sandburg, 1953, p. 315). What remained for the young poet, however, as vividly as the actions of the mob, was the reality that the prisoner received his trial, and the mob leaders were punished. Years later, Sandburg was attending a church service at Joliet prison chapel and saw the man. Still haunted by the vagaries of chance and fate that brought this strong and attractive man to life imprisonment, Sandburg wrote, "'What a pity it was that when your fist hit that man in the saloon he didn't slam into a wooden wall instead of a pane of glass that broke so it cut a leg artery and he died. It was an accident and you didn't mean it to end like it did.' Maybe he read my eyes and had an inkling I [hoped for him a better life]" (1953, pp. 315–316).

What Sandburg also took from the lynch mob and its aftermath, however, was an acute awareness of the countervailing beliefs that punctuated his life in Galesburg: the "howls and yells of the mob, 'Kill the nigger!'" echoed across the same terrain as Lincoln's stand on slavery, articulated in the Lincoln-Douglas Debate and reflected in words of bronze on the door of a local college (Sandburg, 1953, p. 316).

By the time the race riots of 1919 tore apart the city of Chicago, Sandburg the socialist and Sandburg the journalist had written extensively of the city's Black Belt. Interviewing local residents, Sandburg wrote a series of articles underscoring scandalous conditions in housing and employment affecting the city's Blacks. Placing the conditions of Chicago's Blacks and race relations in the context of racial tensions throughout the country, Sandburg tracked the dreams, disillusionment, and devastation facing Blacks immigrating north out of the Jim Crow South in search of a better life, as well as the challenges experienced by Black veterans returning from World War I to face discrimination and rejection at home. For his steadfast eye on conditions facing African Americans, Sandburg was later honored by the NAACP as "a major prophet of Civil Rights in our time" (Niven, 1991, p. 699).

Liberal and socialist that he was, however, Sandburg's conceptions of race were also influenced in other, less benign ways by the era and places in which he matured. As James Banks and others have argued, race is a social construct, one that has differed over the years (1996). The cultural context that nurtured Sandburg's own construct of race was a small Midwestern town in the late 19th century and Chicago of the early 20th century. In the mid- to late 1800s, "race was conceptualized in a way that designated specific groups with clearly defined, biologically inherited phys-

ical and behavioral characteristics. Some groups were defined as inherently superior to others," and "the environment or experiences of individuals
or groups could do little to change their inherited racial characteristics"
(Banks, 1996, pp. 68–69).

"By the late nineteenth century," Banks notes, "rigid and racist ideas
about the inherited characteristics of different racial groups were codified
in established social science in the United States. Groups of color such as
American Indians and African Americans" were considered "inherently
inferior," and "White ethnic groups were perceived as different races, some
inferior to others" (1996, pp. 76–77).

By 1918, within two years of the publication of Sandburg's poems on
Black workers, Robert E. Park, his theories, and his writing were becoming highly influential in the department of sociology at the University of
Chicago. By 1921, in a textbook required by students in the department,
Park had written of Blacks, "The temperament of the Negro, as I conceive
it, consists in a few elementary but distinctive characteristics." These characteristics result in "a genial, sunny, and social disposition, in an interest
and attachment to external, physical things rather than to subjective states
and objects of introspection, in a disposition for expression rather than
enterprise and action." The Negro "is primarily an artist, loving life for its
own sake" (Park, 1921/1937, p. 139, quoted in Banks, 1996, p. 72).

Such views on race held by individuals or academic circles were not
created by them but through their socialization in institutions throughout
the country (Banks, 1996). Further, during the years corresponding to
Sandburg's childhood years, Blacks were not far removed from slavery and
this meant that, objectively, as a group they reflected "high levels of poverty," and "low levels of education" (Banks, 1996, p. 77).

Where does this leave us with the apparent "knowledge" reflected
about race in the writings of Sandburg? Although Sandburg produced
many pages of nonfiction exposing racial injustice affecting Blacks, especially those living on the South Side of Chicago, he wrote few poems
focusing on Black life, and the images of Blacks reflected in those works
appear radically different and quite divorced from the larger framework
of his politics. In one poem, entitled "Nigger," the poet attempts to
describe Black workers in the spirit of Walt Whitman: "I am the nig-
ger/Singer of songs/ Dancer" (Sandburg, 1970, pp. 23–24), but what follows reads like an embarrassing list of stereotypes. In another poem,
"Singing Nigger," the poet purports to know Black workers and to envy
their sense of self and happiness. The poem ends on a note of lament: "I
went away asking where I come from" (Sandburg, 1970, p. 108). But the
poet's romanticism surrounding the images of poor Black workers,
singing and hopeful, rings artificial and ignorant. And the "envy" on the

part of the White poet is hollow and unconvincing.

Although Sandburg's articles written for the cause of justice for Blacks reflect the deeply held values of a social reformer, his poems about Blacks during that era are more akin to prevailing racist ideologies about race at the time, constructed by Whites. The poems in question suggest the influence of these theories. Sandburg the social reformer was also a citizen of his times, vulnerable to prevailing subjective, as well as objective, "knowledge" about race.

A TEACHER'S PERSPECTIVE

But let us examine another aspect of the strains of "knowledge" that come together in these discussions. Like the poet, the English teacher, too, is subject to multiple conditions influencing what he or she knows. Racial or cultural identity, the place and time and nature of his or her upbringing, his or her education, all contribute to what the teacher will bring into the classroom and how effectively he or she will work with students from various backgrounds. Central in what many well-educated English teachers have been taught is the canon of American literature, which until recently represented a gradually expanding, little-changing or -challenged body of writers taught perpetually to the nation's students regardless of those students' own identities or backgrounds. Although not without his critics, and subject to the waxing and waning of popularity accorded most writers, Sandburg's presence in the broader canon of American literature has remained secure. "Like no other writer before or since," one critic notes, "Sandburg was treated as a great national leader. He was often referred to as a living national monument." When Sandburg died, at 89, in 1967, "there was national mourning." President Lyndon Johnson attended a memorial service at the Lincoln Memorial in Washington, D.C., led by Chief Justice Earl Warren. "'Carl Sandburg,' [Governor Adlai] Stevenson [of Illinois] said, 'is the one living man whose work and whose life epitomize the American Dream'" (Yannella, 1996, p. xi).

Sandburg's interest in and descriptions of the lives and concerns of ordinary Americans in a language and verse form average readers could understand gave his work broad appeal. For many of his readers, he was one of them, and his life represented the possibility that one could achieve greatness from modest beginnings (Yannella, 1996).

For his poetry and for his prodigious biography of Abraham Lincoln, Sandburg has retained a place of prominence in American literature, and the broader the grounding in particular aspects of American literature by aspiring English teachers, the more likely his prominence would be deeded on to them, and through them to the next generation. In teaching the significant writers of Chicago, Sandburg's status is doubly assured because he remains one of the most famous voices from a city boasting many famous writers. And so the knowledge the teacher draws on as he or she prepares his or her classes is constructed through the machinery of for-decades-unquestioned literary history passed on by the overwhelmingly White guardians of the canon, in colleges and universities. Moreover, the works of those writers who have been part of the pantheon of significant figures in American literature are often offered forward to university students and then through those students-turned-teachers to their students as "universal" in their focus or concerns. "These writers and their works," the teacher says in effect to the students, confidently opening his or her book, "are deemed worthy of study because they deal with 'universal' concerns. Their work transcends the boundaries that limit writers of lesser stature." So the material arrives in class cloaked in notions of "significance" and "universality"—designations that are offered in such a way as to appear objective, but which have been awarded not only in some ways objectively but also subjectively, out of the position of those who for years have conferred the designations of significance and universality on particular members of their own, broadly speaking, cultural inner circle.

In incorporating this work, these poems, in the class, however, the teacher is now complicit in perpetuating, as "knowledge," the racial stereotypes and erroneous, subjectively constructed racist conceptions of race embodied in the poems. But to reflect on this process can be troubling: once the teacher begins to deconstruct his or her own received knowledge and to ask how he or she knows what he or she knows, then what of his or her knowledge can he or she depend on? In the dialogues of the culture or canon wars, these observations are familiar.

THE STUDENTS' PERSPECTIVES

We must move now, however, to the other side of the desk in our investigation into knowledge construction, cultural contexts, and power, and their relationship to classroom learning. We must sit among the students. Into a multicultural group of students in the late 20th century comes this writer swathed in the context of "significance" and "universality." But what does this mean for students?

For Black students who have established a reasonably trusting relationship with a White teacher, suddenly they are confronted with profoundly contradictory and potentially destructive messages. The same openness in Sandburg's style and language that has won him decades of accolades serves up baldly and boldly stereotypical, ignorant messages about Blacks, and this means Black students are pulled between opposing pressures. To remain actively engaged with the material, they must remain open to messages that are patently destructive in relation to their own racial group. They must engage in or hear a discussion that centers on ignorant and destructive notions of their own racial group and their own racial identity, or they must disassociate themselves sufficiently from their own racial identity to intellectualize their relationship to the material and protect their emotions and vulnerability. Conversely, to support the process of building their own healthy identity, they need to throw off such material, engage in resistance (Nieto, 1996, 1999). But this means, essentially, that to preserve a healthy image of their own cultural group and by extension themselves, they must reject published material coming to them in a classroom setting.

In addition, such works call on Black students to make maneuvers that protect their relationship with the teacher while also protecting their own sense of self. If the students take part in the examination of the offending material, they may be left, at least temporarily, with a somewhat bifurcated sense of self, some might say a false self, as they may find themselves playing—in some ways inauthentically—the game of classroom literary criticism to maintain the teacher's approval, but at the cost of engaging in that which may be overtly self-destructive. If, however, the students reject outright the writer or the work, they may fear that in doing so they will strain their relationship with the teacher or perhaps even lessen their chances of academic success. For the students to reject outright the proffered work is for them to take a stand of defiance that risks the public or private rebuke or ire of the teacher or even stronger disciplinary action. This could jeopardize not only their work on this section of the course, but their working relationship with the teacher. The teacher's "authority" or choice has been publicly—or privately—questioned, and thus, out of a host of reasons associated with such exchanges, the teacher may deem one or more of the students a troublemaker, or at least someone who makes him or her uncomfortable. As a result, the teacher may pull back on future efforts to support the students or engage them in learning. The teacher may cease to be the students' ally to the degree that the students questioned his or her choices as teacher, and this has the potential to disrupt the partnership in learning. In the flow of the course, the students are put into a position to learn material that goes against aspects of a fundamental sense of self, or, theoretically, to "fail." What the students ought to resist—intellectually and psychologically—for their own best interests, they must "learn," or else risk the consequences of a poor grade that can have long-term effects as it affects their school record.

Such moments for the Black students are further complicated by the presence and role of White students in the class. Regardless of the positions taken by Black or White students on the material at hand, heightened consciousness about racial issues in recent years means that the very presence of such material as these poems will most likely inject an uneasiness into the group's tone. For the Black students, this group uneasiness is tied to their own emotional relationship with the material, since now something related to their own racial identity is not only making them uncomfortable but is having an uncomfortable effect on White students around them. And this discomfort may be seen, vaguely, on the part of Black students and White students as each other's fault: If the class were not racially mixed, this could be a less uncomfortable moment. If Black students remain quiet during a discussion of the material, they must listen and watch White students and perhaps other Black students discuss a piece of work that includes material degrading to Blacks. But they may also be spotlighted or marginalized out of discomfort on the part of Whites who sense the discomfort of the Black students whose discomfort is related not only to the material but to the White students' own discomfort.

White students struggle with ways to approach, discuss, and take meaning from a text that is uncomfortable to them as well—but for different reasons. White students are often uncertain how to proceed. Should they engage unquestioningly in complicity with the White teacher to preserve their role in the class with the teacher while discussing something they sense or know is awkward or painful, for them and for their Black classmates? Or should they take a stand and raise questions about the validity of doing the work, which may strengthen their ties to the Black students or place them in opposition to the teacher? Moreover, with such material, in order not to have their attitudes about race adversely affected by the material, White students are put into a position of having to actively reject negative and erroneous cultural messages about Blacks coming to them from an authority figure in a classroom, even while supposedly learning the material in front of them, material that ascribes stereotypical characteristics to Blacks. If, however, they do not throw off the essence of the material, they are essentially engaged in learning that perpetuates racist views.

In discussions of material touching on race in one way or another, both Black students and White students are often aware that the racial identity of their classmates has come under scrutiny, and that creates a sense of public awkwardness. In the face of that awareness, students have been placed in position to somehow manage not only their own feelings but those of other classmates and the group, as well as those of the teacher. And this type of moment calls on them to manage ideas and emotions in particularly demanding ways. In the class discussion centering on Sandburg, the original student seminar leader found a way to construct a framework that might deflect the impact of the images of the Black workers by asking the students to look at them as stereotypes. Another White student in the class asserted that these images would not promote more stereotypes and racism and that in fact the poems showed what Blacks had had to deal with. Black students had to contend not only with the effects of the material, but also with managing their rightful anger and frustration in the face of such material. They also had to manage a discussion on the part of the whole class tied directly to sensitive and complex issues related to their racial identity, including the gestures of White students who felt a need to address the feelings of Black classmates as an uncomfortable discussion unfolded.

In the case of this discussion, by the end of class, for the Black students the pressures remained, the damage was done: Who am I? What does this "significant" and "universal" writer convey about Blacks in front of all these White students and placed before us by this White teacher? Where can I go? Whom can I talk with about how this feels? Whom can I connect with to remove myself from this insult and scrutiny and discomfort?

For these Black students, as they made clear to me, beyond reaching out to the few other students of color seated near them, real support for a moment of pain and anger and confusion would have to wait until they could leave class—that is, leave a site of "learning," and reconnect with friends or mentors or family members who could continue the long-term process of supporting a young Black student's sense of identity and strength in a predominantly White school, in a for-now predominantly White society. Although I had attempted to work with the material in a way that could serve us all, I knew I had created a wide gap between myself and the students of color. For how long, I could not know. I did not know whether they could or should trust me again.

ANATOMY OF A LESSON

What sense can we make of these colliding bodies of knowledge in the context of culture and power? What factors supported a meaningful construction of knowledge? What factors impinged upon that? And how can our understanding such moments enable us to better serve the needs of our students?

EXAMINING DIFFICULT MATERIAL

In originally compiling Sandburg's poems for the students to read, and knowing Sandburg's deep-running commitment to bettering conditions for Blacks, I had wanted to include poems that somehow tapped into this side of his work. But although Sandburg wrote many articles addressing issues related to civil rights, he wrote few poems involving Blacks, and those that he did reflect language and biases embedded in his era. One critic notes that Sandburg's "preoccupation in 'Chicago Poems' was not simply with documenting the travails of the lowly; it was to affirm and glorify them" (Yannella, 1996, p. 65).

But what I mostly felt after class was a failure to have read these poems as my students might read them. I had failed to try to experience the poems through my students' eyes in time to keep the poems from doing harm.

One could argue that the poems could be approached in the contexts of American history, literary biography, or critical thinking, and it is within these contexts that the students and I, during the next class, addressed the problematic poems and their effects on us a group:

1. The texts have grown out of aspects of American history and American life, especially American race relations. The study of traditional American writers or of American history often thrusts a group into confronting uncomfortable, overtly discriminatory or racist attitudes and behaviors, some of which belong more to the past than to today. American literature, reflecting American life itself, especially prior to the 1960s, is filled with pejorative references to Jews, Catholics, immigrants, and people of color. The reality of American racism and bigotry is reflected in much of its literature. We cannot excuse or change the multiple forms of discrimination the literature reflects, but approaching them in the light of history can help us understand them.

2. As we move from neighborhood to neighborhood through reading the works of Chicago writers, there will be many contrasting points of view. Within the literature, at different times, Irish Americans, Polish Americans, African Americans, Chicanos, and Asian Americans have all been tied to forms of prejudice. All of the writers come bringing the stories, the tensions, and the prejudices of their own ages, their own groups, their own neighborhoods, their own lives. Although it is a gradual process, by the end of the course we will have gained some understanding of a wide array of Chicago's racially and ethnically diverse communities as well as their cross-cultural tensions.

3. The poems represent one facet of a writer's life and work, for better or worse. In many aspects of his work as a writer, Sandburg is clearly an ally of Blacks, a fighter for Black causes, especially in the extensive series of articles written about Blacks on Chicago's South Side. As a writer he also drew on received images of his time regarding Blacks, some of which came to him through his long-running interest in American folklore and songs, including songs by Blacks and laborers (Callahan, 1970, p. 105). Although in his own time he distinguished himself in the fight for social justice, the relationship to Blacks rendered in these two poems also represents a facet of who he was, for better or worse. Understanding something of the range of Sandburg's work, including these poems, means for students a broader, more accurate, and realistic understanding of the man and his work, beyond what may be more readily associated with his work. In accurately evaluating a life or in evaluating the work of a writer, it may be useful to know as much as possible. Sandburg did good things in the fullness of his life, but some of the pieces he wrote are more acceptable to us than are others.

4. The poems can help us understand more fully the nature of positions and attitudes that offend and divide. Controversial material can prompt discussion of significant issues. And through a greater understanding of the issues, we can move further in clarifying and strengthening our own positions. We can learn to use the dislocation and pain such material may generate, and turn it into power. Such was one young Black student's position, even as the original discussion of the poems was unfolding: "When someone disagrees with me, I try to learn from them. It's good to talk about [these things]." It was similar gestures that allowed Toni Morrison to gaze on the nature of Blackness at the heart of well-known works of American literature, and turn her feelings into the power of understanding and illumination, not only for herself but for succeeding generations of readers. In her response, *Playing in the Dark: Whiteness and the Literary Imagination,* Morrison (1993) transformed the way we think about the relationship between White writers and Black characters in some of this country's most famous works.

Thus, perhaps in some ways it makes sense to read Sandburg's poetry on Blacks—to explore the breadth of the poet's concerns during that era, and because of the importance of his work as a writer for racial justice reflected in his nonfiction. But given the nature of those poems, we are left working with material that raises significant pedagogical issues in the classroom. Placed beside some of Sandburg's most famous early poems on the lure of the city, the problems of immigration, the lives and losses of workers and women, as well as the romance of the prairie, Sandburg's poetry on Blacks raises multifaceted and disturbing questions.

KNOWLEDGE CONSTRUCTION, CULTURAL CONTEXTS, AND POWER

Part of what this investigation confirms for me and what made teaching the Sandburg poems so difficult is that "how we create, define, and validate social knowledge, is determined largely through our cultural context" (Stanfield, 1985, p. 388, quoted in Scheurich & Young, 1997, p. 8). What Sandburg knew and didn't know and what I as teacher knew and didn't know were influenced by the knowledge surrounding us in our cultural contexts. Similarly, the students before me brought their own cultural contexts into the classroom, and how they responded to the moments and what they took from them was inextricably tied not only to the cultural context they brought to class with them, but the one that Sandburg and I and their classmates created in that space of learning. Together, as teacher, poet and poetry, and students, we ourselves constructed a cultural context that influenced what these students came to know, that is, their knowledge. Given the nature of material such as these particular Sandburg poems and the complex responses they elicit, this is a sobering thought. In teaching these poems, their false images may be perceived as "truth," and contribute in negative ways over time to attitudes, behaviors, and policies. More troublingly, these images might be said to have been "enculturated into those who are the victims of the distortions, especially children, who have less ability to resist," prompting an internal struggle over accepting or rejecting debilitating images tied to the self (Scheurich & Young, 1997, p. 9).

An additional factor that amplifies these types of difficulties in the sharing and pursuit of knowledge is the accompanying unequal distribution of power. Recent studies confirm that the vast majority of classes at the high school level are still conducted in ways that preclude significant input by students: Teachers deliver information to be memorized and repeated by students for evaluation. Even in a discussion course such as this that supports the voice and authority of the students, it is clearly I the teacher who has had the power to select and require the material to be read. Beyond several major independent projects in the course, I have designed the syllabus, created the parameters of the class, and suggested what is good and worthwhile for these students to know about this subject. In this small but significant arena of their lives, I determine what they will learn. As Sandra Nieto explains, "Never neutral, institutional environments are based on certain views of human development, of what is worth knowing, and of what it means to be educated" (1999, p. 15). And, daily, I have the power to judge these students in ways that affect them now and potentially for a long time to come—through grades, evaluations, or recommendations. Even the writer, poet Carl Sandburg in this case, has the power that accompanies the designations awarded him through history, the power of his place in the accepted body of noteworthy American writers, the power of having been published, and the power of having been chosen to be part of the material of the course.

Even in a learning community as democratic as the one in which I teach, students know that although they possess a great deal more power than many of their contemporaries in other schools, those who largely determine what and how they will learn will be the adults around them, and, consistent with present demographics of school staffing throughout the country, those adults are overwhelmingly White. And most students come to schools unfamiliar or uneasy with questioning the authority of adults on matters of curriculum and pedagogy beyond a cursory rejection of a given class, focal point, or opinion.

Thus, when students encounter material such as the Sandburg poems on Blacks, they may well feel they have little real power to raise candidly their legitimate concerns about the point of view and subject matter of the poems, or even about the use of the poems, without feeling that they might weaken their position in the class or in the school. For the student to question the teacher and his or her choices in a way that can serve the student's own needs without alienating the teacher or straining the student's relationship with the teacher requires a poise and strength beyond the years of most students. We must consider what it means, as teachers, to put students in that position.

What all of these factors mean is that as teachers we have types of power beyond what we may have ever imagined—not just to facilitate the creation of community or the sharing of ideas or the texts of good writers, but the power to hurt and to divide in ways we may have little considered. In the face of that power, we must respect the perspectives of our students and their expression of rightful resistance to aspects of curriculum or pedagogy as part of the learning process.

CURRICULUM, PEDAGOGY, AND THE STUDENTS

The choice of the poems raises further disturbing questions for me as well, tied to curriculum, pedagogy, and the psychosocial dynamics of teaching literature in the multicultural classroom.

In retrospect, I can say, "I made a mistake." I can conclude that the poems are racist and should not be taught, or I can conclude that the poems are not worth the hurt they caused the students, the dynamics they triggered in the classroom, and the discomfort their teaching brought to my students or to me. Since I wanted the students to know about Sandburg's work on issues of social justice for Blacks, I should have used his nonfiction writing that addressed directly issues for Blacks on Chicago's South Side. That would have been a better choice pedagogically all around.

But does that choice also imply a type of censorship that may not be such a good thing? Does such a conclusion say that there is a body of material that we should not teach because of cultural factors, tied to specific times and places, that the material reflects, or because of the complex dynamics it results in for students and teacher? And does excluding such material preclude students' learning about particular times, places, writers, and race relations, racism, or racial issues reflected in those times and places?

I can also look back and say that in choosing those particular poems I failed to employ a multicultural perspective in planning. I did not anticipate or think through multiple ways in which the poems might be experienced by students of various cultural identities within the class. The cost of my not doing so resulted in unnecessary harm to my students, a "symbolic violence" (Nieto, 1996, p. 284).

In addition, in our discussion of the poems, one of the White students suggested that students know that the images of Black workers in the poems are from another era, that they are not real, and that they will not have the effect on students of perpetuating stereotypical and inaccurate images of Blacks. But is this the case? In his film examination of "ethnic notions," the images and artifacts of a culture that influence our knowledge of and interactions with each other, Marlon Riggs (1987) includes a segment on the original dance associated with "Jim Crow." The commentator says that many Midwesterners of the time knew little to nothing about Blacks, and images tied to the dance—which were not intended to be accurate—began to constitute that knowledge. Those images, Riggs suggests, had a "devastating" effect on the image of Blacks among Whites. And this affected, for obvious reasons, both Whites and Blacks. Similarly, early racist Southern fiction by Whites contributed to the image of Blacks for the nation (Gross, 1966). Does, then, teaching material that reflects the racism of a particular time and place perpetuate that racism? And if so, in the interest of teaching about race and culture, how does one approach and/or teach material that in and of itself reflects racism or racist views?

Further, if we remove the Sandburg poems from study because of their language and focus, what other works should be removed, given the endless awkward and disturbing ways humans have viewed, lived among, and communicated with each other in their actual lives and as writers have responded to that actuality through literature?

Why do works reflecting or exploring aspects of race pose significant challenges for teacher and students? And what can teachers do to approach such works in ways that turn difficult material and classroom moments into power for our students?

WRITERS ON RACE

In offering broad reading lists to our students, the works of many well-known writers—White writers and writers of color—require us to deal with the presence of race, race relations, or racism; moreover, if we are to engage our students in thinking and dialogues about a central issue of our times, material tied to race and the issues it raises should be confronted. James Banks thinks it crucial that students grapple with multiple aspects of race: "Students should examine the ways in which the construction of race reflects the social context, the historical times, and the economic structure of society" (1996, p. 83). And not to teach works with racial content is to offer our students less information about particular eras, places, and race relations, as well as less understanding of a broad body of writers and material.

But to teach such texts can produce dynamics among students complex and difficult for both students and teachers. Each text dealing in one way or another with race can have a different effect on a class. The nature of those responses is tied to a combination of factors: era and locale represented by the text; cultural identity, point of view, and intent of the author; nature, content, and thrust of the text; cultural identity and multiple histories of the teacher; cultural identities and multiple histories of members of the class; number of students of each culture represented in the class; rationale, pedagogy, and context for using the work; frequency of classes focusing on material that touches on racial or cultural issues or cross-cultural relations; and the way in which the students will be able to respond to the work. Let us look at just some of the factors involved as, for example, White students and Black students encounter White writers and Black writers writing on race.

White Writers and Black Writers on Race

Many works of literature that deal in one way or another with race, whether written by White or by Black writers, share a number of characteristics. They generally reveal, consciously or unconsciously, the language and workings of race from the cultural perspective of the author. They reveal or imply Whites assuming a sense of superiority and power and the effects of that for Whites and Blacks. Writers from each race often portray members of the other race in ways potentially difficult for students to come to terms with. Works by White or Black writers on race can trigger uncomfortable feelings for a group of students as a whole. The nature of such literature means there are reasons for both White students and Black students in the multicultural classroom not to want to read works by White writers or Black writers reflecting racial issues: It's uncomfortable to see one's own culture, or those in another culture, depicted in a negative, inaccurate, or painful light. Even if we teachers refrain from judging literary works' quality "based on the attitudes of an author or whatever representations are made of some group," as Morrison explains that she has refrained from doing in her examination of American literature by White writers (1993, p. 90), all elements of the works nevertheless affect the ways in which students experience and respond to the texts, including, and sometimes especially, whether or not the works reflect racism.

Beyond these common features, however, lie significant distinctions in the ways in which works reflecting aspects of race by White writers and Black writers potentially affect students in the classroom, and those distinctions are traceable in part to the times and circumstances producing the works as well as perspectives the works reflect.

White Writers on Race

In her study of the "ways in which a nonwhite, Africanlike (or Africanist) presence or persona was constructed" in American literature, Toni Morrison (1993, p. 6) explores a number of aspects of literature by White writers that includes Black characters.

Until recently, published major American writers have overwhelmingly been White, and according to Morrison, their focus has been "the architecture of a *new white man*" (1993, p. 15). White writers brought in Black characters not in order to portray those characters fully or realistically, Morrison suggests, but primarily for "meditation on the self," that is, White writers used Black figures to understand or render one's White self and world (p. 17).

There is also, in work after work by White writers, an implied or overt racism in the depiction of Blacks. The works of many White writers fail to depict Blacks fully or accurately, reflecting either an intentional or unintentional bias on the part of the author, or a lack of knowledge and understanding of Blacks. Works by White writers reflect a long history of inaccurate and degrading portrayals of Blacks tied to stereotypes, untruths, or misrepresentations (Morrison, 1993). "The Negroes of fiction are so consistently false to human life," writes Ralph Ellison, "that we must question just what they truly represent" (1966, pp. 115–117).

This phenomenon is so pervasive in American poetry that the pattern of White poets creating demeaning and inaccurate images of Blacks and setting up a privileged and exclusive conversation between White poet and White reader originates in the time of Jefferson and continues into contemporary poetry by mainstream White poets (Nielsen, 1988).

The power accorded published writers in a classroom adds power to the messages these writers deliver, and in the case of White writers, such power is an extension of the relatively greater power still held by Whites in the culture.

Morrison also suggests that young American literature is "antithetical . . . to our modern rendition of the American Dream" (1993, p. 35). But even beyond works emerging from the young country, many works by major White writers—unless they are protest literature—appear to reflect tacitly an immoral social order in relation to race.

Each of these observations holds as true, for example, for aspects of depictions of Whites and Blacks in Mark Twain's *The Adventures of Huckleberry Finn* (1959), many of William Faulkner's novels, Edgar Lee Masters's *Spoon River Anthology* (1914/1962), Upton Sinclair's *The Jungle* (1906/1980), and short fiction by Flannery O'Connor (1971), as they do for Carl Sandburg's poetry on Black workers.

Black Writers on Race

Like White writers, Black writers often offer stories through the lens of their own cultural experience. And, like the works of many major White writers, their works often reflect the effects of the existing power structure. But Black writers' knowledge and vantage point of the victim of the racism they describe leads many Black writers into a realistic depiction of both Blacks and Whites. Contrary to the images of Blacks in works by many White writers, the images of Whites in works by many Black writers tend to be accurate depictions of White attitudes, language, and behaviors in a particular time and place. White readers cannot usually argue with the truth of the representation of Whites.

For Lorraine Hansberry and James Baldwin, one key fact accounts for this difference: Blacks had more opportunity and need to understand Whites more intimately, fully, realistically than Whites ever did of Blacks. "The intimacy of knowledge which the Negro may have of white Americans does not exist in the reverse," says Hansberry. Baldwin explains why: "[Faulkner's Black character Dilsey] knows much more about [the people she works for] than they will ever know about her. Faulkner has never sat in a Negro kitchen while the Negroes were talking about him, but we have been sitting around for generations, in kitchens and everywhere else, while everybody talks about us, and this creates a very great difference." Baldwin also tells us that it gave Black writers "a very great advantage" (Hansberry & Baldwin, quoted in Bigsby, pp. 97–98). Thus, while many works by White writers reflect a more real understanding of Whites than Blacks, the works of many Black writers reflect a real understanding of both Whites and Blacks.

In the classroom, published Black authors take on a position of power in a system that has historically been designed to cut them off from power, and their works often focus on American race relations.

Unlike the tacit descriptions of an immoral system tied to race embodied in many works by White writers, many Black writers are actively engaged in pointing out an immoral system, calling on their audience to take note of injustice, and out of that, to institute change. Works by Black writers often reflect straightforward, overt depictions of abuses of power and racism, and a quiet to impassioned rightful rage. There is throughout the history of Black American literature a moral thrust to the texts: Black writers' descriptions of race relations as they have experienced, observed, or recorded them have the effect of urging a country to live up to its own stated ideals embodied in the American Dream.

These characteristics can be observed in, for example, the slave narratives of Frederick Douglass and Harriet Jacobs, the poetry of Countee Cullen and Langston Hughes, the essays and fiction of James Baldwin, the speeches of Malcolm X, and the fiction of Toni Morrison.

READERS IN THE MULTICULTURAL CLASSROOM

What do these factors mean for our students as readers in a multicultural classroom?

White Writers and Their Audience

Although, according to Henry Louis Gates, Jr., by the mid-1990s "black Americans bought 160 million books" in a single year (Smith, 1996, p. B5), until recently, works by White writers were intended for a White audience, a White audience that did not see itself in racial terms, but rather in terms of being "universal" (Morrison, 1993, p. xii). Works by White writers were not intended to be read by non-Whites. In the writer-reader relationship, White writers were conveying or wrestling with ideas they were sharing with other Whites. On some level this means that many White writers could and did write anything about Blacks, not under the gaze of Blacks themselves, in fact assuming the exclusion of Black readers.

If we consider the implications of Morrison's observation that until recently readers of American literature by Whites were "positioned as white" (1993, p. xii), in the multicultural classroom many White writers are in a type of metaphorical "collusion," a "privileged conversation," with White readers in the class, to the disregard and exclusion of Black readers. And this perpetuates or re-creates the invisibility of Ellison's "invisible man": "I am invisible, understand," says Ellison's famous character, "simply because people refuse to see me" (1947/1972, p. 3). Material such as Sandburg's poems on Black workers, Faulkner's descriptions of Dilsey (1929/1956), Sinclair's depiction of Black factory workers (1906/1980), Masters's character Shack Dye (1914/1962), or O'Connor's fictional southern Blacks (1971), for example, read as though no Blacks are present. And the actions and images of Blacks in the texts may be highly insulting on a regular basis to Black readers. It didn't matter, theoretically, originally, how Black readers might respond to the nature or veracity of the texts, since the texts were not written "for" them.

Simultaneously, however, Black students, unlike White students, even though they have not been thought of as members of the audience, are being asked to engage in texts that present threats to a sense of self through presentations of untruths, distortions, and inaccuracies in the depiction of Blacks. Critic Aldon Nielsen likens reading White American literature to the "incident" in Black poet Countee Cullen's poem "Incident" (1925/1997, p. 1306), in which an eager and joyful Black child is suddenly insulted while riding on a bus in Baltimore. As Nielsen explains, "One sets out upon the project, 'head filled with glee,' only to be assaulted by insult, insult which is no whit lesser because committed sometimes unwittingly" (1988, p. 29).

As we have seen in our analysis of the discussion centering on the poems on Black workers by Sandburg, works by White writers reflecting inaccurate or racist depictions of Blacks often trigger hurt and anger for Black students and discomfort and awkwardness for White students. As we have also seen, Black students may be placed in a position to feel a need to fend off untruths or racism targeted at Blacks within the texts. The texts on some level often mobilize in Black students a psychologically understandable and healthy type of resistance, expressed or not, to the untruths or racism reflected in the text.

Thus as students and teachers read many classical White writers who touch on race, the White writer is still engaged in speaking to White readers to the exclusion of Black readers. The task of a teacher is to engage all of his or her students. But to bring Black students into this type of material is to bring them into material that for many Black students may be psychologically difficult to read, to want to read, or to tolerate: In many ways, why should Black students want to read some of this material given its nature and thrust? They have many reasons to reject it and not study it.

If teachers *are* going to use works by a number of major White writers, they must find ways to intervene in that unequal psychological thrust between a White writer's work dealing in some way with race—originally intended for White readers—and readers from multiple cultural backgrounds in the class. The teacher must mediate the effects of specific content on students that result as the White American writer "speaks to" White readers in the room and, in the presence of Black students, not to those Black students, in fact, to the disregard and "insult" of those Black students—and the hurt and the anger that can be generated in that process. In working with many White writers, teachers need to be able to help Black students manage the effects of the writers' use of racist language and descriptions and the writers' conveyance of implied or overt racist attitudes and behaviors that can understandably generate hurt, anger, and resistance. And in working with White writers, teachers have an additional responsibility. Unmediated, many texts by White writers leave readers with untruths about Blacks, and that should be an aspect of the work that teachers address.

Black Writers and Their Audience

Works by many Black writers trigger a different series of responses. Like White writers, major Black writers have been writing, until recently, for an audience "positioned as white" (Morrison, 1993, xii). But unlike many works by White writers, many works by Black writers read as though they are intended for a broader readership. Both White and Black students can feel included as audience. White characters in works by many Black writers, although often implicated in culpable attitudes or behavior, are not created in a manner that suggests there are no White readers. In fact, given the thrust of many works by Black writers to document racial injustice, reaching White readers as well as Black readers could be important. Whether in nonfiction slave narratives, fiction, poetry, speeches, autobiographies, or plays, over the years Black writers have often recorded historical realities of Black life, and they have called on their audience to take note of racial injustice.

Most Black students enjoy or appreciate reading texts by Black writers (especially since the number of Black writers read relative to the number of Whites writers read in many schools is still small), and they appreciate the fact that many Black writers place aspects of Black history or

Black life before their classmates of other cultures. For many Black students such texts confirm an aspect of historical or present reality. What can be difficult for Black students reading these texts is the sense that White students are "peering into" life among Blacks and commenting on it in discussions in ways that can be uncomfortable for Black students.

Many White readers of works by Black writers experience: the power of the published Black writer's voice, overturning the historical and still-widespread distribution of power involving Whites and Blacks in this society; description of racial wrongdoing from the perspective of those wronged; and a type of "guilt by association" as they consider the implications of descriptions of "their" people in racist gestures and behaviors. In dealing with texts by many Black writers, White readers must come to terms with an ugly truth tied to their culture and cultural history, with Whites often being accurately portrayed in morally corrupt or bankrupt behaviors. Some White students are ready for an examination of their culture's historical and present relations with Blacks, including racist attitudes and behaviors. White students open to issues of social injustice feel they are engaged in the writer's call and find it involving and satisfying to discuss the issues the writer raises. In other White students, the material sets off defenses, anger, resentment, and hostility. Those Whites for whom the material is too threatening may reject the author or the material itself out of discomfort.

Thus in working with many Black writers, teachers need to be able to help White students come to terms with the meaning, reality, and effect of White privilege and White racism. They need to be able to help White students manage comments about Whites and racism made by Black students. And they need to help Black students deal with White students' resistance to understanding White racism, as well as White students' lack of knowledge of Black history, life, and culture—and the naive, uninformed, or insensitive observations and questions that may emerge from that lack of knowledge.

Relative Effects of the Texts on the Students

Although texts dealing with race in one way or another can be hard for both White students and Black students to read or to study, I would suggest that there is nonetheless a lopsidedly difficult effect of texts by many White writers on Black students, one that creates a significant challenge for Black students in working with these texts, especially in the company of White students and teacher.

White readers of many Black writers are being asked to confront and come to terms with embarrassing and shameful but historically accurate material, while Black readers of many White writers are being asked to read and discuss material that is often not only overtly insulting to Black readers—through racist language and images—but also often untrue, reflecting stereotypes, distortions, and misrepresentations of Blacks. Such texts are also harsh reminders for Black students of the nature and effects of White racism that has and continues to hit close to home for many Black students.

In some cases, what many texts by White writers overtly reveal is power in the hands of Whites tied to quiet or subtle racism, and the meaning and effects of that racism are not visible to many White students until and unless they see or understand what such behaviors say about people who do such things or until and unless they see and understand the results for Blacks. For Black students, however, many of those same texts reveal directly the victimization of and harm done to Blacks; the effects of racism are immediately visible and painful. Black students may also see powerlessness on the part of Blacks who are being defined and abused by Whites. Faulkner's portrait of Dilsey (1929/1956), for example, affects many White readers as a warm and affectionate depiction of a Black woman, while it affects many Black readers as a depiction drawn out of a lack of full knowledge of Black life, one that assumes that the central and only feature of a Black domestic worker's life was tending to the well-being of her White employers.

Further, White students can remove themselves more easily from the brunt of the unpleasantness or ugliness of the material in ways that Black students may not be able to. In an essay entitled "Slavery in Hannibal," Mark Twain writes: "There were no hard-hearted people in our town." But his conclusion follows his own observations about slave auctions in Hannibal and about seeing "black men and women chained to each other, once, and lying in a group on the pavement, awaiting shipment to the Southern slave market" (Twain, 1922/1993, pp. 1–2). James Baldwin has explained a similar response on the part of Whites to the harsh reality facing many Black Americans that Richard Wright describes in Native Son: "Americans were now able to look full in the face without flinching the dreadful facts. Americans, unhappily, have the most remarkable ability to alchemize all bitter truths into an innocuous but piquant confection" (1966, p. 238). I would suggest that White students can more easily distance themselves from images tied to White racist attitudes and actions that they can maintain are done by others, than Black students can distance themselves from racist, demeaning, and inaccurate depictions of Blacks that cut to the core of a sense of self and identity.

Thus, White students in reading works by many Black writers are being asked to come to terms with *actions* by individuals in their culture, and while many White students resist seeing themselves implicated in such actions, others are moved by the connection in ways that stir their social conscience. Students who resist such a connection distance themselves by suggesting that they were "not there" or not responsible themselves for such actions. Black students responding to literature by many White writers must encounter and respond to works that pose *a threat to a sense of self*. Many White writers' seemingly tacit depiction of racial injustice versus Black writers' stance of activism leads to many White writers appearing to convey racist images as "truth" (as in the case of the Sandburg poems, Twain's depiction of Jim as human plaything in the final chapters in *The Adventures of Huckleberry Finn* [1959], or Faulkner's depiction of Dilsey strictly as long-suffering and devoted [1929/1956]), and many Black writers conveying racism as wrong (as in Langston Hughes's poems or in Morrison's depiction of Blacks and Whites in *The Bluest Eye* [1972] or *Beloved* [1987]). This leads to different effects on students as students are left in the first instance with not knowing what is in fact the truth of the situation, while potentially being engaged in a thrust toward greater social justice in the latter instance.

In some ways, ultimately, White students do have a significant challenge in working with material that deals implicitly or overtly with racism, since the immorality portrayed rests in the hands of powerful Whites who have structured an immoral system or who perpetrate immoral acts. Conversely, to experience depictions of Blacks in texts by White writers may be harder for Black students initially, but ultimately the Black perspective in most works has moral thrust on its side.

Conversations about the literature are complicated further by the fact that responses to material on the part of students may be experienced by other students as responses to those other students themselves, as they may identify with the cultural perspective reflected in the work. For the group as a whole, students' abilities to engage in healthy discussions of such works suggest, in some ways, a parallel with racial identity development stages. That is, such discussions require White students to be able to recognize White privilege and White racism—and the meaning and implications of that—and for Black students to come to terms with the effects of racism on their sense of self.

One can begin to see accumulating levels of complexity as one adds to these already complicated intersections between students and texts, additional factors that will influence students' responses and classroom dynamics: cultural identity and multiple histories of the teacher; cultural identities and histories of other students in the room; and inexperience on the part of teacher or students in discussing these issues and managing their intellectual and emotional responses in a classroom discussion, or even having the time, support, and inclination to do so.

THE IMPACT OF RACED READINGS
ON THE MULTICULTURAL CLASSROOM

Working with well-known texts dealing with race in the multicultural classroom underscores even more boldly the role and importance of teacher as
"cultural mediator," that is, to help students examine cultural conflicts,
develop sound relationships across cultural lines, and avoid "perpetuating
prejudices, stereotypes, and racism" (Gay, 2000, p. 43). Without effective
teaching, such texts may well serve to further divide our students.

Studying and discussing many well-known texts that reflect or address
aspects of race can bring some of the worst aspects of past or contemporary society or social dynamics into a classroom of young people already
divided by that very past and those dynamics. Most Whites and Blacks in
this society are still engaged in figuring out how to build successful cross-
racial relationships, and this has already led to an "instability in all typical
relationships between [Blacks] and Whites in America" (Klein, 1966, p.
256). Dynamics depicted or implied in many such works—the culpability
of Whites and the abuse of Blacks—are those that are difficult for both
White and Black students to come to terms with. Moreover, similar dynamics are still going on in the culture, and our students know it.

As a result, working with such texts may redivide students by underscoring issues of power and racism. The works underscore chasms between
the races. Further, the difficulty of accepting an ugly truth about one's culture or national past or present can set off defensiveness and distancing on
the part of White students, and this in turn can anger Black students for
whom it is important that Whites acknowledge and accept the truth of
White racism. In the wake of the ideas and emotions such works trigger, it
can be hard for teachers and students to overcome the divisive effects of
such material to build, maintain, or rebuild group relatedness.

Under duress, students may or may not feel a natural cultural affinity
with the teacher. That is, in a complex discussion involving race in a work
of literature, White students may consciously or unconsciously attempt to
align themselves with a White teacher out of a shared cultural identity, and
Blacks may not be drawn to doing so or feel they cannot do so, or vice
versa: Black students may align with a Black teacher and White students
may not be drawn to doing so or feel they cannot do so. Given the complexity of the unfolding discussions and emotions, however, and the vulnerability of any student, it is important for teachers to remain committed
to each student in the class, since an alignment with one or more students
that creates a sense of exclusion for other students will potentially deepen
tensions, frustrations, hurt, and divisions in the class.

What all of these questions and observations address is the potential psychosocial impact of studying material that touches on aspects of race or culture in the multicultural classroom and the significant impact of our choices regarding curriculum and pedagogy. In a monocultural setting, our teaching will have a psychosocial impact. In multicultural settings, I would maintain, that psychosocial impact is deepened. What does that mean, then, for choices regarding curriculum and pedagogy, especially regarding issues surrounding what we do teach and what we do not teach? When is it better to confront, directly in a classroom, material generated out of the muddle of our collective lives and when is it better to avoid that material? In my own teaching, I attempt to hold to a notion espoused by progressive educators for decades: that education is tied to building healthy communities (Dewey, 1916/1966; Parker, 1894/2001), and it is my responsibility, whether in choosing works to teach or in overseeing the dynamics they trigger in a classroom, to facilitate a movement toward the common good. In Parker's words: "Is that work the best for the whole, and at the same time the best for each individual?" (p. 252). But such choices are not always clear or easy, especially if we are committed to working with racial or cultural issues in the classroom.

LESSONS ON TEACHING RACED READINGS

As I reflect on this series of moments in a course on Chicago writers, I recall the image of an old-fashioned scale, teetering back and forth. On the one hand, I know that the history of human experience as it is captured in the disciplines and texts we study today is filled with prejudice and racism. Rather than ignore or censor those texts, in the interest of fuller understanding perhaps it is best to look directly at disquieting language and situations. In such moments in the classroom we can think about and discuss them—their origins, context, and effects. In so doing, perhaps we bring them more under our control and they can have less power to damage us, and they can provide wisdom and impetus for social change. Perhaps they prepare us better to talk of such things, to know the past, to know what gestures support human connectedness and what can destroy it.

On the other hand, I know that I cannot create a classroom situation in which students feel they must choose between actions that protect a fundamental sense of self and actions that promote academic success. Those moments years ago in my afternoon class on one Chicago poet reshaped the way I work with literature in the multicultural classroom.

I take even more seriously the decisions I make to include or exclude material from the classroom, no matter how the material has been regard-ed in the past. I would no longer teach those particular poems by Sandburg unless I were using them to study racial attitudes of a specific time and place or to address problematic aspects of Sandburg's work. As I take into the classroom works that have been born out of prejudiced and racist circumstances—as have many classic works of literature—I make sure I understand clearly my intention in using specific material and ped-agogy, and I make sure I explain those choices clearly to my students. I consider the complex and broad range of responses that racially or cul-turally related material may trigger among my students from multiple racial and cultural backgrounds. I am aware that with some of those responses, my students could simultaneously feel troubled and feel pow-erless to act on those feelings in relation to figures of authority in the class-room or in the school.

In the face of that awareness, in teaching such works as Twain's *The Adventures of Huckleberry Finn* (1959), Upton Sinclair's *The Jungle* (1906/1980), or the short stories of Flannery O'Connor (1971), I estab-lish a context ahead of time for approaching biased, distorted, or sensi-tive material. I explain why we are reading a particular work and why we are approaching it in the manner we are. As we study the work, we focus not only on the artistry involved, but on the background, environment, influences, and values of the writer and the ways in which aspects of the work can instruct us about attitudes toward race in a particular time and place as well as what those attitudes can teach us about that society. I help students understand the factors and milieu that gave rise to such material and how the work may affect us as readers today. I provide suf-ficient time and opportunity for students to express and to examine fully and candidly their ideas and understandably complex and confusing emotions as we read and discuss the work, and, through conversations or explanations, I support students individually and as a group in that process. We debate head-on the power and problems of such works and the advantages and disadvantages of studying them, not in a bow to "political correctness," but in an effort to forge an effective, thoughtful, and inviting pedagogy for each of the students before me. I anticipate and support students' honest responses, including a healthy resistance to aspects of curriculum or pedagogy, as part of the learning process. And in the face of those honest responses, I use my own power to support and promote a healthy, emerging power on the part of each of my students as they broaden their background and understanding of our complex past and the types of thinking and writing it gave rise to. I tell my students that they, like Toni Morrison, can use their growing wisdom to change the way others think and act.

CONCLUSION

Within several weeks of our encounter with the race-based poems of Carl Sandburg in the course on Chicago writers, one of the Black students most offended by the pieces wrote the following as part of an examination on early writers in the course: "[Sandburg writes,] 'I am the Nigger/Singer of songs.' Not only is society responsible for conjuring up these harmful illusions but society is very much responsible for keeping them alive and leaving many blacks to wonder [as Sandburg writes in the poem,] 'I went away asking where I come from.' Society's strong grip has everlasting effects in being the blockade against blacks in search of happiness."

Later, she and another young Black woman were the tour guides who took us to the home of poet laureate Gwendolyn Brooks on our literary tour of the city, inviting us into her world, her verse.

In the end, I am left with one overriding thought: Given the history of American race relations and the thrust of writers as they have described those relations over the years, even with a growing awareness of how texts affect students from multiple cultures in a classroom, we have much to learn before we can believe we are offering an equally sound and inviting educational experience for each of the students before us.

But if we are successful in working with race-related material in the multicultural classroom, we can take the immorality and pain sometimes all too apparent in these works—and the discomfort experienced by our students in response—and turn that combination of factors into power tied to writer and reader. In the face of what is a natural increase in tension among individuals and groups of individuals over the issues these types of texts raise, students and teacher can come together in the classroom and use these texts as the basis of discussions that can lead us toward change, toward constructing a society among us that will move us beyond a racist past and present.

PART II

Principles and Practice(s): Thoughts on Curriculum and Pedagogy

CHAPTER 7

A Breadth of Materials: Reading Within and Across Cultural Lines

As the ragged end of summer approaches, I turn once again to designing reading lists for the students I will meet in a matter of weeks. It is an annual ritual I savor, a chance to revisit old friends—writers whose works I have taught for over 20 years—and writers whom I've met only recently. As I shape the list into a meaningful whole, the voices of students as well as those of educators and critics hover.

I see my students as they gather from neighborhoods all over Chicago, some born in this quintessentially American city, some having immigrated from Mexico, Russia, the Baltics, Vietnam. I see them enter the room in the fall—eager, anxious, somewhat awkward in their new clothes and shoes and carrying notebooks bulging from already overstuffed backpacks. I see them wondering what our time together will be like. Some of these students have known each other for years. Some are coming to this school for the first time. I do not yet know their names, their faces. I do know they will bring widely varied backgrounds into our room. Their life experiences and values, their racial or cultural identities mirror the shifting demographics of contemporary America, and each of these factors will contribute to our shared experience over the next months.

Sometimes I tremble at the responsibility of teaching—the trust of these open-eyed adolescents and their parents that somehow I will offer them an experience with reading and writing that will engage them or even linger after the course is over. Although I cannot know yet how our time together will unfold, I do know that what I will offer to these students will be a reading list culled from multiple literary histories. The works will be artistically intricate and demanding. The writers will be, among others, Latinos, Asian Americans, Native Americans, African Americans, European Americans, and Middle Eastern Americans, as well as religiously diverse.

I know the criticism such a pedagogical choice elicits: about "misguided liberals" and "dangerous multiculturalists," about teachers who substitute politics or baseless pop therapy for education and therefore "will never, ever teach their children how to read" (Hymowitz, 1999, p. 124). And I know that the choices I make unavoidably constitute a political choice, no matter what cluster of writers I eventually assemble. I also know that having made a commitment to working with writers from a wide array of backgrounds, the discussions in my classroom will not be easy ones to lead or perhaps even to participate in. These writers will tax my students and me and will make us work hard—on our own and as a group. But I also believe that the journeys we will take over the next several months will be in some ways infinitely more satisfying because through these writers we will be able to explore our own worlds and the worlds of others more fully.

The decision to build broadly based reading lists draws on, in many ways, the nature of the reading experience itself and the fact that one cannot separate the academic, the personal, and the social aspects of reading. Reading in school is a personal and a social act, and it contributes to who we become as individuals and as members of a community.

Those of us who work closely with young readers as well as those of us who attend to the nature of our own relationship to reading know that the act of reading inhabits both the private and public spheres of human experience. Reading facilitates journeys into the self and into the world, alone and with others. All of these journeys are reflected in myriad moments as students choose, inquire into, and respond to books. The private, the personal, the individual, the public, and the communal are all part of the reading process, especially in classrooms.

Contrary to the vocal, bristling, and at times vicious critics of multiculturalism, I continue to believe that course reading lists grounded in multiple cultures represent a good and necessary response not only to what I know of the needs of my students but also consistent with enduring arguments of classical and contemporary humanists. Such choices are grounded as well in broader questions concerning how we learn, why we read, and the ways in which cultural identities are related to reading, writing, and learning.

What might such choices look like in a classroom?

MULTICULTURAL READING LISTS IN THE CLASSROOM

The first few weeks of school. My freshmen are newly coming together in a course called "Self and Community: Reading and Writing Across the Genres." Typical of classes at this school, a number of these students have been together since Junior Kindergarten; others are just now joining the class, as ninth graders. Some are timid as they try out the newness of these halls; others boast the boldness of a longtime acquaintance with classmates and the environment. Given the power of the group that takes root during all those shared years of elementary and middle school, as well as the multiple neighborhoods, cultural identities, and histories represented among us, it is particularly important to help bring these students together, to help each of them find a home in this school.

"Self and Community: Reading and Writing Across the Genres" is a yearlong required course that allows students to explore the ways in which literature and writing can offer us an understanding of individuals and the contexts in which they evolve, and for these students to develop their own voices as young writers. Through the year, we will read classic and contemporary works from multiple cultures, and the students will gain practice in developing their voices as critics, playwrights, poets, and fiction and nonfiction writers.

In our exploration of literature for the stage, we examine Shakespeare's *Romeo and Juliet* (1992), August Wilson's *Joe Turner's Come and Gone* (1988), and David Henry Hwang's *FOB* (1983), turning first to *Romeo and Juliet* (1992). As students finish reading the text and simultaneously seeing Franco Zeffirelli's (1968) film version in class, I ask them to craft their first piece of analytical writing. They should develop a thesis based on any area of interest to them in the play. Their ideas do not disappoint. One young White student woman draws analogies between this Renaissance play and the American pastime of baseball. A young Black woman compares the pressure on Shakespeare's couple to the pressures on interracial couples, pulling together material from the play and a number of interviews from an article in *Essence* magazine. A young Latina compares the story of Romeo and Juliet to an ancient Latin American legend. Another Black student compares the family dynamics of Shakespeare's two warring families to a recent incident in which an Asian Indian couple eventually slay their daughter as a result of her entering into a relationship with a young Indian of whom they disapproved. Allowing the focus of the papers to emerge from students' own passions, our weeklong writing workshop in the computer lab is animated and engaged.

Within days of their submitting the first paper of the course, students are bringing to class not only what they are learning, but also their interests that extend beyond this classroom. The young woman who has written on the similarities between Romeo and Juliet and interracial couples brings in news of Chicago aldermen discussing reparations for Blacks for slavery and discussing financial liabilities of insurance companies that had participated in slavery.

We move next to reading August Wilson's story of Southern Blacks moving north during the Great Migration in *Joe Turner's Come and Gone* (1988). Before students begin reading the play, I initiate a conversation about language and the power of words. Knowing that the word "nigger" will appear in the text, I want to open up issues surrounding the word before it can take us by surprise and create moments of awkwardness, uncertainty, or insensitivity among these students together now for only a few weeks. I mention that some words hold extraordinary power over us and that this word is one of the most potent words in our language. We look at the word in the context of American history and in the context of contemporary usage among Blacks and among Whites, and I ask them how they would like us to work with this word in our readings aloud or in our conversations. Should we use the word? An abbreviation? One young White student suggests that readers should use the word they feel most comfortable with. But this immediately raises the question: What if that choice isn't okay for others? A number of Black students and White students mention that they encountered this issue as they read *The Adventures of Huckleberry Finn* (1959) and *Black Boy* (1945) in middle school. In the case of this play, they think it's okay to say the word because the author is Black, and because he has used it knowing it would be spoken openly on stage. We agree to raise the issue again if our approach doesn't feel like it's working for us all. A Jewish student notes the way in which other words have that same power historically for Jews. In initiating a conversation about such words and their power, we place the issue into the open, explore it together, decide as a group how we would like to handle it, and establish a context through which we know we can raise questions about such issues in days to come.

As students read the play outside of class, in class we view a documentary called *The Promised Land Vol. I: Take Me to Chicago* (Badour, 1995) to give us a context for understanding Wilson's characters, their pasts, and their needs. Through the voices of Blacks who remember this time and place, the film takes us deep into the South of tenant farming, Jim Crow laws, and the decision of millions of rural Blacks to move north to escape daily humiliation and exploitation.

As we discuss the play, students move back and forth between the film and the text of the play in their observations, some mystified by aspects of this history. The humiliating and criminal extremes in the system of tenant farming are new to many of these young urbanites, and for some, the broad spiritual ties of characters, expressed in visions and rituals, are perplexing. The next day one young Black woman comes in excited. Seeing the film and our discussions of the play have prompted a conversation at home. Her father has talked of past difficulties traveling in the South and recounted stories of those days. The daughter says, "I never knew they went through that."

Our third play in this trio of pieces for the stage is David Henry Hwang's *FOB* (1983). The play concerns three young Chinese and Chinese-American students at UCLA coming to terms with their varying relationships to the United States. Hwang wrote the play as an undergraduate at Stanford, where he premiered the play. The play went on to win numerous national awards.

Prior to our beginning to read the play in class, I ask each of the students to write down responses to several questions about cultural identity: Do you or do members of your family identify with a particular culture? What are some of the ways that culture is expressed in the context of your family or your own life? Describe briefly a moment or incident when an individual excluded or was unkind to you or someone else on the basis of cultural identity. When that moment occurred, what did you think or feel at the time? What did you do? Why do you think the moment occurred— why do people do this? Can this type of moment or incident take place within the same cultural group? The conversation is rich and broad, bringing forward observations about language, foods, customs, and holidays, from Norway, Poland, the Philippines, Jamaica, Germany, Mexico, and Puerto Rico. We all have these ties, some more overt, others more submerged.

As students turn to the question of a moment in their past, the conversation becomes more disturbing, more somber. For one young Puerto Rican, her worst encounter occurred unexpectedly at Disney World, in an environment more tied in the mind of a child with images of Mickey Mouse and his floppy feet. A series of cruel remarks hurled at her family leaves her parents quiet, her sisters and herself frightened and confused. Her parents refuse to explain the moment, frightening her further. It hurts still, she tells us.

Our conversation also lingers on the gains and losses of assimilation and on aspects of cultural adaptation. Some of the White students point out the advantages—of feeling like an American, of knowing more about how things work here. But one young Chicana speaks out sharply against assimilation. She has been raised to understand not only the beauties and power of Mexico in her daily life in Chicago, but the value of her ethnic neighborhood, holding on to Spanish, and never assimilating. Another student speaks of family moves among extended family homes in Brazil, Chicago, and England. We also hear from one young Puerto Rican student of the way in which friends in his own culture can move from jokes to cruelty about maintaining or distancing oneself from one's own culture. "Yeah," he says, "people in your own culture can definitely call you names." The conversation has brought forward stories from many house-holds, many lives.

For the next two days we read the play aloud, my own students intrigued with this piece about these students in Los Angeles: one young man who is a second-generation Chinese American, a young woman whose family brought her from China to the United States at age 10, and a young man "fresh off the boat."

As we finish reading the play, I ask them to think of the play from the perspective of those involved in producing it: How would you play the young woman's role? What would you emphasize about this play? Based on ideas you want to bring forward for the audience, how would you light this piece? And then I pose a question to the young Chicana who has spoken so eloquently about the importance of holding on to one's culture: Let's say you were sitting in the audience that night when Hwang opened this play at Stanford. You are intrigued with the issues it raises about assimilation, and as a director, you decide to mount a production yourself, casting each role with Latino/a actors. What might this result in for the audience?

We play with various color-blind casting possibilities: What about a White director directing three Black actors in the play—what might this put forth for the audience? Language under slavery? Not even the possibility, during slavery, of assimilation? What then emerges from our conversations is not only the ways in which multiple cultural groups do or do not experience similar challenges, but the ways in which artistic choices such as nontraditional casting can help tackle cultural issues.

We leave our exploration of the texts of these plays charged with the possibilities of exploring our own lives and cultures in the context of art across three distinct cultural traditions.

The next week, as we turn to playwriting ourselves, I am deeply satisfied to see one of the Latinas as playwright moving seamlessly in her script between English and Spanish as she renders the speech of a young father from Mexico attempting to understand his life in America. She knows that to make this choice is valuable for herself and her relationship to multiple languages and to her art, and she knows that to produce a bilingual script will be valued in this classroom. Just as do writers such as Julia Alvarez, Maxine Hong Kingston, and Leslie Marmon Silko, she is drawing on her bicultural experiences to inform her art.

The following week, in the last project of our work on literature for the stage, students select one of the plays we have read and work together in small groups to imagine a production. In each group, one director, two actors, set and costume designers, and an individual responsible for marketing will develop a clear concept for their production and share their ideas through a presentation to the class.

One group decides they will produce *FOB* (1983) in China, set it at a McDonald's with workers wearing Chicago Cubs shirts, and explore the ways in which Americans might face challenges and choices tied to assimilation in China. Two other groups develop diametrically opposed production concepts for *Joe Turner's Come and Gone* (1988). For one group, bright lights and brilliantly colored costumes will accentuate the hope and sense of possibility that accompany Southern blacks moving north. The other group designs a marketing poster that highlights a quote from Malcolm X on oppression. In this group, White and Black students work together to imagine a production that emphasizes not hope, but the fact that oppression follows Blacks out of the South into urban Pittsburgh. Another group offers a hip-hop version of *Romeo and Juliet* (1992) set in a high school in Chicago, the balcony scene now an alley's fire escape cantilevered over a dumpster, the young lovers still torn apart and destroyed by social differences. Their poster advertises ticket sales in the language of rap.

By the time we conclude our section on writing for the theater, we have been together for a little over a month. But I know the choices of these three works by some of our most recognized classic and contemporary writers, emerging from three different cultures, have helped to bring us together. They have given us stories that have prompted the telling of our own stories. We have talked of language and its power to hurt and to isolate, as well as its power to deepen our ties to the culture of home or to cross borders through art and the imagination. We have shared histories, we have shared something of who we are, what we care about and what, sometimes, has hurt us. The students' writing—monolingual and bilingual, and emerging from their own lives and experiences—has found a real and appreciative audience within our classroom and in exhibits beyond our room. We are on our way to being a group that will more and more understand the multiple values of our being together.

The reason this series of choices worked is because offering our students reading lists from multiple cultures is consistent with some of the most fundamental elements of engaged learning and reading.

HOW WE LEARN

Progressive educators have repeatedly located the most effective learning in the expanding interests and curiosity of the child. For Dewey, learning best proceeds from the present experiences of the child through his natural and constantly emerging curiosity: We must start with the child. If the focus of the lesson is tied to the ever-expanding interests of the child, if it emerges from "his own past doings, thinkings, and sufferings," then he will remain engaged (1902/1971, pp. 9, 27). Similarly, W. E. B. Du Bois argued in speaking of "The Negro College," education begins with the "present condition" of the students (W. E. B. Du Bois, 1933/1995, pp. 69–70, quoted in Nussbaum, 1997, p. 168).

Conversely, a lack of real connection to the child's life "makes the material purely formal and symbolic" (Dewey, 1902/1971, p. 24). From the child's point of view, "the great waste in the school" comes from his not being able to use life experiences in school or to use what he learns in school in his day-to-day life (Dewey, 1900/1971, p. 75).

In addition, in *How We Think* (1910/1991), Dewey maintains that the best teaching and learning occur as the child experiences a combination of materials from "the far" and the "close by," that is, material that is new or "strange" and material that is "familiar."

A curriculum rooted solely in what is alien to the student means that most of the learning experience relies on interaction with what is potentially, for the student, the "far" or the "strange," or, as Dewey further describes it, the "difficult." The danger in that, he explains, is that "too much of the hard renders inquiry hopeless." Conversely, a curriculum rooted solely in the "familiar" means that the student may find the material approachable but missing in the potential stimulation created by studying the new or "strange" (pp. 221–222).

But let us examine for a moment the relationship between Dewey's and Du Bois's concepts and cultural identity as it relates to reading. Cultures and cultural identities are an integral part of students' experiences with reading and with discussing the books they read. Individual cultures provide the particular, the base from which any story emerges and rises toward the sphere of the universal. The cultural milieu of the story is one factor that initially invites in or causes hesitation in the reader. And the relationship between the cultural identity of the reader and cultural identity reflected in the text will become part of the reading experience. Whether emerging from continuity of cultural identity between reader and text or from discontinuity, the nature of those cultural identities plays a role in the reading experience and potentially influences the degree to which the reader connects with the text. Connections can be made equally powerfully within or across cultural lines, and each type of connection is significant.

Countless testimonies exist about the ways in which texts have the power to reach across cultural boundaries to engage and to move us as readers. White students cling to the work of Toni Morrison and Leslie Marmon Silko, Black students have said their thinking has been transformed by reading Thoreau, Latino students say that James Baldwin has spoken directly to their lives. In the works of these writers, students connect with aspects of human experience that transcend cultural boundaries. For one young Black woman, the appeal of Ruben Navarrette's *A Darker Shade of Crimson* (1994) came from a sense of shared experiences across cultures.

But countless testimonies exist as well that confirm the power of cultural familiarity in the reading experience. Henry Louis Gates, Jr. has described what his discovery of James Baldwin meant for him: "Finding James Baldwin and writing him down at an Episcopal church camp during the Watts riots in 1965 (I was fifteen) probably determined the direction of my intellectual life more than did any other single factor" (1992, p. 21).

Historically, however, the nature of reading lists has precluded many students from finding the familiarity of their own cultures in the texts they have been offered in schools. To prevent students from being able to read within a familiar cultural domain narrows the opportunities for them to connect meaningfully with texts and perpetuates a loss described by some of our most famous writers. As James Baldwin himself has explained:

> The most crucial time in my own development came when I was forced to recognize that I was a kind of bastard of the West. . . . I might search in ["Shakespeare, Bach, Rembrandt"] in vain forever for any reflection of myself. I was an interloper; this was not my heritage. At the same time, I had no other heritage which I could possibly hope to use—I had certainly been unfitted for the jungle or the tribe. I would have to appropriate these white centuries, I would have to make them mine—I would have to accept my special attitude, my special place in this scheme—otherwise I would have no place in any scheme. (Baldwin quoted in Gates, 1992, p. 110)

And as Gates notes about Baldwin's fear, "having no place in any scheme" is a form of "terror" (1992, p. 110).

Novelist Paule Marshall has described how, denied knowing her own literary tradition in the public schools, she one day stumbled on a whole new world in her neighborhood public library in Brooklyn:

> Something I couldn't quite define was missing. And then one day, browsing in the poetry section, I came across a book by someone called Paul Laurence Dunbar, and opening it I found the photograph of a wistful, sad-eyed poet who to my surprise was black. . . . And I began to search then for books and stories and poems about "The Race," . . . about my people . . . I started asking the reference librarian . . . for books by Negro writers. . . . No grade school literature teacher of mine had ever mentioned Dunbar or James Weldon Johnson or Langston Hughes. I didn't know [Zora Neale Hurston or Frederick Douglass, Harriet Tubman or Sojourner Truth]. What I needed, what all the kids . . . with whom I grew up needed, was . . . someplace we could go after school—the schools were shortchanging us—and read works by those like ourselves and learn about our history. (1983, p. 35)

Poet Audre Lorde found "there was no one saying what I wanted and needed to hear. I felt totally alienated, disoriented, crazy. I thought that there's got to be somebody else who feels as I do" (1984, p. 261).

What Baldwin, Marshall, and Lorde suggest they were searching for was literature that reflected familiar experiences, a yearning for what Dewey referred to as the "close by."

For our students, to be able to read within and across specific cultural realms significantly broadens the opportunities for them to connect meaningfully with texts in ways that Baldwin, Marshall, and Lorde tell us they felt they could not. Books from a wider range of cultural backgrounds offer students more opportunity to locate themselves—their "own past doings, thinkings, and sufferings" (Dewey, 1902/1971, p. 27)—in their readings, to move forward from their present experiences. In culturally mixed groups of students, what is "close by" for one may be "far" for another. And, Dewey explains, students need both: at times it is the "close by" they need; at other times it is the "far." Consider the following responses, recorded in their journals, by two of my own students: For one young Latina, *The House on Mango Street* (Cisneros, 1989) clearly engaged and delighted her through its reflection of the "close by":

> *The House on Mango Street* has my culture embedded into every word. After reading every vignette I found myself saying, "Damn, that happened to me!" I loved that book. My favorite line was when Esperanza declares that she refuses to grow up tame laying her neck "on the threshold waiting for the ball and chain." I love that. I also refuse to "grow up tame." As Esperanza is growing up she is fighting to leave her home on Mango Street and she is fighting the traditional role of a Mexican woman. I am also fighting.

For a biracial student identifying herself as Asian and White and responding to the Native American novel *Ceremony* (Silko, 1977), "the far" had equal power:

> [Reading] *Ceremony* was a lot like being trapped in a great nightmare. I somehow felt a panic while reading it. I don't know if that was due to the content of the story or just Silko's narration, though I am inclined to think it's the latter. Once Tayo stepped into the jungles of war, it's like it was impossible for him to find a way out. I was reading a poem (I think it was Emily Dickinson's) and she said something which reminded me of Tayo, something about how sometimes we descend into pits so deep in our mind that even we can't rescue ourselves from them. Somehow, that's how *Ceremony* made me feel, at least in the early parts of it.

By moving among materials drawn from multiple cultures, students will, optimally, find the familiar as well as the new, the "close by" as well as "the far." Providing students from multiple cultures with writers from multiple cultures means more potential for establishing what Dewey and Du Bois considered optimal conditions for learning.

WHY WE READ: THE SELF AND THE WORLD

Reading and the Self

As teachers, we rediscover every day that reading is a supremely personal and individual enterprise, and we are intersecting with lives in significant ways when we engage in teaching it. One of the most powerful and intimate processes associated with reading is the building, comprehension, and sustaining of the self. Few authors have explored this process more convincingly or more lyrically than Robert Coles in *The Call of Stories* (1989), whether he is recalling the lingering images of his parents reading to each other, the effect of reading in his own life, or the role of reading in the lives of his students. As Coles's stories so clearly attest, books become both the prompting and the companion for journeys into the self. So, too, for our own students.

Students' conversations repeatedly reveal the depth and degree to which reading has assisted them in constructing their notion of who they are. Books provide, for all of us, conversations, images, paradigms, and models for constructing the self throughout our life. They speak to us directly, offering illumination, guidance, direction, comfort, instruction, and solace, whether we are, in Coles's words, "starting out" or learning how to die. Those of us who work closely with students and good literature are privy to such moments on a regular basis. An essay by Michael Dyson on the problems confronting Black men (1998) offered one young Black student a way of thinking about his own future: "After reading Dyson," he wrote, "I've realized that no matter what, the world will never let me forget that I am black, but it is up to me to change the depiction they already [have] of me. Some years from now, as a young black man, I will be able to do as Dyson did in his essay, which was tell stories, which, in my case, motivated me."

Reading also facilitates an examination and understanding of the self as it comes into being. Books help to initiate and to sustain the process of self-examination that Socrates felt was crucial to a life "worth living." Psychologist Mihaly Csikszentmihalyi says that "the written word allows us to understand better what is happening within ourselves. By reading . . . we can savor the images and their meanings and thus understand more accurately how *we* feel and what *we* think" (1996, p. 238). Looking back on a semester of reading, one young Latina explained that reading *The House on Mango Street* (Cisneros, 1989) and *Sula* (Morrison, 1973) had enabled her to explore the connection between her neighborhood and her identity and role as a woman. The books had helped her to discover herself.

Sometimes these processes occur privately. At other times they occur as part of the dialogues that emerge when we share what we read with others. Construction and examination of the self is furthered through discussions of what we read. Such discussions become part of the lifelong "dialogues" (Taylor, 1994) that contribute to the shaping of our identity. Through discussions prompted by reading good works from multiple cultures, students come to know, to further construct, or to adjust the private and public self.

Beyond the Self: Reading and the Public Sphere

Reading takes us beyond the self as well; reading good works from multiple cultures equips each of us more fully for thinking about and living in the world. Works from multiple cultures and discussions about them broaden our base of understanding as the stories of lives different from our own and the multiple responses to those stories take shape in front of us.

These books give us a larger and broader understanding of the human community. Social observers repeatedly note the necessity of equipping this generation of students for navigating the terrain of a multicultural society. And, Susan Wolf reminds us, the "other" is us. Literature of America is multicultural literature, and to deny that fact is to fail to recognize in the most basic sense who "we, as a community are" (1994, p. 85). For White students to read Asian-American writers, for Black students to read Latino writers, enables them to cross borders. In the words of one White student who was drawn to works by Chinese-American writers, "*Donald Duk* [Chin, 1991], similar to 'Eat a Bowl of Tea' [Wang, 1989], was interesting reading because it immersed me in a culture that is not my own."

Reading good works and engaging in dialogues about them help form us not only as individuals but as social beings. Woven amidst the hours students spend alone with reading are the times we gather to wrestle out the meanings of literature in classroom discussions. The nature of works from multiple cultures contributes to the depth, vivacity, and power of these discussions and the way they affect us as individuals and as a group. In a nation of cultural divides, these writers offer us one of the most natural ways to come to know others—whether through the knowledge we gain in reading works from multiple cultures or through the discussions the works evoke. Works from multiple cultures facilitate journeys beyond the self into the larger world. They help us understand the self in the world and aspects of the larger world itself. And they connect us with others. For one White student, pleasure in reading Gish Jen's "What Means Switch" (1993) was tied to the fact that, in her words, "it made me view myself through different eyes." For another young White woman, reading a Latino novel helped her learn more about her own city: "After having lived in Chicago all my life, I feel that I know the city and its people fairly well. However, after reading *The House on Mango Street* [Cisneros, 1989], I saw a whole different side of the city." One young Latina suggested broader implications of reading works from multiple cultures: that learning of other cultures helps us to draw parallels between lives across the borders that separate us.

The choices we make as teachers model for our students the way we as adults approach the larger world. Through espousing the works of writers from multiple cultures, we are employing a broader view of the world. And so, as we build our reading lists, we must ask ourselves: Will we offer our students that broader view? Will we move beyond the ethnocentrism at the heart of hierarchical thinking about multiple cultures and their works of literature and beyond a confining "idolatry" (Gutmann, 1994, p. 15) in our relationship to writers?

CRITICAL THINKING IN A DIVERSE WORLD

Works from multiple cultures also have the capacity to make students stronger readers. They stretch their capacity to know, to understand, and to interpret. Broad reading among the works of multiple cultures yields a more comprehensive understanding of the past (Lauter, 1983) as well as the present. Texts like Toni Morrison's *Playing in the Dark* (1993) open up whole new paradigms for considering aspects of familiar disciplines.

The study and discussions of these works also deepen our strengths as critical thinkers. In the face of competing perspectives, students must sift through multiple ways of thinking about an issue made almost palpable in the animation of a group discussion, weigh each perspective, and assemble the parts for themselves into a meaningful whole. As the works and words of diverse writers accumulate week after week from an array of converging and diverging worlds, the parts that students have before them to assemble become fuller and more complex. Being able to absorb, interpret, and respond thoughtfully to multiple perspectives is increasingly essential in a global society and in a world flooded with information. "Talking about Cisneros' work [1989]," one White student wrote, "made me search for new ways to look at every situation I come across. I learned to have more empathetic eyes, which is a lesson hard to teach and hard to understand."

The nature of these works means that during discussions, students engage in the sharing and testing of complex and often competing ideas. In many instances, they hear views of others that are distinctly different if not contrary to their own. They attempt to find and interpret threads of what they see as a writer's form or stance, but they also need to withstand, with a kind of public decorum, the free play of contradictory ideas. The process demands that they be increasingly able to articulate ideas about complex and at times uncomfortable aspects of human experience. Sometimes their responses will have emerged from the reading, sometimes from what they have learned in other courses, sometimes from the life they observe around them, and sometimes from the often too-complex fabrics of their own lives.

Thus, contrary to some critics' notion that multicultural reading lists cripple critical thinking, reading good literature from multiple cultures deepens it. Considering human experiences and issues from the multiple points of view afforded by works from multiple cultures forces our students to weigh and examine competing views of the world around them, and there are no ready or easy responses. To support the work of these writers is not to support a lessening of demands on our students; if anything, the diverging and sometimes colliding worldviews brought forward in these texts make students work harder.

Such reading and thinking also involve students in education based in social worth. In looking to the future in his observations on subject matter, Dewey explained, "With the wide range of possible material to select from, it is important that education . . . should use a criterion of social worth." For Dewey, a good education involves students in problem-solving that can better society (1916/1966, pp. 191–192). Given the focus of many writers of color in this country, grounding curricular materials in literature from multiple cultures provides students with myriad opportunities to explore complex and vexing social issues. Critics of multicultural education, in fact, often denounce multicultural literature for presenting too "negative" a view of American society (Stotsky, 1996).

For classicist Martha Nussbaum, a multicultural focus in teaching helps us better prepare our students for living in the global society. Studying diverse cultures is complex, yet essential to "help us become more rational beings." Yet she worries that few American intellectuals now have "cross-cultural expertise" (Berube, 1997, pp. 55–56). And this is troubling:

> It would be catastrophic to become a nation of technically competent people who have lost the ability to think critically, to examine themselves, and to respect the humanity and diversity of others. It is therefore very urgent right

now to support curricular efforts aimed at producing citizens who can take charge of their own reasoning, who can see the different and foreign not as a threat to be resisted, but as an invitation to explore and understand, expanding their own minds and their capacity for citizenship. (Nussbaum quoted in Berube, 1997, p. 57)

Nussbaum sees such skills as having immediate and far-reaching, practical applications: "Whether we are discussing the multinational corporation, global agricultural development, the protection of endangered species, religious toleration, the well-being of women, or simply how to run a firm efficiently," more and more we need a multicultural knowledge "to answer the questions we ask." To the degree that we do not develop such skills, we are apt to suffer. Of one young professional working abroad whose education had not helped her develop satisfactorily these skills, Nussbaum explains, her "education had not equipped her to live as a world citizen, . . . 'her imaginative capacity to enter into the lives of people of other nations had been blunted by lack of practice'" (Nussbaum quoted in Berube, p. 57).

We need not travel beyond our own borders to know the crucial need for skills in cross-cultural understanding and communication. Anne Fadiman's (1998) depiction of one immigrant family attempting to provide appropriate health care for their epileptic daughter is a case in point. Fadiman's portrait of communication failure among individuals in White and Hmong communities in California all too devastatingly conveys the need today throughout this country for cross-cultural knowledge, respect, and skills in communication.

RESPONDING TO THE CRITICS OF MULTICULTURAL READING LISTS

Because of the power of works from multiple cultures to invite us into reading, to develop a broader understanding of ourselves and others, to develop an ability to understand and converse about issues across cultural lines, and to develop more fully our powers of critical thinking, we must stand up to attempts to keep them from our students and attempts to discredit their use in classrooms.

Critics of multiculturalism suggest that different ("lesser") standards are invoked in choosing the ("lesser") works of these writers for inclusion in course materials and through offering multicultural ("less demanding") readings to students of color to boost rates of achievement. Although it is a generally agreed upon virtue to be broadly read, creating a broader reading background through the works of writers from multiple cultures is often described as, somehow, of "lesser" intellectual merit or of converting the study of literature into "merely" the study of social problems. Such observations would be unusual indeed in relation to courses in World Literature or Comparative Literature. Thus it appears inconsistent when Harold Bloom, professor of literature emeritus of Yale University and a staunch defender of the traditional literary canon, observes: "We are destroying all intellectual and esthetic standards in the humanities and social sciences, in the name of social justice. The Balkanization of literary studies is irreversible. I do not believe that literary studies as such have a future." At the same time, the writers Bloom celebrates as most worthy of study are those he sees as not only the "most original" but as the "most representative of their cultures" (Fruman, 1994, p. 9). And as Bloom himself knows, art itself has never been immune to reflecting or rendering perspectives on cultures and issues, and thus, to discuss the art is to discuss the issues. Respect accorded to works of literature that directly confront social issues has waxed and waned over the decades in the flow of the vagaries of literary tastes among critics and readers: While one generation applauds the work of Dos Passos or Steinbeck, another decries it. But such art has its roots in the most revered writers of centuries past and has continued to represent a vital and central creative presence throughout the history of literature. Why is it, then, that contemporary writers of color, many of whom are concerned with pressing social issues, are now so broadly maligned for somehow "destroying" the humanities "in the name of social justice"?

Beyond the artistic integrity of good texts from multiple cultures is their value for us as thoughtful citizens. Critics of multicultural reading lists are fond of associating their use with a pandering to "lesser" standards and tastes. Such a response represents a gross failure to appreciate not only the merit of such works from multiple cultures on their own as texts but also the value of involving ourselves in the tenets and ideas of these artists. Connected in a very real way with Dewey's concern for the social motive, we have much to gain from the lessons of these works, because they often address our humanity—or our lack of it. Nussbaum makes one such case in explaining the importance of teaching Ralph Ellison's *Invisible Man:* "Our nation has a history of racial obtuseness and this work helps all citizens to perceive racial issues with greater clarity" (1997, p. 110). Henry Louis Gates, Jr. describes a similarly significant goal in teaching writers from multiple cultures: to educate "students to think, to read, and to write clearly, to expose false uses of language, fraudulent claims, and muddled arguments, propaganda, and vicious lies—from all of which our people have suffered, just as surely as we have from an economic order in which we were zeros and a metaphysical order in which we were absences" (1992, p. 80). "'Minority studies' (so-called)," Gates continues, "are not 'for' minorities, any more than 'majority studies' (let's say) are for majorities. . . . Truly humane learning can't help but expand the constricted boundaries of human sympathy, of social tolerance" (p. 117). Reading and discussing Cisneros's novel *The House on Mango Street* (1989) left one young Black woman thinking about such gestures: "Esperanza's character," she wrote, "reflects the strength and subtlety of genuine human kindness, an indispensable attribute for survival in today's society."

Further, writers of color have been maligned by anti-multiculturalists for their use of language; yet critics and readers have cheered the verisimilitude of similarly accurate dialect from Mark Twain's "irascible" boys along the Mississippi (1959), from William Faulkner's Snopes family in the rural South (1963), or from James Joyce's workers and lovers in Dublin (1959). The accurate use of such language by these celebrated writers to create realistic characters, situations, dialogues, and sense of place—flowing from the strength of a writer's ear for natural dialogue—has never been accused of ruining students' ability to learn correct English or to imply the corruption of standard English. And yet criticism is regularly leveled against a number of noted writers of color who have similarly relied on the accuracy of language to develop strongly crafted fiction. Critics of the speech of the young girl in the picture book *Nappy Hair* (Herron, 1997) have suggested that the use of such a text compromises children's ability to learn standard English (Hymowitz, 1999). Critics of Asian-American works have, according to several Asian-American scholars, "forgotten that the vitality of literature stems from its ability to codify and legitimize common experience in the terms of that experience and to celebrate life as it is lived." As a result, critics have cited as "bad English" the language found in some works by Asian-American writers. But new people in a new land using a new language will not write or speak it as native speakers. The writer wanting to capture authentically this experience must be faithful to the way the language is being used and spoken (Chan, Chin, Inada, & Wong, 1982, pp. 216–217). In working with these texts, if anything, students are gaining a more sophisticated understanding of language—its breadth, its power, its relationship to culture and region and life experiences, its variability and significance.

Critics have also suggested that building reading lists that acknowledge and serve the diverse backgrounds of the students is a narrowing and casting out, a lessening, a loss of other significant titles. Including the works of writers from multiple backgrounds need not be, however, an either/or process. For any of the pictures of human experience that works of literature provide, each offers a single image that must be deepened, broadened, challenged by others. It was Ralph Waldo Emerson who noted, "none is quite perfect" (Emerson quoted in Gutmann, 1994, p. 16).

Neither Mark Twain, William Faulkner, Frederick Douglass, nor Toni Morrison alone can give us a complete understanding of American race relations. And by extension of writerly point of view and the nature of human nature, some characters will behave in more moral and felicitous ways than others. By reading a broad array of writers, however, our students will suffer neither from the absence of whole groups of individuals in our readings nor from individuals or groups being repeatedly portrayed in a lopsided, inaccurate, or potentially damaging fashion.

Multicultural reading lists need never "take away" from the classics, but rather add to them, as, in fact, the writers from these cultural backgrounds take their own places of distinction among the most revered writers from the past. Writer Michael Dyson has described his own childhood reading, a blend of classic and contemporary writers from multiple cultures made possible by the wisdom of teachers who knew the value of reading from a broad range of writers: "My own early education might serve as an illustration of the way in which the black and white traditions together shape a course of wide learning." For Dyson, discovery of the "Harvard Classics" and the works of Alfred, Lord Tennyson; Thomas Gray; Benjamin Franklin; and John Milton followed vivid memories of learning the poetry of Paul Laurence Dunbar, Langston Hughes, and Margaret Walker Alexander through the guidance of his fifth-grade teacher (1995, p. 47). By having our students move steadily among the contrasting points of view and visions that broader reading lists provide, our students can begin to assemble a more trustworthy image of themselves and others as these writers explore—for better or worse—our limited and stumbling and somehow gallant attempts to build lives and to make our way through the world. To do this, these voices are crucial.

Some vocal and leading critics of multicultural reading lists suggest that the works of these writers are damaging to the development of a civic consciousness since they describe Americans, especially White Americans, in a negative light (Stotsky, 1996). And yet it would be difficult to imagine writers who describe Whites more negatively than some of the most famous White writers: when every one of Huck Finn's (Twain, 1959) landings on the banks of the Mississippi—and the scenes of behavior he observes there—take us further from decency, and when, as Toni Morrison has noted, neither Twain nor his readers could have even imagined or permitted—"because it would not have been possible"—Huck's and Tom's human plaything in the terrible actions of the last chapters—Jim—to be White (Morrison, 1993, p. 57). Similarly, it would be hard to find a reading experience more "damaging to the development of civic consciousness" than that described by critic Aldon Nielsen (1988) when Black students encounter a number of major White American poets and their descriptions of Blacks.

Contrary to those critics who suggest that writers from multiple cultures are a threat to a proper civic education, Giroux suggests, "What [academic] life should be all about [is] dreaming a better future, and dreaming a new world" (1993, p. 92). For Dewey, education allowed individuals to immerse themselves in society's problems and to equip themselves for participating in democratic public discourse (Giroux, 1993, p. 97).

The contemporary thrust toward using texts from multiple cultures strengthens rather than damages the reach and power of education for today's students. And a clear distinction must be asserted between the rigors of such an approach, and education founded on shoddy curriculum or pedagogy. The form of "multicultural education" described by and so alarming to critics such as Sandra Stotksy, and its threats to a sound education (1999), have, in fact, little to do with the essence of a thoughtfully constructed multicultural approach to learning. Good literature is good literature and "pseudo literature" (p. 20) is "pseudo literature," no matter how it is taught or what purpose it serves. And poor teaching will disarm the power of even the most significant works of literature. Sound multicultural education is in no way synonymous with either "pseudo literature" or poor pedagogy. Thoughtful approaches to multicultural education foster critical and humane thinking about universal aspects of human life as well as multiple perspectives on the particularities, intersections, divergences, similarities, or collisions of cultures. Indeed, working successfully with students as well as texts from multiple cultures in the same classroom places significant additional intellectual, psychological, social, and pedagogical demands on teachers and students.

An education grounded in significant works and perspectives from multiple cultures thus deepens and broadens individual and group reading experiences. Reading lists grounded in multiple cultures assist our students with knowing more fully themselves and others. Good works of literature from multiple cultures promote critical thinking and involve our students in issues of importance on a national and global scale, on a daily basis. In the face of these factors, efforts to prevent them from entering classrooms or efforts to pull them from classrooms are not only counterproductive for our students, the emotion behind the gestures is simply not grounded in fact. Nussbaum asserts of such emotion, the disdain "is inaccurate" (1997, p. 298).

The private and public experiences with reading facilitated by these works are consistent with enduring tenets of liberal education in a democracy. Interests in examining and addressing overarching human and social needs through education at the beginning of the 21st century recapitulate those same interests articulated at the beginning of the previous century and during centuries past (Addams, 1910/1981; Dewey, 1900/1971,

1902/1971; Parker, 1984/2001). Similarly, the thinking of contemporary humanists mirrors the thinking of leading humanists of centuries past. Ideas and ideals of philosophers and writers from ancient Greece, and those of John Dewey, W. E. B. Du Bois, Robert Coles, Henry Louis Gates, Jr., Walter Massey, and Martha Nussbaum, share broad humanitarian values that transcend individuals, cultures, and eras. As Nussbaum notes, Massey, president of historically Black Morehouse College, cites the work of Dewey in describing the goals of a liberal education: "hospitality of mind, generous imagination, trained capacity of discrimination, freedom from class, sectarian or partisan prejudice and passion, faith without fanaticism" (Massey quoted in Nussbaum, 1997, p. 180).

And so, in fact, perhaps we have come full circle. In her philosophical examination of reform in liberal education, Nussbaum (1997) points out that contemporary multiculturalists have much in common with philosophers of centuries past upon whom our most trusted thinkers have relied over the centuries to continue to craft this modern democracy. The tenets at the heart of multicultural education reflect and embrace and even underscore, rather than nullify or replace in some essentially damaging fashion, central humanitarian values at the heart of the "great books." Even the movement's harshest critics should be able to see what transcendent values lie at its core.

CONCLUSION

The decisions I make about writers to include and exclude in a course reading list will not occur in a vacuum. Those decisions are intrinsically political. But I have also come to know and to trust that the choice of including works by writers from multiple cultures is a good and decent one, consistent with the ideals of the most thoughtful and generous among us: those who have understood well the processes of learning and the nature of reading, and those who have championed the dignity of the human community.

Memorable experiences in reading come when the reader can attach personal meaning to an author's story because something in that story is an extension in some way of the reader—the story offers something familiar, or something unfamiliar for which the reader is ready, curious, hungry. As teachers, sometimes we can guess what that readiness consists of, but often neither we nor our students can predict it. But our students know it when it happens. In selecting the books they read, we are opening or closing doors on the possibility of our students' connecting meaningfully with books and with reading. And so we must cast the net of our choices wide, allow as many opportunities for as many students as possible to make that personal connection out of need or hunger or delight. Did Robert Coles's students, did he himself, did his parents, find their "self-esteem" boosted by their reading? If by such a phrase we mean a sense of well-being that comes from savoring works of literature that matter in our lives or that comes from understanding more clearly something about ourselves or the world, then yes.

Once students have left our classrooms, their reading the books many of us treasure will be optional as their lives unfold. It is only by allowing books to feed the broad-based hunger of human curiosity when our students bring it before us that these students will be drawn into books, and will come to know books as friends, as companions who can nurture them through a sense of the familiar, or invite them beyond the confines of their own experiences into the larger world, and then, once there, help them to understand it. For each of our students—for those who come to us craving the next book or for the most tentative students before us—this is what must be done.

Beyond the value of these works for enriching students' individual experiences with reading, choosing to work with literature from multiple cultures reflects a commitment to supporting artistic integrity, to deepening in our students the practice of critical thinking, to broadening their understanding of the world and themselves in the world, to fostering cross-cultural dialogues and communication, and to embracing the ideals through which we have sought to define ourselves as a nation.

I eagerly await the students who will come before me in a few weeks and the moment when we begin our months of reading, together.

CHAPTER 8

A Pedagogy of Belonging: Toward a Pedagogy of Multiculturalism

Each year, my students and I begin a journey. From greetings to good-byes. From uncertainty toward familiarity, and from the familiar into the unknown. And if our days go well, from the solitary toward a sense of belonging: from you and me, to us. In some ways, our journey evokes a journey made decades ago by another student, six-year-old Ruby Bridges, as she integrated a Southern elementary school. Hers was a journey solitary and yet crowded, from the familiar to the unknown, from uncertainty toward a growing familiarity, and from cultural segregation toward what many had hoped would be a broader sense of community. As psychiatrist and author Robert Coles came to know Ruby, over the years he was to reflect on many meanings of her journey. His mentor Anna Freud had suggested that as children mature, they move from a self-centered view of the world and others to "empathy, mutuality, and companionship with [their] contemporaries." For Ruby and other children integrating Southern schools, that process became tied to, Coles suggests, a "long march" from "legally enforced, racially connected egocentricity to a knowledge of 'others,' a daily experience with those 'others' that had all sorts of personal meaning and consequences for them" (1992, p. 76). Connectedness, a sense of belonging, is no small thing as it relates to education, especially in a multicultural and divided nation.

Throughout the 20th century, progressive educators have agreed that a primary aim of education is to enhance participation in the larger culture. Although similar thinking took some educators down disastrous paths of forced assimilation, for others, communal notions tied to education provided for an essential respect for individuals, their roots, and the manner in which they found satisfactory membership in the larger culture. Jane Addams (1910/1981), John Dewey (1916/1966), and Francis W. Parker (1894/2001) maintained that the social motive and social engagement lay at the heart of meaningful education.

Today, a century later, instincts and commitments of those educators have been reconfirmed by Vivian Gussin Paley (1995, 1997), Geneva Gay (2000), Gloria Ladson-Billings (1994), Sonia Nieto (1999), bell hooks (1994), and others. For each of these educators, attentiveness to the cultural moorings of our students, connectedness among teachers and students, a sense of caring, and the fostering of community become core values in the shaping of curriculum and pedagogy.

A recent article reviewing research on "students' need for belonging in school" described a series of benefits accruing to students who experience a sense of relatedness in their schooling. Students' sense of belonging has been associated with higher degrees of motivation, independence, investment in learning, positive interactions with others, positive attitudes toward school, and sense of their own inner resources and social strengths. Relatedness is a basic and essential human need (Osterman, 2000). The link between education and social connectedness is an enduring one, and perhaps more essential now than ever.

In some ways, students today are being asked to continue the journey Ruby Bridges began in 1960. They, too, may travel alone and uncertain through the unfamiliar with those both like and unlike themselves. They, too, are being asked to take us into an America in which we can move forward with greater wisdom and understanding of each other across significant cultural divides. Their journey is not always easy. And many of our students, similar to Ruby, feel a solitariness in the midst of a crowd. As was the case for Ruby, it is up to us, the educators who surround our students, to assure that their journey is a safe and productive one, a journey that serves both the self and the larger community, a journey, I would argue, toward "empathy, mutuality, and companionship" (Anna Freud quoted in Coles, 1992, p. 72), facilitated by a pedagogy of belonging.

Why? What are the experiences of some of our students today? What does a pedagogy of belonging look like, and why is it important?

I would like to suggest five components to a pedagogy of belonging: Understanding and responding to the pressures and choices that can tug us apart in the multicultural classroom. Engaging in thoughtful planning. Understanding and drawing on the power resident in a multicultural group of students. Understanding what might be expected in the flow of a course. And creating a supportive environment.

UNDERSTANDING THE PRESSURES AND CHOICES THAT DIVIDE US

Worlds Apart: Effects of Cultural Difference

As students from multiple cultures gather in classrooms, many factors militate against their feeling part of one cohesive group. Students come together in schools wary of those unlike themselves, uncertain how to learn about each other, and inexperienced with creating multicultural communities. Recent studies show that high schools tend to be "less supportive and more impersonal than elementary schools" (Osterman, 2000, p. 353) and that high school teachers tend to provide few opportunities for students to interact (Goodlad, 1984, in Osterman, 2000). In either case, schools are less likely to foster a sense of belonging among students. In addition, the efforts of teachers and students to build a strong and lasting sense of belonging across cultural lines unfold in a milieu characterized by a powerful interplay of factors related to cultural difference and social dominance.

Each of the factors we have examined thus far—the journey between home and school, the presence of history, the role of racial or cultural identity, multifaceted discussions, a shared and shifting nature of authority, and the impact of curriculum or pedagogy—can reflect the power of cultural difference and can work against our students' experiencing a sense of belonging in the classroom.

In multicultural communities, students' travels between home and school often reflect differences in students' cultural affiliations and the values, assumptions, challenges, or privileges that may accompany those affiliations, and these differences emerge as students interact with each other on a daily basis. Further, the nature of the relationships students establish between home and school affects how they interact at school.

Students for whom the culture of home and the culture of school are contiguous more easily and readily feel a sense of belonging in school and in class than do those students for whom the cultures of home and school represent different worlds. Moreover, studies have shown that students who feel secure in school by virtue of the similar nature of the cultures of home and school may find it difficult to relate to those unlike themselves. In their discussion of students' "multiple worlds," Phelan, Davidson, and Yu explain:

> Students who are secure and comfortable within the bounds of their congruent worlds may have an especially difficult time connecting with peers unlike themselves. Many have little opportunity or reason to practice or acquire border crossing strategies. Distanced from students in other groups, it is these stu-

dents who are particularly at risk for developing spurious ideas and stereotypes about others. Some of these students are not interested in getting to
know or working or interacting with students who achieve at different levels or who have different backgrounds. . . . In a sense, their view is limited
and bounded by the congruency of their worlds [of home and school].
(1993, p. 83)

Simultaneously, those students for whom the worlds of home and
school are quite different may be marginalized in the world of school. In a
study of Black students in a primarily White independent school in
California, Horvat and Antonio found there was a sense among the Black
students that:

"It is [the White students'] school." . . . Thus while the black middle-class students were formally members of the school community, . . . their status
remained peripheral. . . . This distancing and lack of recognition as full members of the school profoundly affected their experience at the school. . . .
Despite the fact that these young women tried to change [essential aspects of
themselves], they could never achieve the unquestioned comfort and sense of
belonging that came so easily and innately to many of the white and privileged
girls. (1999, pp. 333, 335)

The presence of history can also serve to divide our students. Students
from multiple cultures may bring to the classroom widely diverging histories, as well as experiences and responses that emanate from those histories. One of our White students noted that as a country we have historically
driven apart cultures in ways that are hard to remedy; our actions in the
past have left resentments between cultures that have had unequal access
to advantages, and an ongoing animosity between racial or cultural groups.

Differing racial and cultural identities also predispose students to seg-
regate. Racial or cultural identity can play a central role in influencing the
connections that students are able and likely to build with their classmates.
Experience and studies tell us that students tend to gravitate toward those
within their own racial or cultural group. One Latina in our course on
issues of race and culture suggested that bringing people together across
cultural lines involves finding something that they share, and it involves
work. Given current demographic trends, the challenges facing students in
building satisfactory relationships across cultural lines will increase.

In a similar respect, aspects of multifaceted discussions and a shared
and shifting base of authority in the classroom can also work against bringing together students in the classroom. Diverging opinions growing out of
diverse cultural identities, histories, or experiences can strain students'
relatedness. Issues related to cultural identities and histories may well come

to the foreground in class discussions, and this may lead to conflict. Points of view that are shared or not shared on given issues can create, strengthen, or shift subgroup alliances within the class, and this can deepen already existing divisions among students. As students' experiences are respected as a valid and powerful form of knowing, differences among students can easily lead to competing voices of authority. Negative emotions tied to conflicting points of view about issues close to students' lives may be potent in class and after, and these strong emotions may lessen a feeling of connectedness among students across cultural lines.

Further, the ways in which students experience curriculum and pedagogy emerge in part from cultural identities and histories, and, just as with difficult or complex discussions, this can lead to divisions among students. A text that succeeds in capturing a significant aspect of reality for one student or group of students may inflame or alienate other students. Similarly, one way of approaching a text or material may excite some students and cause discomfort for others, based on culturally influenced styles of learning. A number of scholars, for example, note that Asian or Asian-American students' respect for the authority of the teacher may diminish their familiarity or comfort with questioning a teacher's point in a discussion; for other students, questioning teachers' proffered points of view can create an exhilarating atmosphere of debate and discovery in the classroom.

A Hierarchical Society: Effects of Social Dominance

Potential divisive effects of cultural differences in the multicultural classroom are compounded by the effects of attitudes or behaviors linked to "social dominance." In their day-to-day interactions in the classroom, our students' attitudes and actions often reflect the effects of living in a society in which, presently, power exists disproportionately among Whites and people of color. The effects of social dominance tied to Whites can become a constant force against which we make our efforts at bringing students together. Four phenomena tied to social dominance affect and may well serve to divide our students: Minor differences among individuals can lead to prejudice and discrimination. Our society is hierarchical in structure. This hierarchical structure results in an unequal distribution of privileges. And our views of the world emerge from our relative positions of dominance or subordination in society (Howard, 1999).

Many of our students are well aware that such forces exist beyond and within school. As one White student explained, many White Americans value a sense of superiority and disdain for those in other cultures, and such feelings drive the culture; they have no interest in equality.

Additionally, this student pointed out, whole areas of art would disappear without such dynamics at their core. One young Black woman posed a key question about such forces to her classmates:

> Sometimes I have to wonder if we as a society really want everything desegregated and for racism to really not exist. Do we fully realize what the world would be like without racism? [Individuals from] all races would be CEOs and corporate businessmen. Who would do the "dirty work?" Since there'd be no racism and segregation, everyone would have the best education. So who would clean the pool at your condo in Florida? I don't think we can even begin to imagine life without racism. And as long as humans try to do something [about it], it won't work.

The ripple effects of social dominance may be reflected in students' affiliation with each other; casual encounters or formal discussions; subtle or overt gestures, remarks, or observations; or assumptions, choices, attitudes, or behaviors on the part of cultural-majority and cultural-minority students. Although Allport's "contact" theory (1958) suggests that enabling students to work together can facilitate cross-cultural relations, Helms cautions that because of the overriding racism of the country, which seeps into the schools (1990), interaction among students in ostensibly "equal" roles in shared activities cannot be assumed to automatically promote healthy cross-cultural relatedness. bell hooks shares Helms's concern: "The politics of domination are often reproduced in the educational setting. . . . Many students, especially students of color, may not feel at all 'safe' in what appears to be a neutral setting. It is the absence of a feeling of safety that often promotes prolonged silence or lack of student engagement" (1994, p. 39). Consider the following moments among my own students: A young Black woman's hair elicits curiosity and comments from her White classmates that make her uncomfortable. With seeming impunity a young White male discredits a young Black female during a class discussion. Some White students are incensed by affirmative action programs operant in university admissions, claiming that admissions spots that should rightfully be "theirs" have gone to students "less deserving."

Two other concepts related to social dominance can be useful to us as well. In her work exploring the ways in which individuals' developing racial or cultural identities affect their behaviors and attitudes, Beverly Tatum has referred to "the smog of racism." According to Tatum, all of us breathe an atmosphere polluted with racism. The fact that racism is a reality of American life means that we ourselves and our students will inevitably exhibit aspects of racism as we interact in our schools and class-rooms (Tatum, 2001).

But let us examine one more paradigm that may help us understand group dynamics that may emerge in front of us in the multicultural class-room and that may make it difficult for our students to come together as a group. Researcher Janet Helms examines group dynamics that result from a combination of the effects of cultural identity and social dominance. She warns her readers that empirical data on such dynamics are rare, and that she is offering a tentative framework for thinking about multicultural group dynamics.

Multicultural groups are more complex than are culturally homoge-neous groups, and the cultural makeup of the group influences the charac-ter of the group (Helms, 1990). The interaction of a number of factors tied to racial or cultural identity may influence the direction and tone of a given group: the proportion of members of the cultural majority to the propor-tion of those in the cultural minority; the stage of racial or cultural identi-ty development of each member of the group, including the teacher; and the coalitions that may form as individuals in similar stages of racial or cul-tural identity development are drawn together out of a sense of shared per-spective. In addition, each individual brings the norms of his or her own group to the larger group. Members of the cultural majority, however, bring to the group the "zeitgeist" (atmosphere) of the larger society, which, similar to Tatum's notion of "the smog of racism," presumes White "supe-riority" and person-of-color "inferiority" in this historically racist country. This racist atmosphere is a powerful factor that may inform the assump-tions, attitudes, observations, and actions brought to the group by mem-bers of the cultural majority, even though those same individuals may or may not be aware of it. If members of the cultural majority also make up the numerical majority in the classroom, minority culture members will have a difficult time influencing the tone and direction of the class as a whole (Helms, 1990).

This series of dynamics directly affects how all students experience being members of the class, but it is particularly salient for students from minority cultures. Although coalitions of like-minded students in the cul-tural minority may give those students more power, if, over time, they feel they have little to no influence over the larger group, they may wish to withdraw—in one way or another—from the class altogether.

All of these factors affect the cohesiveness of the class. Statements, ideas, or gestures of students in the cultural majority may wittingly or unwittingly reflect the larger American racist zeitgeist and alienate students in cultural minorities. Students may form coalitions that increase the strength and power of their members' voices but that subdivide the class. Tension may develop between members of the cultural majority and cultural minority or among those in separate coalitions. Power may shift among those in the cultural majority, outspoken individuals, and strong coalitions of like-minded students (Helms, 1990). But the result may be a fractured class with little movement toward cohesion across racial or cultural lines. Our own experience with multicultural groups of students in our course on issues of race and culture bears out Helms's ideas. For that reason, her work has been most helpful in giving us additional understanding of group dynamics within the class, as well as an understanding of various dynamics that may emerge between teachers and the class as a whole.

Thus, although we and our students may yearn to create a sense of belonging across cultural lines in our classrooms, many factors militate against doing so. Students do not initially feel connected to one another across cultural lines. They are wary of each other. Pressures related to cultural difference and social dominance operate in ways that can tug them apart. Students themselves have little to no experience building a multicultural community. And they may have few opportunities and little support for interacting with each other in meaningful ways. For all of these reasons, our students are dependent on us, their teachers, to help them to do so.

Learning from Experience: Choices That Help/Choices That Hinder

Beyond factors tied to cultural difference and social dominance, factors tied to our own pedagogical choices can diminish a sense of belonging in the classroom, whether in choosing overall approaches or in our interactions with individual students.

The curiosity of the child predisposes him to enquire (Dewey, 1916/1966; Parker, 1894/2001). Thus, to tell students what to think in relation to cross-cultural issues or dynamics is, potentially, to foreclose, to shut down, the possibility of choice and of a student's vital participation in problem-solving. Didacticism on the part of a teacher may be appealing, but experience suggests that such an approach denies students the need for and pleasure of inquiry. Perhaps more importantly, didacticism often produces resistance, backlash, or withdrawal on the part of students. Particular moments among students unquestionably require clear, overt directives, as, for example, when one student deliberately exhibits cruelty toward another. But in our own experience, in the flow of a course, allowing students to explore and debate ideas related to racial or cultural dynamics as they are presented in significant texts, films, or discussions— that is, to engage in inquiry—leads more readily to enduring inclusive thinking. Students, especially adolescents, are always sensitive to being "told what to do," and this sensitivity is deepened if they feel they are being told what to think. They resent questions that appear loaded in any way, designed to bring about a particular, desired response. In our experience, students are much more likely to give serious thought to these issues when they can examine and debate them in an open-ended manner.

As with reliance on didacticism, in our experience two other approaches have proven less effective in bringing together groups of students from multiple cultures. One is allowing discussions to drift into competitions of victimization. Another is allowing dialogues to create a cycle of "blame and guilt" (Howard, 1999, p. 110). Such focal points most often lead to greater degrees of resistance rather than an openness of thought and conversation through which, together, we can address significant issues. Although all of us in the classroom may be affected by factors related to larger social forces that pull us apart, we are better served by strategies that enhance rather than diminish our students' engagement in the process of building group relatedness. For students to establish a competition by which the victimization of one people is measured against that of another or for students to engage in a cycle of blame and guilt can easily cause anger, defensiveness, and retreat among students, and this works in opposition to relatedness.

As our students come together before us, they are trusting us to create an environment in which each of them feels secure in the learning process. Tied to that need is the way in which we come to know each of the students before us and the way in which we interact with them as individuals as class unfolds. Although there will be much about our students we do not know, their lives, their identities, their histories, their needs, their challenges, and their joys are far too complex to conform to our uninformed speculation. Making assumptions about any of our students is to rob them of the essence of an emerging and compelling uniqueness of the self. And as class unfolds, singling out or ignoring any student—tied to cultural or racial identity—as part of the teaching experience can stress a student's feeling of membership in the group. In the flow of classroom interactions, to spotlight a student based on his or her identity is to rob that student of privacy, and to do so can create an uncomfortable, unjustified intrusion into the private world of the individual in a public space. Nor do we want any of the students among us to feel excluded as class unfolds.

Thought should also be given to the management of reading aloud or presentations in multicultural classrooms. Cultural identity or history can affect, in multiple ways, students' relationships to classroom material. What are the effects of calling on or not calling on, for example, a young Black male or a young White male to lead a seminar on an essay on the dangers facing the young Black male in America? In some instances both White students and Black students have found it uncomfortable when White students have been asked to read passages from Zora Neale Hurston's novel *Their Eyes Were Watching God* (1937/1978). White students are generally unfamiliar with the dialect Hurston employs, and sometimes they feel awkward or may stumble in reading it. Black students sometimes feel that White students are ridiculing the language itself. At the University of Pennsylvania, a White professor of law was suspended for singling out a Black student and referring to him as an "ex-slave" as he asked him to read a segment of the Constitution related to slavery (Pack & Prizer, 1993). In our choices, we do not want to create awkward or embarrassing moments for individual students or for the class as a whole.

Each of our students is there to learn, and to learn of and from each other through the shared give-and-take of ideas is a privilege. But no students in a given culture enter our classroom in order to educate those around them. Many students of color feel they are saddled with educating their White peers as an extension of their membership in a particular culture. And this can lead to resentment. Thus, while some of the richest learning will result from our students' interacting, sharing their perspectives, and telling their stories, we cannot *expect* students in one culture to be responsible for educating those in another culture.

Similarly, we need to protect students from being placed in unwanted positions as spokespersons for their cultures. Such moments can make students intensely uncomfortable, whether those moments originate with teachers or classmates. We all deserve acknowledgement of the uniqueness of our own experience and voice. And the complexity of any aspect of a culture defies summation by an individual. In the flow of classroom discussions, however, students may turn to each other and expect their classmates to "speak for a whole culture." For one biracial student in our class on racial and cultural issues, *not* being put in that position was noteworthy: "For the first time in my career [at this school], I was in a class with other minority [students], so I didn't feel like I had to defend my race."

Neither we ourselves nor our students want to carry away from our time together an overriding sense of regret, embarrassment, anger, hurt, or shame, nor do we want to lose any of our students into isolation or withdrawal. Negative experiences in cross-cultural learning can cause students to back away from such involvement in the future. Learning is not always easy, nor should it be. Inevitably, some classes unfold and end with unsettled and unsettling emotional edges. But we must work toward establishing a context for such discomfort—to help our students locate it in an understandable and understandably complex process. Arcing over moments of disequilibrium in a class should be a student's confidence in the reliability of the process we are engaged in, and the opportunity we hold to construct something we can all find rewarding. We need to enable our students to leave us each day wanting to return.

Our explorations need to acknowledge our shared and our individual needs: the overarching commonalities that intrigue us all as well as the specific interests, needs, passions, or challenges that drive each of us as individuals. And as caring adults, we need to shepherd our students through the natural conflicts that emerge as we bring together our disparate lives and values. We cannot absent ourselves from the need to guide, support, and set limits for our students from the time they enter our door until they leave us. We cannot turn aside if students violate the sanctity of each other with words or gestures. We must be there, unaligned, for each of them. They are depending on us to do so.

Creating a sense of belonging in a classroom comes about obliquely, and it takes time, nourished by a steady and shared engagement with texts and activities, the sharing of responses and ideas, the gradual revelation of who we are to each other, and the pleasure of having one's needs recognized and attended to by individuals and the group. And some students need more space apart from the group than others. In our effort to support group relatedness, we must not deprive any student of the space necessary for private and independent growth. Nor can we be impatient. Developing a sense of connectedness in the classroom can be neither forced nor rushed.

PLANNING IN A MULTICULTURAL ENVIRONMENT

How we and our students experience our time together in the multicultural classroom begins in part before we open the classroom door. Good teaching often originates in thoughtful planning. In creating meaningful experiences for students in multicultural classrooms, however, that process can be more complex and essential. In order to create a vital and useful experience for each student, and in the face of so many factors that can easily divide us, what considerations should enter into planning for the multicultural classroom?

At the center of our thinking about pedagogical choices in the multicultural classroom should be a commitment to learning that is relevant in the lives of our students. As with a shared commitment to the social component of education, progressive educators have long underscored the importance of relevance in learning. bell hooks remembers how crucial that connection was in her own schooling. Looking back on her early education in the Black schools of the South made her "forever dissatisfied with the education I received in predominantly white settings, . . . with an education that in no way addressed my social reality" (hooks, 1994, p. 51). Countless moments among our own students reaffirm the importance of students' being able to connect their lives with what occurs in the classroom and to take learning from the classroom and apply it to their lives beyond. When students can make that connection, their excitement is palpable. For one young Latina, this meant that discussions in the course on issues of race and culture always carried over into conversations with friends and family, and that the course had enabled her to reconnect with aspects of herself.

But planning classes and courses around the expanding consciousness of the child is more complex when planning for a group of students from multiple cultures. Students' starting points, what they know, their compelling interests and priorities, and the nature of the "cultural capital" students bring to the group may vary considerably from child to child. Each student comes bearing a unique fund of knowledge, and each student bears the potential for a unique response to our efforts. Thoughtful planning, therefore, must begin with a multicultural perspective on the part of the teacher. Some of my own worst or most uncomfortable moments as a teacher have arisen from my failure to consider multiple and distinctly different ways in which students from diverse backgrounds might react to a single piece of curriculum.

Given the diversity of the students before us, in selecting works to read or activities to engage in, we need to consider a wide range of backgrounds, interests, values, and experiences on the part of our students. And we need to consider the potential impact, tied to racial or cultural identity, of our choices. What choices will constitute, over the course of a week or a year, a healthy combination of, to return to Dewey's phrase, "the far and the near" (1910/1991, p. 221) for each student? What choices will enable us, as well, to examine aspects of human experience that transcend the cultural particularities of our diverse origins?

Although researchers are reluctant to link specific learning styles with particular cultures, research on individual learning styles, some of which may be culturally influenced, suggest the usefulness of a variety of approaches. In order to engage and further develop the strengths of each of the students before us, we can move among use of: the verbal, the visual; the written, the oral; the concrete, the abstract; the private, the public; small- and large-group work; and individual and collective approaches. We need to facilitate students' work individually, in small groups, and in the larger group to foster growth related to skills and concepts as well as an ability to work together successfully in multicultural teams. We need to provide students with the opportunities to engage in a shared focal point as a class, and we need to give them repeated opportunities to make personal choices in reading and writing that appeal to individual interests and needs and that lead to individual growth. Reliance on a broad array of approaches to reading, discussions, writing, and working together should lie at the core of the pedagogy.

Good literature from a variety of cultural traditions embodies and reflects Dewey's concepts of "the near" and "the far," as well as overarching aspects of the human experience. Reading and discussing, as a class, significant texts emerging from a variety of cultures enable students to explore lives and ideas close to home and far away, the unique and the universal. Such activities provide opportunities for identification with what is familiar and for exhilarating journeys into the new and unknown. They can offer us understanding about ourselves and others. And as we explore a wide range of texts, we can draw on and depend on the involvement and responsive of our students to bring the texts alive. For one young Black student in our course on issues of race and culture, a sensitivity to the assimilationist nature of American education meant to her that schools *must* offer a balanced curriculum, one that acknowledges and reflects students' own experiences and histories and, at the same time, educates them about worlds beyond their own.

Discussion among members of the class as a whole and within smaller groups supports the further development of the individual and the group. Opportunities for students to talk with each other, just as do broadened reading experiences, enable them to learn more about themselves and each other. They can begin to understand and further develop their own voice of authority based on their own background and experience. Drawing on that voice in discussions enlarges the sphere of shared knowledge, as well as, at times, a sense of the magic of storytelling, for all of us. Students can begin to learn something of the difficulty and the practice of civic discourse. They can learn to mediate conflicts and to manage the power of multiple opposing positions on significant topics. In many schools, high schools in particular, students have surprisingly few opportunities to interact with each other in classrooms (Goodlad, 1984, in Osterman, 2000). Yet sound interaction at the heart of classroom discussions has been found to be among the most effective approaches yet for fostering healthy cross-cultural relationships (Tharp, 1994). Well-facilitated discussions enable our students to construct a vibrant multicultural community before our eyes. "We are learning so much—through literature, videos, [the teachers], but also from each other," wrote one White student about the role of discussions in our class on issues of race and culture. "I love the conversations and sometimes arguments that we have in class; they really make me think, and sometimes even change my mind about what I believe."

All of our students enter the classroom with unique perspectives and experiences, rich ground for yielding compelling points of view and stories that can move and engage their readers. In recognition of and in response to those strengths, we need to give students repeated opportunities to write, and to write about what is important to them; we need to support them in developing their own voices as young writers and to give them repeated opportunities to draw on that voice, as critics or as storytellers. Writing allows for reflection, for an ordering of ideas, and for an ordering, sometimes, of chaos. In the public space of a classroom, writing allows for privacy and intimacy. For our students, just as for ourselves, to experience the power of writing is to experience the power of the individual and his or her voice.

Students should also be encouraged to share their writing with each other, in the classroom and beyond, in exhibits, presentations, publications, the news media, or responsible social action. We have seen classes of students mesmerized and moved to silence by the power of a classmate's words. Such times enable young authors to share their experiences as well as to savor the power of their own words. They see firsthand that their writing can engage, entertain, and educate others. And at times their writing enables them and members of their audience to feel less alone with their experiences. As students share their writing in the classroom, we come to know one another's voices; we pay attention to one another.

Teachers and students can find it useful to keep course journals. Students' journals allow them to engage in a private, ongoing dialogue with a supportive adult. Their journals become repositories of powerful feelings that students may be reluctant to share in class discussions but that press for understanding. Reviewing students' journals allows us teachers to know individual and group interests, concerns, and responses to curriculum and pedagogy. This information in turn enables us to be more sensitive and responsive to individual and group needs as a course unfolds. Keeping a teaching journal allows for recording and understanding facets of teaching and learning in the classroom. What worked, and why? And especially important, what did not, and why?

Students should also be encouraged and given the opportunity to work together. Engaging students in projects involving teams of students from multiple cultures is repeatedly mentioned among researchers as having the potential to promote better cross-cultural relations. For one of our White students, working in a group altered the whole experience of studying a major text: "[Working on the presentation for the novel *The Joy Luck Club* (Tan, 1989)] gave me a chance to work with 'new minds.' [Group work] really brings the class together. My group and I would work for a while then take a break. We all had dinner together. It was definitely a good productive experience for all involved."

Effective planning for the multicultural classroom, however, is always complex. As is the case for any group of students, what works for one individual does not necessarily work for another. Such distinctions are deepened, however, as students gather from culturally varied backgrounds. As we have seen in the examination of my own decision to teach several poems by Carl Sandburg, aspects of culture and power can significantly affect a lesson in the multicultural classroom. By considering a number of the elements that will come together in a single lesson, however, we can anticipate the potential cultural complexity of that lesson (Figure 8.1). To do so requires that we assess several distinct components of the lesson: 1) What is the cultural mix in the classroom: Is the class culturally homogeneous or culturally heterogeneous? 2) What is the nature of the material under consideration: Is the material devoid of or does it focus on issues tied in one way or another to race or culture? Further, do students have a choice in working with the material: Is the material elected or required? 3) What is the nature of the approach to the material: Will the material be delivered by lecture, thus allowing little to no conversation? Or will the material be approached through discussion, thus inviting multiple viewpoints into the forum? And who will be involved in the discussion? Such factors exist on a continuum from a low degree of potential for cross-cultural complexity to a high degree of potential for cross-cultural complexity. The combination of these elements predisposes a lesson to have lesser or greater potential for complex cross-cultural dynamics in the classroom. For example, a Black teacher lecturing about James Baldwin in an elective course to an all-Black class has a low degree of potential to generate cross-cultural tension or volatility. On the other hand, a White teacher leading a discussion of affirmative action in a required course with White students and Black students has a high degree of potential to generate cross-cultural tension or volatility.

Particular types of activities also lessen or deepen the potential intensity of cross-cultural dynamics of a lesson. Activities done individually—lecturing or reading silently in class—tend to lessen the potential for volatility. Activities done as a group—panel presentations, group discussions, reading aloud in class—tend to increase the potential for volatility.

Understanding something of the link between pedagogical choices and dynamics in the classroom can enable us to modulate the potential for tension in a class. To make one choice or another in planning is not intended to control or suppress either responsiveness or engagement on the part of students, but rather to allow us as teachers some measure of understanding about what type of lesson we are constructing and what type of response it may elicit, that is, to enter a classroom more knowingly.

Figure 8.1. Anticipating the Cultural Complexity of a Lesson

CONTINUUM OF COMPLEXITY

Classroom Mix

Cultural convergence:	Cultural divergence:
Teacher, students, students' families, material, author share same culture or assumptions.	Teacher, students, students' families, material, author represent a mix of cultures and assumptions.

Material

Material less focused on racially or culturally sensitive circumstances or issues.	Material more focused on racially or culturally sensitive circumstances or issues.
Course and material elected.	Course and material required.

Approach

Teacher's voice dominates.	Teacher's voice is resource or guide.
Students' families' voices, students' voices, responses, opinions play little to no role in the learning process.	Students' families' voices, students' voices, responses, opinions play significant role in the learning process.
Little to no openness of expression.	Broad openness of expression.

Potentially less complex	Potentially more complex
Potentially less volatile	Potentially more volatile

Teachers can anticipate the potential cultural complexity of a lesson by thinking ahead about the cultural mix in the classroom, the focus of material being used, whether or not the material is required, and the approach being taken.

One example of what can happen when teachers little understand the effect of components of a lesson occurred in Brooklyn in 1998. This particular incident resulted in media coverage from Seattle to Boston. A young White teacher in a public elementary school read aloud a picture book called *Nappy Hair* (Herron, 1987)—by a prize-winning Black author—to her predominantly Black and Latino students. After a parent discovered xeroxed segments of the book—a book about a historically sensitive issue in the Black community—in her child's folder, the teacher was summoned by school officials to an emotional meeting with frustrated parents. Unsatisfactory communication among school officials, parents, and the teacher resulted in the teacher being assigned to a desk job and then being granted a request to transfer to another school. After leaving to attend the meeting with parents, the teacher never saw her students again. To be caught off guard by cross-cultural tensions, volatility, or conflict is to be less prepared to address or mediate such moments satisfactorily for all involved.

Given the complexity of students' responses to materials and approaches in the multicultural classroom, establishing a context for curriculum and pedagogy can be helpful for our students and for ourselves. In an arena in which point of view or social context can be important, students often want to know about the identity and background of authors, scholars, or artists they are studying. They also want to know—and deserve to know and understand—the reasons behind curricular or pedagogical choices. We need to know clearly ourselves the reasons for our choices, and to be able to explain and to justify them to our students.

Helpful also is an atmosphere in which students can be honest with themselves and with us about the work they are engaged in. For one young Black woman in our course on issues of race and culture, this meant backing off of reading a text the focus of which was difficult for her to confront at that particular time in her life. Her being able to be honest with us about her needs meant that later the work was able to have much more meaning for her. To enable students to be candid and open about the process of learning makes for a fuller, more honest partnership between us and our students as well as among the students themselves.

As with any good teaching, we need to be alert to the responses of each of our students to a given lesson. What has been the impact on the students of the choices we have made? What worked for whom, and why? What has not worked for whom, and why? And what has been the effect on the group as a whole? We need to be attentive to the individual and the group, and allow the lessons of each lesson to inform our next ideas in planning.

DRAWING ON THE POWER AMONG US

As we have seen, the factors explored throughout this book—students' journeys between home and school, their histories and identities, discussions and the nature and locus of authority, and the impact of the choices we make about what we will teach and how—are factors that remain salient during our time with students, and they are factors that can divide our students. In our planning and once we are in the classroom, however, we can use our understanding of these factors to turn them into a source of power and connectedness.

Students' ties to the cultures of home; passions or fears they experience in relation to history; the experimentation, the joys, and the confusions of growing up, all can be regarded as the collective cultural capital of the group. Experiences embedded in these factors become the source of students' authority. They enrich students' relationships to reading, writing, discussions, and collaboration. Students' communication and partnerships with one another, in turn, can begin to narrow the gaps among them. Students' awareness of their differences as well as their similarities can make possible a growing understanding of themselves and those around them and begin to give them skills in navigating the rocky terrain of a multicultural America. In this way, students' grounding in the languages and cultures of home provides a valued and respected foundation for their continued growth and development.

Further, as psychologists have long understood, aspects of ourselves beyond our conscious understanding can exert power over our attitudes and behavior. To be able to name or describe those elements, however, is to release them into light. And this can lead to a fuller understanding of ourselves and others, as well as to more power and control over our decisions. Something not unlike that process occurs in multicultural classrooms as students seek to relate to each other and create a harmonious group without knowing of or understanding the forces that may be at work within themselves or throughout the group. For students to understand that their connections between home and school can significantly affect their lives as students—and that there are ways to strengthen those connections—can help them feel less confused or alone in what may be a series of daily challenges. For students to know of the power of history to shape our responses in the present can enable them to gain more understanding of their own responses and the responses of those around them. To know that developing a racial or cultural identity is a complex, sometimes puzzling, and perhaps lifelong process can enable students to grasp more consciously a host of confusing emotions, responses, and experiences. For students to know that all of us may have difficulty engaging in significant cross-cultural conversations and that yet, with practice, this is a process we can come to engage in with less fear and awkwardness, enables them to believe they can go forward into new settings with more tools for communication and more hope of reaching across divides. For students to know that moving among competing voices of authority on a given issue can be difficult but can also both enlarge their thinking and give them valuable skills for their futures can help them better manage the confusion such moments can generate. Knowing that all of us, teachers and students, are vulnerable to the impact of prevailing social dynamics in the larger culture—the effects of cultural difference and the effects of social dominance—can help us understand those forces in the classroom. Helping students understand the intangible forces at work in our midst can help them better understand their own attitudes and behaviors as well as the moments that may occur unexpectedly and puzzlingly around them. And this can give them not only understanding but the power to alter those forces.

THE COURSE OF THE COURSE: WHAT CAN WE EXPECT?

Even with careful planning, there will be days and periods of time that feel more or less successful than we had hoped. Some of those ups and downs are natural. To expect them may help us as we encounter them. If we are to remain involved in the process of fostering engagement, cohesiveness, and trust, knowing what we may encounter can help.

In multicultural schools, more so than in culturally homogeneous schools, every class of students is unique. Teachers and students will experience each group of students differently, depending in part on the cultural makeup of the class. Any one student's voice, as well as the voices of groups of students, has the power to affect the dynamics of a class or a course on a daily basis. In our experience, for example, discussing Latino fiction in the absence of Latinos lacks a breadth and fullness that comes when Latinos are members of the class. When both young Black women and young Jewish women enter a discussion on the impact of cultural images, the conversation is richer than if voices from one of those cultures are missing. Students' personal experiences of a class, too, are shaped in part by the makeup of the class. "It's good for White students to be in the minority in a class," one White student observed about a time when she was in the cultural minority in a class, "the discomfort is a learning experience." Classes in which there is a clear cultural majority with one or two students from a cultural minority will yield different dynamics than will a class that has a high degree of cultural mix or a class that is culturally homogeneous. The racial or cultural identity of each student, the racial identity of the teacher, and the stage each of us inhabits as we are establishing our racial or cultural identity affect, potentially, the way in which each individual as well as the group as a whole experiences the class.

Materials offered at the beginning of a course will be experienced differently than materials offered later in the course; thus, the cultural makeup of the class may affect the optimal way of designing a course. As any experienced teacher knows, in course design, material A followed by material B followed by material C does not produce the same series of effects as material B followed by material C followed by material A. What we teach when, the sequence of our materials, can influence the impact materials have on students and the ways in which students respond to them. Sequence can also determine, to some degree, whether material succeeds or fails, indeed whether a course itself may succeed or fail. This is particularly the case in classrooms of students from multiple cultures and particularly the case with materials that offer a confrontational tone or controversial stands on sensitive issues. At the beginning of a course, students may bring a rich and varied cluster of responses to material and little shared background. As students share one reading or concept after another, however, they begin to build a broader base of shared knowledge from which to experience and respond to each subsequent piece of material. Gradually, that shared and broadening base of knowledge will begin to inform not only their responses to new material but the way in which they respond to each other, their growing shared wisdom and vocabulary easing the challenges of cross-cultural communication among them.

Given this predictable path, opening courses with material that may be less culturally threatening for the class can help establish group cohesiveness. As students develop a shared base of understanding, a shared vocabulary, and a greater sense of connectedness with each other, however, they find it easier to work with material that may be culturally more sensitive. Knowing of ongoing cross-cultural tension in the larger school may point to an optimal way, too, of structuring a course. Material that taps into known cross-cultural tensions may best be handled at a later time in a course, when students have had the opportunity to develop more trust in each other and in us. Students in early stages of cross-cultural learning tend to be more shy, hesitant, uneasy, and vulnerable. As they grow accustomed to sharing their own ideas with others and to the give-and-take of discussing opposing positions, however, they become more relaxed, comfortable, and confident about the process. Students also respond well when they are given the opportunity to explore issues tied to their own cultural experiences in the process of being asked to be open to perspectives grounded in other cultures. As a result, supporting students at each step of cross-cultural exploration enables them to begin to embrace the process on their own, to be more comfortable with the risks and uncertainties of such explorations, and to realize that they are gaining skills that will serve them well in their futures.

Cross-cultural learning, nonetheless, is difficult for teachers and for students; it involves—almost unavoidably and by definition—uncertainty, discomfort, and risk. In the face of this discomfort, teachers need to be sensitive to the vulnerabilities of their students and respond to the needs of individuals as they encounter concepts or challenges that unsettle their sense of themselves or the world. Such responsiveness on the part of the teacher can be crucial to maintaining students' trust and engagement and the equipoise of the class as a whole.

Students' initial weeks together may feel tense, artificial, uneasy, as though they are walking on eggshells with each other. They may not know what to think about each other or how to act with each other. If in fact study turns to what is real among us, as it should, it may mean that issues close to the students' lives become the subject of inquiry. Over time, their sense of self, perspectives, values, and assumptions may be challenged. They may discover an uncomfortable distance between the way they perceive themselves and the way they are perceived by others. Their conversations may nudge them away from prior assumptions. There is perhaps, in a journey such as this, a necessary iconoclasm. But that is not reassuring to students in the process of ordering their world. They may move from certainty to uncertainty; in the face of multiple competing perspectives, they may feel the ground crumble beneath them. All of these factors can lead to difficult private or public moments. And such moments may be more difficult for students who feel that few to no other students share their perspective. None of that is easy.

Students may also resist elements of a shared multicultural experience. Our differences and the issues and pressures that divide us are significant. They emerge from who we are, where we have come from, and what we care about. To have those aspects of ourselves brought, unavoidably, into question and examination and scrutiny—either by the materials we explore or by the observations we generate in the natural process of being and talking together—may well set off resistance. As a result of that resistance, students may play down differences, withdraw, reject the source of the difference, or become defensive (Barker-Hackett & Mio, 2000). If we can help our students understand, ahead of time, our choices involving curriculum and pedagogy, as well as the nature of cross-cultural discussions—and the advantages as well as the challenges that may be involved in such engagements—we can invite them into such inquiry and reduce the likelihood of resistance. And if we can help students understand the nature of resistance as it involves education across cultural lines, they can begin to understand more fully their own responses and remain more open to ideas or perspectives that may broaden their knowledge.

One young Latina described a conversation with a Latina friend who had experienced significant frustration in a predominantly White school. Our student identified with much of what her friend had gone through, and this prompted a reflection on her own experiences—including moments of defensiveness—in a predominantly White school: "[Since coming here] I have learned much more of other cultures and how [individuals in] those cultures perceive me. But most importantly, I have learned so much more about myself and what my culture means to me and how it defines who I am. I used my experience and grew from it. It took me awhile to learn to lower my defenses, but I realized that if I wanted to grow and if I wanted people to understand me, then I had to."

Although some discomfort or risk is involved in any learning, too much risk can hamper learning. Students whose discomfort or sense of risk reaches unmanageable levels may grow angry and take out their frustration on classmates or teacher, or they may withdraw in one way or another—remove themselves from discussions, disengage themselves from activities of the course, or, if possible, drop the course altogether and take away from the experience a cluster of negative feelings. By modulating the challenges involved in day-to-day explorations, however, we can maintain an engaging focus and a manageable experience for the students before us.

Just as there are ups and downs for individuals in the class, there may be highs and lows for the class as a whole as a course unfolds, a pattern known as "the school romance" (Frank, 1998). Most students and teachers enter classrooms each fall with optimism and hope. Fall represents a new beginning for all of us. This class, this course, this term will be an exciting one. But then one moment goes awry; particular material doesn't work; an idea that seemed so good fails. Students get frustrated with one another's differences or the effects of larger social patterns tied to aspects of race or culture. We may all experience a period of time when we feel not more wise, but less, and that's not the way that education is supposed to reward us. Experience has shown, however, that if we can help our students understand the difficult moments and understand that we will continue to be there for them, we can move beyond disillusionment toward a renewed sense of involvement. One of our White students described experiencing a series of ups and downs linked to the tenor of the class as a whole during our course on issues of race and culture:

> My emotions and attitude toward the class changed several times. In September I came into class enthusiastically, but by late October I was frustrated. I didn't feel like we were accomplishing anything in class and we never got to the bottom of an issue. The frustration was compounded by what I felt was a lack of respect for the other classmates' perspectives. I remained interested in the literature and the history but when the discussion turned to contemporary issues I felt like everyone's cooped up emotions boiled over. By December my focus was changing a little [again]. It's going to be hard, I thought, changing attitudes in a class, much less a country.

As teachers, we need to be aware of the level of comfort or discomfort, ease or tension, that individuals and the class are experiencing, whether in a given activity, in a particular period of a course, or in the course as a whole, and to be able to make choices that support students' continued engagement.

Such moments are not restricted to students. In our class on issues of race and culture, it was several years before I realized that, predictably, by November I was feeling overwhelmed by a sense of inadequacy as a teacher. Why had I taken on this course and this focus? And yet, equally predictably, by January, as our students readied to leave us, I knew that not only was part of me sad to see the course end, but by fall I would be eager to take on again all of the challenges—and the pleasures—the course entailed.

One reality, however, in navigating the challenging terrain of multicultural teaching and learning is that there *will* be difficult moments: moments of tension, conflict, or confusion; moments that fail in front of us; moments we did not understand or know how to prevent or avoid; moments of regret on the part of our students and ourselves.

And no matter how conscientious we are as teachers, controversy will most likely occur. Multicultural teaching and learning are too complex to avoid it. Choosing materials, choosing approaches, interacting with students across differences, negotiating cross-cultural classroom dynamics— any one of these aspects of life in the multicultural classroom is rife with opportunities for controversy. What will we teach, and why? What will we not teach, and why? How will we teach what we teach, and how will that affect each of our students and the group as a whole? In multicultural teaching, more so than in culturally homogeneous classrooms, what works for one individual may not at all work for another. And we are going to make mistakes. If, however, we are cognizant of the myriad complexities that constitute multicultural teaching and learning, we can anticipate many of those moments. For the moments that do catch us by surprise, we can learn from them and trust that if they do not break us, they may, as Hemingway has suggested, make us stronger—even, perhaps, wiser.

CREATING A SUPPORTIVE ENVIRONMENT

If we value connectedness and a sense of belonging in the classroom, we need to create an environment where students can trust us and trust each other.

We need to recognize the value of students' relationship to the culture of home and to support our students in ways that support the journeys they take each day between home and school. We need to affirm the power of proficiency with multiple languages as well as the skills in translation many of our students develop as they serve as interpreters for members of their families. We need to understand and address the factors, related to their daily journeys, that keep students from feeling a sense of belonging to their school and with each other.

We need to understand and to be responsive to the significance, variability, power, and tenacity of history in each of our students' lives and the complexity of coming of age in a time and place that has given considerable emphasis to racial and cultural identity.

We need to give students opportunities to talk with each other about ideas that have importance in their lives, and to support and guide them in that process. We need to support the existing and emerging authority of each of our students as they examine and reflect on the world they have inherited. We must respect the knowledge that each of them brings to the group, as well as the limitation to that knowledge—and the difficulty for all of us, sometimes, of talking about what we know and do not know.

We need to design curriculum that appeals to students from multiple cultures and that aids them in understanding and constructing meaning in their world. We need to be cognizant of the various ways in which our choices of curriculum and pedagogy may engage and affect them and be prepared to understand and address the effects of those choices.

We need to anticipate, understand, and mediate the effects of cultural difference and social dominance among our students. We need to help students understand the origins, nature, and effects of such cultural patterns in order to demystify and dismantle their power among us. We need to protect students from their own and one another's capacity to do harm out of ignorance, thoughtlessness, or malice.

We need to offer attention to the growth and well-being of each student. We need to remain connected with each child as the vicissitudes of difference divide the larger group in moments of tension, disagreement, or misunderstanding. We need to respect the solitariness of the individual, give him or her room to grow, room to be alone, room to say "no," room to be a rightful resister, and room to find the optimal path of his or her own growth.

We need to understand our own strengths and weaknesses, the power and limitations accorded us by our own histories and identities.

We need to be available to each student and we need to be reliable listeners, to support growth from below rather than impose direction from above. Our room needs to be a place where each student can be heard, a place without fear, a place where histories can visit and linger, a place for identities to emerge. A place where students can build bridges from the island of the self, to each other, to us, and to the joys and mysteries of the world before us.

*   *   *

I began this book and this chapter with descriptions of students' journeys, contemporary and more distant. I would like to end, as well, on words of a journey.

The last day of class in our course on issues of race and culture. Students exuberant over ending first semester of senior year have gathered for potluck lunch to be followed by sharing key points from final papers. Bowls of hummus, platters stacked with pita, a baking pan of Indian rice, bagels, sushi, and chocolate chip cookies spread across our makeshift table. A congenial gathering unfolds, students laughing, remembering moments in the course, and sharing thoughts of becoming spring-term seniors, relieved that college applications are behind them. After clearing our plates, we turn to hearing segments of their writing. Black, White, Latino, Russian, Middle Eastern, and Asian-American students read from their final papers. They speak of the power of history, challenges involving identity, tensions of assimilation and separatism, ties of friends and family to culture, problems in the American educational system, and what it means to be an American.

Prior to the final day, one of the young Black women had decided that she might, during the last class, read a poem she had written detailing the challenges she has faced as a Black student from Chicago's West Side in this predominantly White school. "I'd like to read a poem," she says to the class, "I may need some help. It's hard to read." At one point she falters. As she finishes, the room is silent. Gradually, students begin saying goodbye, many of them gathering around the young poet. "A lot of people heard you, LaShandra. We heard what you were saying." Then, backpacks slung onto shoulders, the students are gone. After all the months of readings, discussions, papers, lectures, films, speakers, the ups and downs for all of us, we leave this morning, in stillness—through memory, poetry, individuals' voices—a place where, however tenuously, we all belonged. Lingering in the empty room, I miss every one of them.

CONCLUSION: WHERE'S IT ALL GOING?

If a pedagogy of belonging works, what does that mean?

From our early days together, perhaps tense and awkward, more aware of the gaps that divide us than the overlaps that unite us, uncertain how we will all fit together, we have gradually constructed a shared vocabulary, language, history, and even identity, founded on the strength of who we are as individuals. Our explorations of ideas and concepts, our speaking and listening to each other, have given us new words, and from those new words, we have built a language we share. Time has given us shared memories, a growing knowledge of one another's histories, and a new history we have built together. Woven from the solid strands of our own strong and separate identities, we have built together an identity we share for a while. As one biracial student observed near the end of the course, "I felt comfortable because [these students] were my classmates."

We have moved toward greater ease in managing multicultural perspectives and cross-cultural communication. We've heard new perspectives. From the confusion of being surrounded by multiple perspectives, the students have moved toward embracing the richness of multicultural perspectives themselves. We have learned more about ourselves and each other. We have learned to be less afraid of each other; we have learned something about how to ask the questions we've wanted to ask, how to talk with each other, how to listen, and why.

During our time together we have journeyed toward understanding and belonging, from ethnocentrism and feeling separated by difference, fear, uncertainty, and biases to a fuller, more compassionate awareness of others. Our time together has allowed a coming together of worlds, from which we have built a new world. We have moved from "you" and "me" toward "us." Some would say that such movement is important not only for individuals, but as well for communities that lie beyond our room. Some of our students would agree. As one Russian-American student wrote at the end of the course, "Sometimes I feel that, in a way, each student who takes this course almost has a sort of responsibility to take the information from the class and teach others. You owe it to the authors that produced the material you read to go out and pass it on."

At least, this encircling sense of connectedness is what we hope for. It does not always occur. Although many of us believe that knowledge can enable us to address the significant divides that accompany us into the classroom, that will not always be the case. The distances and the differences among us are significant. Not all individuals want to leave behind the attitudes and pressures that divide us. For whatever reason, some embrace them. And for some, knowledge can be used to hurt. To know another better is to know his or her vulnerability. Attitudes, language, and behaviors whose power we have come to respect because of their ability to cause harm can be used to do just that: to underscore difference, to reinforce the paradigms of dominance. Prejudice, stereotypes, discrimination, and racism are not simply the products of ignorance, and so they defy being dismantled solely through the power of knowledge. For many, self-interest keeps such forces alive.

Or for some students, perhaps little of what we have done together will matter. Maybe this has been neither the time nor the place for this type of growth to occur. Learning is a fickle thing. As significant as our own readiness is the readiness of our students.

But if it does work, when we leave, we will miss this time and place and what happened here, as together we explored the world. We will have come to understand, at least for a while, what John Donne (1624/1962, pp. 794–796) meant so many years ago: "No man is an island, entire of itself; every man is a piece of the continent, a part of the main." We will miss each other when we go, when the journey we shared is over.

References

Adams, M., Bell, L. A., & Griffin, P. (Eds.). (1997). *Teaching for diversity and social justice.* New York: Routledge.

Addams, J. (1910/1981). *Twenty years at Hull-House.* New York: New American Library.

Adler, B. (Ed.). (1997). *Growing up Jewish.* New York: Avon.

Akash, M., & Mattawa, K. (Eds.). (2000). *Post Gibran: Anthology of new Arab American writing.* Syracuse, NY: Syracuse University Press.

Allport, G. W. (1958). *The nature of prejudice.* Garden City, NY: Doubleday Anchor.

Anaya, R. (1972). *Bless me, Ultima.* New York: Warner.

Andersen, M., & Collins, P. H. (Eds.). (1995). *Race, class, and gender.* New York: Wadsworth.

Andrews, S. (Director). (1994). *School colors* [Video]. Alexandria, VA: PBS Video.

Archibold, R. C. (1999, December 20). Minority growth slips at top private schools. *The New York Times,* pp. A1, A35.

Augenbraum, H., & Stavans, I. (Eds.). (1993). *Growing up Latino: Memoirs and stories.* New York: Houghton-Mifflin.

Badour, D. (Producer). (1995). *The Promised Land Vol. I: Take me to Chicago* [Video]. Bethesda, MD: Discovery Channel.

Baldwin, J. (1966). Many thousands gone: Richard Wright's "Native Son." In S. L. Gross & J. E. Hardy (Eds.), *Images of the Negro in American literature* (pp. 233–248). Chicago: University of Chicago Press.

Banks, J. (1996). The historical reconstruction of knowledge about race: Implications for transformative teaching. In J. A. Banks (Ed.), *Multicultural education, transformative knowledge, and action: Historical and contemporary perspectives* (pp. 64–87). New York: Teachers College Press.

Barker-Hackett, L., & Mio, J. S. (2000). Addressing resistance in large groups. In J. S. Mio & G. I. Awakuni, *Resistance to multiculturalism: Issues and interventions.* Philadelphia: Brunner/Mazel.

Beck, E. T. (1998). From "Kike" to "Jap": How misogyny, anti-Semitism, and racism construct the "Jewish American Princess." In M. L. Andersen & P. H. Collins (Eds.), *Race, class and gender: An anthology* (3rd ed.) (pp. 430–436). New York: Wadsworth.

Bendau, M. C. (Producer/Director). (1992). *Gangs: Dreams under fire* [Video]. Cincinnati, OH: Franciscan Communications.

207

Benson, A. (Director). (1987). *Toni Morrison* [Video]. Chicago: Home Vision Entertainment.

Berman, P. (1994). The other and the almost the same. In P. Berman (Ed.), *Blacks and Jews: Alliances and arguments* (pp. 1–28). New York: Dell.

Berube, M. (1997, September). Citizens of the world, unite!: Martha Nussbaum's campaign to cultivate humanity. *Lingua Franca,* pp. 54–61.

Bigsby, C. W. E. (Ed.). (1971). *The Black American writer, Vol. I: Fiction.* Baltimore: Penguin.

Bowen, W. G., & Bok, D. (1998). *The shape of the river: The long-term consequences of considering race in college and university admissions.* Princeton, NJ: Princeton University Press.

Callahan, N. (1970). *Carl Sandburg: Lincoln of our literature.* New York: New York University Press.

Casas, J. M., & Pytluk, S. D. (1995). Hispanic identity development: Implications for research and practice. In J. G. Ponterotto, J. M. Casas, L. A. Suzuki, & C. M. Alexander (Eds.), *Handbook of multicultural counseling* (pp. 155–180). Thousand Oaks, CA: Sage.

Chan, J. P., Chin, F., Inada, L. F., & Wong, S. H. (1982). An introduction to Chinese-American and Japanese-American literatures. In H. A. Baker, Jr. (Ed.), *Three American literatures: Essays in Chicano, Native American, and Asian American literature for teachers of American literature* (pp. 197–228). New York: The Modern Language Association of America.

Chin, F. (1991). *Donald Duk.* Minneapolis: Coffee House Press.

Cisneros, S. (1989). *The house on Mango Street.* New York: Vintage.

Coles, R. (1989). *The call of stories: Teaching and the moral imagination.* Boston: Houghton Mifflin.

Coles, R. (1992). *Anna Freud: The dream of psychoanalysis.* New York: Addison-Wesley.

Colin, C. (1999, November 8). The n-word. *Salon.com* [On-line]. Retrieved December 31, 2002, from http://www.salon.com/books/it/1999/11/08/nword.

Collins, P. H. (1991). *Black feminist thought: Knowledge, consciousness, and the politics of empowerment.* New York: Routledge.

Cone, J. H. (1991). *Martin and Malcolm and America: A dream or a nightmare?* Maryknoll, NY: Orbis.

Csikszentmihalyi, M. (1996). *Creativity: Flow and the psychology of discovery and invention.* New York: HarperPerennial.

Cullen, C. (1925/1997). Incident. In H. L. Gates, Jr. & N. Y. McKay (Eds.), *The Norton anthology of African American literature* (p. 1306). New York: W. W. Norton.

David, J. (Ed.). (1992). *Growing up Black.* New York: Avon.

Davidson, A. L. (1997). Marbella Sanchez: On marginalization and silencing. In M. Seller & L. Weis (Eds.), *Beyond Black and White: New faces and voices in U.S. schools* (pp. 15–44). Albany, NY: State University of New York Press.

Delpit, L. (1995). *Other people's children: Cultural conflict in the classroom.* New York: The New Press.

Dewey, J. (1900/1971). The school and society. In J. Dewey, *The child and the curriculum, the school and society* (pp. 1–159). Chicago: University of Chicago Press.

Dewey, J. (1902/1971). The child and the curriculum. In J. Dewey, *The child and the curriculum, the school and society* (pp. 1–31). Chicago: University of Chicago Press.

Dewey, J. (1910/1991). *How we think.* Amherst, NY: Prometheus Books.

Dewey, J. (1916/1966). *Democracy and education.* New York: The Free Press.

Doillon, J. (Director). (1998). *Ponette* [Video]. New York: Fox Lorber Home Video.

Donne, J. (1624/1962). Devotions upon emergent occasions, meditation XVII. In M. H. Abrams, (Ed.), *The Norton anthology of English literature, Vol. I* (pp. 794–796). New York: W. W. Norton.

Du Bois, W. E. B. (1933/1995). The Negro college. In D. Lewis (Ed.), *W. E. B. Du Bois: A reader* (pp. 69–70). New York: Henry Holt.

Dyson, M. (1995, November 19). Shakespeare and Smokey Robinson. *The New York Times Book Review,* p. 47.

Dyson, M. (1998). The plight of Black men. In M. L. Andersen & P. H. Collins (Eds.), *Race, class and gender: An anthology* (3rd ed.) (pp. 136–146). New York: Wadsworth.

Ellison, R. (1947/1972). *Invisible man.* New York: Vintage.

Ellison, R. (1966). Twentieth-century fiction and the Black mask of humanity. In S. L. Gross & J. E. Hardy (Eds.), *Images of the Negro in American literature* (pp. 115–131). Chicago: University of Chicago Press.

Engebretson, M. (2000, July-August). Suburbia goes global: Cultures collide outside the city limits. *Utne Reader,* p. 15.

Evans, G. (1988). "Those loud Black girls." In *Learning to lose: Sexism and education.* London: The Women's Press.

Fadiman, A. (1998). *The spirit catches you and you fall down: A Hmong child, her American doctors, and the collision of two cultures.* New York: Noonday.

Faulkner, W. (1929/1956). *The sound and the fury.* New York: Vintage.

Faulkner, W. (1963). *Three famous short novels: Spotted horses, old man, the bear.* New York: Vintage.

Feinberg, W. (1998). *Common schools, uncommon identities: National unity and cultural difference.* New Haven, CT: Yale University Press.

Fordham, S. (1988). Racelessness as a factor in Black students' school success: Pragmatic strategy or Pyrrhic victory? *Harvard Educational Review, 58(1),* 54–84.

Fordham, S. (1991). Racelessness in private schools: Should we deconstruct the racial and cultural identity of African-American adolescents? *Teachers College Record, 92(3),* 470–484.

Fordham, S. (1997). "Those loud Black girls": (Black) women, silence, and gender "passing" in the academy. In M. Seller & L. Weis (Eds.), *Beyond Black and White: New faces and voices in U.S. schools* (pp. 81–111). Albany, NY: State University of New York Press.

Fordham, S. (1999). Dissin' "the standard": Ebonics as guerrilla warfare at Capital High. *Anthropology and Education Quarterly, 30(3),* 272–293.

Fordham, S., & Ogbu, J. (1986). Black students' school success: Coping with the burden of "acting White." *Urban Review, 18,* 176–206.

Frank, D. (1998). The live creature: Understanding the school and its passions. *Child and Adolescent Social Work Journal, 15(6),* 419–438.

Freire, P. (1971). *Pedagogy of the oppressed.* New York: Herder and Herder.

Frosch, M. (Ed.). (1994). *Coming of age in America: A multicultural anthology.* New York: The New Press.

Fruman, N. (1994, October 9). Bloom at Thermopylae [Review of *The Western canon: The books and school of the ages* by Harold Bloom]. *The New York Times Book Review,* p. 9.

Fuss, D. (1989). *Essentially speaking: Feminism, nature and difference.* New York: Routledge.

Gates, H. L., Jr. (1992). *Loose canons: Notes on the culture wars.* New York: Oxford University Press.

Gay, G. (2000). *Culturally responsive teaching: Theory, research, and practice.* New York: Teachers College Press.

Gillan, M. M., & Gillan, J. (Eds.). (1994). *Unsettling America: An anthology of contemporary multicultural America.* New York: Penguin.

Gillan, M. M., & Gillan, J. (Eds.). (1999a). *Growing up ethnic in America: Contemporary fiction about learning to be American.* New York: Penguin.

Gillan, M. M., & Gillan, J. (Eds.). (1999b). *Identity lessons: Contemporary writing about learning to be American.* New York: Penguin.

Giroux, H. A. (1993). *Border crossings: Cultural workers and the politics of education.* New York: Routledge.

Goodlad, J. I. (1984). *A place called school.* New York: McGraw-Hill.

Griffin, J. H. (1961). *Black like me.* London: Panther.

Gross, T. L. (1966). The Negro in the literature of the Reconstruction. In S. L. Gross & J. E. Hardy (Eds.), *Images of the Negro in American literature* (pp. 71–83). Chicago: University of Chicago Press.

Gursky, D. (2002, February). Recruiting minority teachers: Programs aim to balance quality and diversity in preparing teachers. *American Teacher 86(5),* 10–11, 19.

Gutmann, A. (Ed.). (1994). *Multiculturalism: Examining the politics of recognition.* Princeton, NJ: Princeton University Press.

Helms, J. E. (Ed.). (1990). *Black and White racial identity: Theory, research, and practice.* Westport, CT: Praeger.

Helms, J. E. (1995). An update of Helms's White and people of color racial identity models. In J. G. Ponterotto, J. M. Casas, L. A. Suzuki, & C. M. Alexander (Eds.), *Handbook of multicultural counseling* (pp. 181–198). Thousand Oaks, CA: Sage.

Herrnstein, R. J., & Murray, C. (1996). *The bell curve: Intelligence and class structure in American life.* New York: The Free Press.

Herron, C. (1997). *Nappy hair.* New York: Knopf.

Hinojosa, R. (1987). *This migrant earth.* Houston: Arte Publico Press.

Honan, W. H. (1999, January 29). Nearly fifth of teachers say they feel unqualified. *The New York Times,* p. A10.

Hong, M. (Ed.). (1993). *Growing up Asian American*. New York: Avon.

hooks, b. (1994). *Teaching to transgress: Education as the practice of freedom*. New York: Routledge.

Horvat, E. M., & Antonio, A. L. (1999). "Hey, those shoes are out of uniform": African American girls in an elite high school and the importance of habitus. *Anthropology and Education Quarterly, 30(3)*, 317–342.

Howard, G. R. (1999). *We can't teach what we don't know: White teachers, multiracial schools*. New York: Teachers College Press.

Hurston, Z. N. (1937/1978). *Their eyes were watching God*. Chicago: University of Illinois Press.

Hwang, D. H. (1983). *FOB and the house of sleeping beauties*. New York: Dramatists Play Service.

Hymowitz, K. S. (1999, Spring). Multicultural illiteracy [Review of *Losing our language: How multicultural classroom instruction is undermining our children's ability to read, write, and reason* by Sandra Stotsky]. *The Public Interest, 135*, 124–128.

Jean-Paul Sartre—Biography. (2002). From *Nobel lectures*. [On-line]. Retrieved December 31, 2002, from http://www.nobel.se/literature/laureates/1964-/sartre-bio.html

Jen, G. (1993). "What means switch." In M. Hong (Ed.), *Growing up Asian American: An anthology* (pp. 235–254). New York: Avon.

Joyce, J. (1959). *Dubliners*. New York: Viking.

Kerwin, C., & Ponterotto, J. G. (1995). Biracial identity development: Theory and research. In J. G. Ponterotto, J. M. Casas, L. A. Suzuki, & C. M. Alexander (Eds.), *Handbook of multicultural counseling* (pp. 199–217). Thousand Oaks, CA: Sage.

Klein, M. (1966). Ralph Ellison's "Invisible Man." In S. L. Gross & J. E. Hardy (Eds.), *Images of the Negro in American literature* (pp. 249–264). Chicago: University of Chicago Press.

Ladson-Billings, G. (1994). *The dreamkeepers: Successful teachers of African American children*. San Francisco: Jossey-Bass.

Lauter, P. (Ed.). (1983). *Reconstructing American literature: Courses, syllabi, issues*. Old Westbury, NY: The Feminist Press.

Lee, H. (1960). *To kill a mockingbird*. New York: Warner.

Lee, S. J. (1996). *Unraveling the "model minority" stereotype: Listening to Asian American youth*. New York: Teachers College Press.

Ling, A. (n.d.). Teaching Asian American literature. Retrieved December 10, 2002, from http://www.georgetown.edu/tamlit/essays/asian_am.html.

Lopez, T. (Ed.). (1995). *Growing up Chicana/o*. New York: Avon.

Lorde, A. (1984). My words will be there. In M. Evans (Ed.), *Black women writers (1950–1980): A critical evaluation* (pp. 261–276). New York: Anchor.

Malamud, B. (1983). The jewbird. In B. Malamud, *The stories of Bernard Malamud* (pp.144–154). New York: New American Library.

Marshall, P. (1983, January 9). The making of a writer: From the poets in the kitchen. *The New York Times Book Review*, pp. 3, 34–35.

Martinez-Serros, H. (1988). *The last laugh and other stories*. Houston: Arte Publico Press.

Masters, E. L. (1914/1962). *Spoon River anthology.* New York: Collier.

McDermott, R. P. (1977). The cultural context of learning to read. In S. F. Wanat (Ed.), *Papers in applied linguistics* (Linguistics and Reading Series 1, pp. 10–18). Arlington, VA: Center for Applied Linguistics.

McIntosh, P. (1998). White privilege and male privilege: A personal account of coming to see correspondences through work in women's studies. In M. L. Andersen & P. H. Collins (Eds.), *Race, class and gender: An anthology* (3rd ed.) (pp. 94–105). New York: Wadsworth.

Momaday, N. S. (1989). *House made of dawn.* New York: Harper & Row.

Morrison, T. (1972). *The bluest eye.* New York: Pocket.

Morrison, T. (1973). *Sula.* New York: New American Library.

Morrison, T. (1987). *Beloved.* New York: New American Library.

Morrison, T. (1993). *Playing in the dark: Whiteness and the literary imagination.* New York: Vintage.

Navarrette, R., Jr. (1994). *A darker shade of crimson: Odyssey of a Harvard Chicano.* New York: Bantam, Doubleday, Dell.

Neiman, A. M. (1986). Education, power, and the authority of knowledge. *Teachers College Record, 88(1),* 64–80.

Neira, C. (1988). Building 860. *Harvard Educational Review, 58(3),* 337–342.

Nielsen, A. L. (1988). *Reading race: White American poets and the racial discourse in the twentieth century.* Athens, GA: University of Georgia Press.

Nieto, S. (1996). *Affirming diversity: The sociopolitical context of multicultural education* (2nd ed.). White Plains, NY: Longman.

Nieto, S. (1999). *The light in their eyes: Creating multicultural learning communities.* New York: Teachers College Press.

Niven, P. (1991). *Carl Sandburg, a biography.* New York: Charles Scribner's Sons.

Nussbaum, M. C. (1997). *Cultivating humanity: A classical defense of reform in liberal education.* Cambridge, MA: Harvard University Press.

Nyberg, D., & Farber, P. (1986). Authority in education. *Teachers College Record, 88(1),* 4–14.

O'Connor, F. (1971). *Flannery O'Connor: The complete stories.* New York: Farrar, Straus, and Giroux.

O'Hearn, C. C. (1998). *Half and half: Writers on growing up biracial and bicultural.* New York: Pantheon.

Omi, M., & Winant, H. (1986). *Racial formation in the United States: From the 1960s to the 1980s.* New York: Routledge and Kegan Paul.

Osterman, K. F. (2000). Students' need for belonging in the school community. *Review of Educational Research 70(3),* 323–367.

Ovando, C. J., & Gourd, K. (1996). Knowledge construction, language maintenance, revitalization, and empowerment. In J. A. Banks (Ed.), *Multicultural education, transformative knowledge, and action: Historical and contemporary perspectives* (pp. 297–322). New York: Teachers College Press.

Pack, M. (Producer/Director), & Prizer, J. (Co-Producer). (1993). *Campus culture wars: Five stories about pc* [Video]. Santa Monica, CA: Direct Cinema Ltd.

Paley, V. G. (1995). *Kwanzaa and me: A teacher's story.* Cambridge, MA: Harvard University Press.

Paley, V. G. (1997). *The girl with the brown crayon.* Cambridge, MA: Harvard University Press.

Palmer, P. J. (1998). *The courage to teach.* San Francisco: Jossey-Bass.

Park, R. E., & Burgess, E. W. (1921/1937). *Introduction to the science of sociology.* Chicago: University of Chicago Press.

Parker, F. W. (1894/2001). *Talks on pedagogics: An outline of the theory of concentration and other writings.* Chicago: The Francis W. Parker School.

Phelan, P., Davidson, A. L., & Yu, H. C. (1993). Students' multiple worlds: Navigating the borders of family, peer, and school cultures. In P. Phelan & A. L. Davidson (Eds.), *Renegotiating cultural diversity in American schools* (pp. 52–88). New York: Teachers College Press.

Phinney, J. S. (1993). A three-stage model of ethnic identity development in adolescence. In M. E. Bernal & G. P. Knight (Eds.), *Ethnic identity: Formation and transmission among Hispanics and other minorities* (pp. 61–79). Albany, NY: State University of New York Press.

Potok, C. (1972). *My name is Asher Lev.* Greenwich, CT: Fawcett.

Riggs, M. (Producer/Director). (1987). *Ethnic notions* [Video]. San Francisco, CA: California Newsreel.

Riley, P. (Ed.). (1993). *Growing up Native American.* New York: Avon.

Rodriguez, L. (1993). *Always running: La vida loca: Gang days in L.A.* New York: Touchstone.

Rodriguez, R. (1982). *Hunger of memory, the education of Richard Rodriguez: An autobiography.* Boston: Godine.

Rodriguez, R. (1997). Asians. In B. Schneider (Ed.), *Race: An anthology in the first person* (pp. 58–73). New York: Crown.

Sandburg, C. (1953). *Always the young strangers.* New York: Harcourt, Brace.

Sandburg, C. (1970). *The collected poems of Carl Sandburg* (rev. and exp. ed.). New York: Harcourt, Brace.

Sarason, S. B. (1990). *The predictable failure of educational reform: Can we change course before it's too late?* San Francisco: Jossey-Bass.

Sartre, J.-P. (1956). Existentialism is a humanism. In W. Kaufmann (Ed.), *Existentialism from Dostoyevsky to Sartre* (pp. 287–311). Cleveland, OH: Meridian.

Sasaki, R. A. (1993). First love. In M. Hong (Ed.), *Growing up Asian American* (pp. 379–392). New York: Avon.

Scheurich, J. J., & Young, M. D. (1997). Coloring epistemologies: Are our research epistemologies racially biased? *Educational Researcher, 26(4),* 4–16.

Schlesinger, A. M., Jr. (1992). *The disuniting of America: Reflections on a multicultural society.* New York: W. W. Norton.

Sengupta, S. (2000, November 6). A literary diaspora toasts one of its own. *The New York Times,* pp. B1, B6.

Shakespeare, W. (1992). *Romeo and Juliet.* New York: Washington Square Press.

Shaw, C. C. (1996). The big picture: An inquiry into the motivations of African-American teacher education students to be or not to be teachers. *American Educational Research Journal 33, (2),* pp. 327–354.

Silko, L. M. (1977). *Ceremony.* New York: Viking Penguin.

Silver, J. M. (Director). (1984). *Hester Street* [Video]. Stamford, CT: Veston Video.

Sinclair, U. (1906/1980). *The jungle*. New York: New American Library.

Sleeter, C. E., & Grant, C. A. (1987). An analysis of multicultural education in the United States. *Harvard Educational Review, 57*, 421–444.

Smith, D. (1996, December 12). Centuries of writing by Blacks distilled. *The New York Times,* pp. B1, B5.

Sodowsky, G. R., Kwan, K.-L. K., & Pannu, R. (1995). Ethnic identity of Asians in the United States. In J. G. Ponterotto, J. M. Casas, L. A. Suzuki, & C. M. Alexander (Eds.), *Handbook of multicultural counseling* (pp. 123–154). Thousand Oaks, CA: Sage.

Sophocles. (1977). Oedipus rex. In D. Fitts & R. Fitzgerald (Trans.), *Sophocles: The Oedipus cycle* (pp. 1–78). New York: Harcourt Brace Jovanovich.

Spiegelman, A. (1991). *Maus II, A survivor's tale: And here my troubles began.* New York: Pantheon.

Stanfield, J. H., II. (1985). The ethnocentric basis of social science knowledge production. *Review of Research in Education, 12,* 387–415.

Steele, C. M. (1992, April). Race and the schooling of Black Americans. *The Atlantic Monthly,* pp. 68–78.

Steele, C. M. (1997). A threat in the air: How stereotypes shape intellectual identity and performance. *American Psychologist, 52(6),* 613–629.

Steele, C. M., & Aronson, J. (1995). Stereotype threat and the intellectual test performance of African Americans. *Journal of Personality and Social Psychology, 69(5),* 797–811.

Stonequist, E. V. (1937). *The marginal man.* New York: Scribner & Sons.

Stotsky, S. (1996). Multicultural literature and civic education: A problematic relationship with possibilities. In R. K. Fullinwider (Ed.), *Public education in a multicultural society: Policy, theory, critique* (pp. 231–264). New York: Cambridge University Press.

Stotsky, S. (1999). *Losing our language: How multicultural classroom instruction is undermining our children's ability to read, write, and reason.* New York: The Free Press.

Suarez-Orozco, M. M., & Suarez-Orozco, C. E. (1993). Hispanic cultural psychology: Implications for education theory and research. In P. Phelan & A. L. Davidson (Eds.), *Renegotiating cultural diversity in American schools* (pp. 108–138). New York: Teachers College Press.

Takaki, R. (1993). *A different mirror: A history of multicultural America.* Boston: Little, Brown.

Tan, A. (1989). *The Joy Luck Club.* New York: Ivy.

Tatge, C., & Lasseur, D. (Directors). (1992). *Bill Moyers: Beyond hate trilogy* [Video]. New York: Mystic Fire Video.

Tatum, B. D. (1992). Talking about race, learning about racism: The application of racial identity development theory in the classroom. *Harvard Educational Review, 62(1),* 1–24.

Tatum, B. D. (1997). *"Why are all the Black kids sitting together in the cafeteria?"* (rev. ed.). New York: Basic Books.

Tatum, B. D. (2001, March 15). *Interrupting the cycle of racism: What parents, teachers, and students can do.* Talk given at the Francis W. Parker School, Chicago, IL.

Taylor, C. (1994). The politics of recognition. In A. Gutmann (Ed.), *Multiculturalism: Examining the politics of recognition* (pp. 25–73). Princeton, NJ: Princeton University Press.

Tharp, R. G. (1994, September). *Research knowledge and policy issues in cultural diversity and education* [On-line]. Systemic Reform: Perspectives on Personalizing Education. Retrieved December 31, 2002, from http://www.ed.gov/pubs/EdReformStudies/SysReforms/tharp1.html.

Three Rivers, A. (1991). *Cultural etiquette: A guide for the well intentioned.* Indian Valley, VA: Market Wimmin.

Twain, M. (1922/1993). Slavery in Hannibal. In K. Whittemore & G. Marzorati (Eds.), *Voices in Black and White: Writings on race in America from Harper's Magazine* (pp. 1–2). New York: Franklin Square Press.

Twain, M. (1959). *The adventures of Huckleberry Finn.* New York: New American Library.

Villanueva, I. (1997). The voices of Chicano families: Life stories, maintaining bilingualism, and cultural awareness. In M. Seller & L. Weis (Eds.), *Beyond Black and White: New faces and voices in U.S. schools* (pp. 61–79). Albany, NY: State University of New York Press.

Wang, W. (Director). (1989). Eat a bowl of tea [Video]. Burbank, CA: RCA/Columbia Pictures Home Video.

Waters, M. C. (1998). Optional ethnicities: For Whites only?. In M. L. Andersen & P. H. Collins (Eds.), *Race, class and gender: An anthology* (3rd ed.) (pp. 403–412). New York: Wadsworth.

West, C. (1993). *Race matters.* Boston: Beacon.

Who's in the classroom. (1998, April 5). *The New York Times Education Life,* p. 28.

Wilson, A. (1988). *Joe Turner's come and gone.* New York: Plume.

Wolf, S. (1994). Comment. In A. Gutmann (Ed.), *Multiculturalism: Examining the politics of recognition* (pp. 75–85). Princeton, NJ: Princeton University Press.

Wright, R. (1945). *Black boy: A record of childhood and youth.* New York: Harper & Row.

Yannella, P. R. (1996). *The other Carl Sandburg.* Jackson, MS: University Press of Mississippi.

Zeffirelli, F. (Director). (1968). *Romeo and Juliet* [Video]. Hollywood, CA: Paramount.

Zhou, M. (1997). Social capital in Chinatown: The role of community-based organizations and families in the adaptation of the younger generation. In M. Seller & L. Weis (Eds.), *Beyond Black and White: New faces and voices in U.S. schools* (pp. 181–205). Albany, NY: State University of New York Press.

Index

Achebe, Chinua, 10
Activism. *See* Social action
Adams, M., 107
Addams, Jane, 127, 177, 181
Adler, B., 83
Affirmative action, 46, 68, 116, 194
Akash, M., 83
Alexander, M. W., 176
Algren, Nelson, 128
Alienation, 29, 45, 53, 122, 184, 186
Alliances, 63, 77–78, 86, 97, 139, 184, 186–87
Allport, Gordon, 15, 51, 185
Alvarez, Julia, 164
Anaya, Rodolfo, 83
Andersen, M., 5
Andrews, S., 37, 98
Angelou, Maya, 35
Antonio, A. L., 29, 183
Archibold, R. C., 7
Aronson, J., 75
Assimilation, 25, 26–27, 37, 45, 72, 76, 163, 180, 192, 203
Augenbraum, H., 83
Authority, 3, 6, 9, 109–26; "an," 112, 113, 119; challenges concerning, 115–19; conferring of, 113; and curriculum and pedagogy, 120, 121, 125–26, 135, 136, 141, 154; and discussions, 110–12, 125, 126; as "earned," 113; of experience, 109–11, 114, 119, 120, 123, 124; freedom from, 115–16; and history, 9, 109, 110, 116–17, 121; and identity, 9, 109, 110, 111, 112, 116, 123; "in," 112, 119; insider vs. outsider, 116–17, 120, 121–22, 126; limitations on, 119; and pedagogy of belonging, 183–84, 192, 196, 197, 203; questioning of, 121–22, 123, 141, 184; sharing, 9,

118–26; sources/voices of, 110, 116–19, 121–22, 123, 126, 197; and "truth," 122. *See also specific topic*
Authors: students as, 123–24, 126. *See also* Writers; *specific author*

Badour, D., 162
Baldwin, James, 145–46, 150, 165, 167, 168, 194
Banks, James, 120, 130, 131–32, 143
Barker-Hackett, L., 100, 200
Beck, E. T., 49–50
Bell, L. A., 107
Belonging, 6, 10, 180–206; and authority, 183–84, 192, 196, 197, 203; and culture, 182–84, 191, 194, 198; and curriculum, 182, 184, 191, 192, 193, 194–96, 203; and discussions, 182, 183–84, 192, 194, 196, 197, 200, 203; and history, 182, 183–84, 188–89, 196, 197, 203, 205; and home and school, 21, 24, 28–30, 36, 182–83, 196, 197; and identity, 69, 76, 182, 183–84, 185, 186, 188–89, 191, 196, 197, 198, 203, 205; and learning, 187–90, 191–92; pedagogy of, 181–206; and planning, 190–96; and power, 184–87, 193, 194, 196–98, 203; and reading, 188–89, 191–92, 197; and social dominance, 184–87, 197–98, 203; and what we can expect, 198–202; and writing, 191–92, 193, 197. *See also* "Fitting in"; Inclusion
Bendau, M. C., 53
Benson, A., 52
Berman, P., 42
Berube, M., 172–73
Bigsby, C.W.E., 146
Biracial students, 64–66, 69, 71–72, 74–75, 76, 77, 168, 189, 205

202–03; bridging of school and, 23, 33–36; community of, 21–24; and culture, 17–19; and curriculum, 28, 33, 34, 35; distancing from, 30; and family/parents, 14, 15, 17–19, 21, 22, 24, 26, 29, 30, 31, 32, 37; and "fitting in," 14, 26, 27–28, 30; and identity, 14, 15, 16, 22, 25, 26, 27, 30, 66, 72, 73; journeying between school, 13–15, 21–22, 33, 34; and language, 24–26, 35; leaving, 36–37; lessons from, 14, 17–19, 34; patterns of relationship between school and, 22–23, 34; race-conscious, 15–17; and race-conscious society, 14, 15–17, 18; and reading, 162–63, 165; returning, 30–32. *See also* Family/parents

Honan, W. H., 7

Hong, M., 83

hooks, bell, 10, 95, 113, 116, 120, 181, 185, 190–91

Horvat, E. M., 29, 183

The House on Mango Street (Cisneros), 32, 83–84, 123–24, 168, 170, 171–72, 175

Howard, G. R., 114, 184, 188

Hughes, Langston, 146, 151, 167, 176

Hurston, Zora Neale, 167, 189

Hwang, David Henry, 161, 163–64, 165

Hymowitz, K. S., 160, 175

Identity, 3, 5, 8, 9, 58–89; and authority, 9, 109, 110, 111, 112, 116, 123; "code-shifting," 73; constructing, 83, 87; and curriculum and pedagogy, 59, 78, 80, 83–85, 87, 88, 130, 135, 136, 137, 143, 151, 152; denial/downplaying of, 30, 72; and discussions, 78, 79, 81, 83, 84, 85–86, 88, 91, 92, 93, 96, 97, 98, 99, 102, 103, 105, 107; emerging, 8, 58, 61–66, 78, 82, 85, 87, 102, 103, 203; emphasis on, 77–78; and extensions of myself, 66–67; and "fitting in"/belonging, 8, 67, 69, 75–77, 86, 182, 183–84, 185, 186, 188–89, 191, 196, 197, 198, 203, 205; and history, 41–43, 46, 60, 64, 71, 79, 85–86; and home and school, 14, 15, 16, 22, 25, 26, 27, 30; hyphenated, 68–69; and labels, 5, 68–71, 82; and language, 25, 71, 72, 76, 82, 87; and names, 59–61, 71, 85, 87; "oppositional," 73; and others, 58, 59, 61, 62, 65, 67–75, 77, 84, 88, 92; and

power, 16, 61, 63, 71, 86; and race, 61–66; and "racelessness," 72, 73, 86; and reading, 9, 161, 163, 166, 170; stages of, 78, 81, 151; theories/models about, 65–66, 80–83; as threat, 59. *See also specific topic*

Inada, L. F., 175

Inclusion, 17, 26, 29, 35, 86, 100. *See also* Belonging

Individual history, 38–41, 42, 44, 45, 46, 47, 49, 50, 51, 52, 54, 56

Inquiry approach, 187–90

Insiders vs. outsiders, 105, 116–17, 120, 121–22, 126, 162

Invisibility, 6, 76, 114, 147, 174

Isolation, 24, 27, 29, 36, 37, 74, 76, 97

Jacobs, Harriet, 146

Jen, Gish, 83, 171

Joe Turner's Come and Gone (Wilson), 161, 162, 165

Johnson, James, 167

Johnson, Lyndon, 133

Journals, 4, 5, 44, 78, 92, 95, 96, 105, 125, 193

Joyce, James, 35, 175

Kennedy, Donald, 113

Kerwin, C., 61, 65

King, Martin Luther, Jr., 115

Kingston, Maxine Hong, 164

Klein, M., 152

Knowledge, 42, 88; and authority, 9, 111, 112, 113–14, 119, 125; and belonging, 192, 199, 203, 205; construction of, 9, 129–37, 140–41; and curriculum and pedagogy, 9, 129–30, 140–41; and discussions, 91–92; about neighborhoods, 19–20; and pedagogy, 140–41, 192, 199, 203, 205; Sandburg's perspective of, 130–33; shared, 36, 192, 199; sources of, 111, 112; of students, 129–30; students' perspective of, 134–37; of teachers, 88, 129–30, 133–34; teacher's perspective of, 133–34

Kwan, K.-L. K., 61

Labels, 5, 68–71, 82, 90

Ladson-Billings, Gloria, 10, 120, 181

Language, 8–9, 143, 153, 175; and belonging, 189, 203, 205; and discussions, 9,

(continued)

About the Author

Mary Dilg has taught in public and private high schools in New York City, Boston, and Los Angeles; at Northwestern University; and at Washington University in St. Louis. She currently teaches English at the Francis W. Parker School in Chicago. Her publications include *Race and Culture in the Classroom: Teaching and Learning Through Multicultural Education* (Teachers College Press, 1999) as well as numerous articles on multicultural education. She received the Paul and Kate Farmer *English Journal* Award for writing in 1995 and 1998. Her presentations and faculty development workshops at schools, universities, and conferences focus on understanding dynamics and supporting students in the multicultural classroom.